Written for and dedicated to all who seek the truth
And who love the God of Abraham, Isaac, and Jacob

"For there shall be a day
When watchmen will cry on Mount Ephraim,
Arise, and let us go up to Zion,
To the Lord our God."
Jeremiah 31:6

Acknowledgements:

To my wife — God was exceedingly gracious to me when He put you in my life. Thank you again for being my best friend and helpmate on our amazing journey.

To my family — thanks for putting up with me during the many hours I spent researching and writing and thank you for your excellent help with proofreading and editing.

Table of Contents

Foreword — A Word of Love

*I*t was after spending several months putting this book together that I was at last able to get some feedback from my brother Chris. Growing up together and being only one year apart in age, we remain very close despite our geographic separation. Not only my younger brother in the flesh, but also my brother in the Lord, I look forward to the deeper levels of conversation that he and I often share. Chris had been working in the Middle East for the past three years for a major oil company and had not visited the U.S. for over a year. He had moved his wife and children to a Muslim country, and I had gotten them in a little trouble once before because of the "religious" nature of some of my e-mails so I had not yet been able to send him the chapter drafts. My brother was finally back in the States and we were able to connect on the phone. At last, after the birth of his fifth son and after getting settled into a house and a new job, he had a little time to look over some of my thoughts.

"Well, have you had a chance to get into my book yet?" I inquired.

Silence…

"Well, I have only gotten through the first few pages, but…*I don't like it,*" he replied.

There was silence on the phone. I had worked diligently on this project — and I wanted to hear what else he had to say.

"Don't take this wrong, but… it sounds like you are trying to say, 'Everything you've ever learned is wrong, and now I'm going to set you straight'"

There was again silence on the phone as I thought about his criticism. "Well," I replied, "that *is* what I'm sort of saying." After an awkward moment we both chuckled. I appreciated his comments so much, and his point was not lost.

Since having that conversation I have thought about what he said. I wondered, *how do you* let people you love and care about know that *we all* may have been taught something that is terribly wrong, without sounding like you are a "know it all" big brother?

After my conversation with Chris, I decided to write this short preface to be placed in front of the original introduction in hopes of somehow conveying the purpose and motivation behind this work. To that end, some explanation is due. It is because of a heartfelt burden for fellow believers that I have felt compelled to write. It is not as though I am a formally trained Bible scholar, yet I do believe that God[1] has graciously given me an understanding that I *must* share. I know all too well the sting of realizing that you have been misinformed and taught the word of God incorrectly.

On a personal level, I have been through at least a couple of periods in my life where God's correction of both my doctrine and my life became obvious. These words penned by the writer of Hebrews have at times been a great comfort to me: **"My son, do not despise the chastening of the Lord, nor be discouraged when you are rebuked by Him; for whom the Lord loves He chastens, and scourges every son whom He receives." Hebrews 12:6.**

It was during those difficult years that my studies grew more serious and my love for the Father increased. I began to have many questions about what the church was teaching and just how it lined up with the word of God. It is not an exaggeration to say that I earnestly sought the Lord to answer my questions. It is truly amazing how our eyes can be opened when we make such a request. **"If any of you lacks wisdom, let him ask of God, who gives to all liberally and without reproach, and it will be given to him." James 1:5**

Because the natural man has inherited a tendency to rebel against God it can be difficult at times to receive the wisdom that God freely gives. Often, matters of God aren't as we had expected and sometimes the things that we discover demand a response.

When God does impart something of Himself, some understanding, it is indeed strong medicine. Now, when I step back and consider the majesty of God's redemption plan for mankind, and how that plan is unfolding before our eyes, I have a true sense of *"Shock and Awe."*

This book is my response to a heartfelt concern for those who might not presently see the whole reality concerning our Creator's marvelous work of Love. After gaining an understanding of just who the people of Israel are and why it makes a difference, I wanted to shout this truth from the mountaintops! I felt that if I did not get this word out I may literally burst! I *had* to write this book.

This is *not* a text of condemnation directed toward those who might be unaware of the matters presented herein, for who am I to point a finger or condemn anyone? This book is meant to be an exhilarating look at God's Plan for God's people. It is intended to spur the reader on to a more "set apart" and Holy life by increasing one's love for the Father and one's faith in Jesus Christ.

It is my hope and prayer that the reader will not be turned off by my inability to convey the true feelings that I have about this matter. My hope is that the reader could somehow understand that what has been penned on the pages that follow was written with a broken heart — a heart that is broken over the plight of God's people — a heart full of love and compassion and not blame. This book was not written by a perfect person, but simply someone who has been given a wondrous gift — a gift that *must* be shared.

I am happy to report that despite his initial reservations, my brother Chris did go ahead and finish reading this book. I hope that you too will also grant sufficient attention to the case that is put forward to allow its full presentation. My brother's feelings about this book changed dramatically as he began to comprehend the overwhelming scriptural proofs that are presented in this volume. He was able to overlook my inability to write because he knows my heart about the subject matter presented. It is my earnest prayer that you the reader would also understand the love that I have for all the brethren who know the Messiah of Israel, but are unaware of their own identity. What follows is an expression of that love and was written simply to bless the reader and to magnify God.

Introduction

A preacher friend once lamented to me about his own congregation, "This church is a mile wide and one inch deep!"
Sadly, his assessment of the body that he was shepherding may be
true for most churches today. Without knowledge, God's people
have become a flock of sheep that are easily misled. When we look
at the church today, evidence is all around us that "ravenous wolves"
have already come into the flock. It is just as Paul predicted in Acts
20:29, **"For I know this, that after my departure savage wolves
will come in among you, not sparing the flock."**

This book was written in response to an inner urging — a passion
that God has given me for His people who are being led astray,
because they do not know their *identity* in Christ. My own journey of
discovery began after personal failures led me to a realization of the
magnitude of God's Grace, and the futility of man's laws.

God then granted that I would have a hunger for His word,
particularly in the area of biblical prophecy. My studies led me to a
startling realization of just *who I am in the Messiah* and have culmi-
nated in a new found love for the Father and *His* commandments.
My prayer is that through the work of this book, the reader will also
find a new passion for Holy living, and a new found love for the
Father and His Word, both the neglected Old Testament and the
New Testament alike. After studying the contents of this book, the
reader will understand why many Christians today have a love for
Israel that is explainable only as "intuitive." [2]

My personal journey began with a closer look at Biblical
prophecy. Thus, this book will trace the footsteps that have led me
to a deeper understanding of the things of God.

End times studies are fraught with varying opinions and positions. On the surface, it seems that it doesn't really matter what a person believes about the end times, as long as one "Trusts Jesus." I am certain that in the past I have even proclaimed such a half truth. Yes, of course one has to trust Jesus, but is biblical prophecy really open to private interpretation? Using the Bible as our guide, let's see what the word of God says:

"Knowing this first, that no prophecy of Scripture is of any private interpretation, for prophecy never came by the will of man, but holy men of God spoke as they were moved by the Holy Spirit." 2 Peter 1:20

In order to unravel the mysteries of the end times, we must come to the realization that we need to rely on that same Holy Spirit to enlighten us and to lead us into the truth. It is my sincerest prayer that as I pen these words I am led by the Holy Spirit. It is not my desire that I convince you of what I believe to be the truth. Rather, I pray that you will come to knowledge of the *real* truth being led by the Spirit of God. To this end I ask that you would also seek the leading of the Holy Spirit and that you would do as those mentioned by Luke in Acts 17:11. I plead with you to *be a Berean*, who **"were more fair-minded than those in Thessalonica, and that they received the word with all readiness, and they searched the Scriptures daily to find out whether these things were so."** Indeed, this book was meant to be read with your Bible opened so that you, being led by the Spirit of God, may prove for yourself the things that are presented.

I have often heard it said, and in fact have also been guilty of saying: *"it will all turn out okay in the end,"* or *"We know* who's *going to win anyway... so what does it matter."* In fact, Timothy Lahaye in *Rapture: Under Attack* makes this very claim, "Premillennialist eschatology provides the promise that eventually Jesus will win, even in a world that seems to be totally out of control. It guarantees that ultimately everything will make sense and that everything will be fine (p. 227)"

Unfortunately, these kinds of statements seem contradict some pointed warnings spoken by our Savior who said **"He who has an ear let him hear"**[3] and **"Here is wisdom."**[4] These words spoken by Jesus Himself were made in direct reference to end time prophetic events and make clear the importance of a careful study of the word of God pertaining to the end times.

The Real Issue — the Possibility of Falling Away

Even so, you might be wondering, what is the big problem? Sure, the Lord said that we should understand and have wisdom — but we should understand the whole Bible, right? Like a rebellious child, many of us will ask *"Why is it so important? Why is this issue of prophecy any different than any other biblical subject?"*

The Bible indicates that there will be a great "falling away" during the last days. **"Let no one deceive you by any means; for that Day**[5] **will not come unless the falling away comes first"** 2 **Thessalonians 2:3.** An honest look at this verse tells us that there will be those who were once part of the church who for some reason fall into apostasy. It is important to ask the question, what happens to those who fall away? Do they lose their salvation?[6]

Putting aside the issue of eternal security for now, we still must honestly face this simple question: If a "falling away" occurs in the last days, *will it really all turn out okay?*

We find another verse confirming this problem in Matthew 24:12. Speaking of the end times, Jesus proclaims, **"because lawlessness will abound, the love (agape) of many will grow cold."**

Dear brethren, we know that the word used in this verse for love is "agape." Agape means *the love of God.* This should startle us. The implications are staggering. *The love of God of many will grow cold*! If our Agape grows cold, are we still saved? 1 John 4:7-8 tells us, **"Beloved, let us love one another, for love is of God; and everyone who loves is born of God and knows God. He who does not love does not know God, for God is love."** This verse seems to indicate that if our Agape has grown cold, then we do not know God. This is indeed a sobering thought.

I am in hopes that the mere posing of these questions will be enough to stimulate the reader to continue the journey through this book. I am fully aware many Christians believe that these verses do not apply to the modern church, and it is to these brethren in particular that I am writing.

If it is true that "a falling away" will occur and if it is true that the Agape of many will grow cold, then this topic is of *utmost importance*. The concepts presented in this book will most likely challenge the reader's long held beliefs, but please look at these ideas closely. They are biblically sound and based firmly in the Word presented as proof within these pages. This book will reveal the marvelous hand of God and show that He continues to control world history, and that He is bringing His Word to pass even in our day.

CHAPTER 1

Overview of End Time Viewpoints

So what do we Christians think about the end times? And how did we come to our conclusions? As we will come to see, one's view of the "last days" will be very important as this present age comes to a close. What follows is a very brief overview of the different schools of thought with respect to the end times. This groundwork must be laid so that the later chapters can be understood in their proper context.

How Do We Interpret the Bible?

First, so that the reader will understand from where the author is coming, an explanation is due. It seems that many disagreements about doctrine and theology stem from what formally trained Bible scholars call their "hermeneutic," which is just a fancy way to say "ones method of interpretation."

Understanding one's hermeneutic is an important issue, as it would be almost impossible to come to like-minded conclusions regarding biblical matters without at least some agreement on foundation issues, particularly the means of interpretation that one ought to use.

I believe that scripture *first* ought to be approached using a "face-value" interpretation method. In this way we show that we take the word of God seriously. If the plaintext seems to make sense, then we ought not to try and twist it to mean something *different,* although we may at times find a *deeper* meaning imbedded in the plaintext.

The ancient rabbinical tradition has defined these deeper levels of meaning. They hold that there are four levels of understanding that can be found in the scriptures and these levels are known by the acronym PaRDeS.[7] This understanding does seem to have merit when it comes to discussing the deeper things that are communicated in scripture. According to this rabbinical tradition the first level of understanding God's word is called the *pashat* interpretation and refers to the face value meaning of the text. This face value interpretation is the foundation for all other interpretations.

The next level of understanding is called in Hebrew, *remez* (which means hint). Remez refers to the implied meaning of the text. When we find something in the text that seems out of place or doesn't fit, it often is a hint or "remez" that there is a deeper meaning to be comprehended than is conveyed by its plaintext meaning.

The third level of interpretation according to the rabbinical tradition is the "drash" (meaning "search"). This is the allegorical or typological application of the text.[8] Regrettably, over the centuries well meaning theologians have thrown out the first level of interpretation, the level on which all other interpretation ought to hinge and have jumped to the *drash* level. They then inserted their own "politically correct" ideas and beliefs. These ideas may have seemed expedient at the time, but were opposed to the pashat (plain text) interpretation. The correct drash interpretation must not contradict the plaintext message of the whole of the Word of God. We occasionally find examples of "drash" interpretations used in the Bible when we find the Bible writers and characters interpreting and teaching the Old Testament in the New Testament.

The fourth and final level of understanding the Scriptures is called Hebrew "sod" meaning "hidden." This understanding is the hidden or secret meaning of the text.[9] I believe that when the Messiah returns, we will stand in awe as He reveals to us the deeper mysteries, the "sod" understandings that are embedded in His Word.

Different Schools of Thought

Presented below is a brief dissertation explaining the different viewpoints concerning matters of the end of the age. This is background material that must be introduced, but it is not the intent of this book to fully investigate these positions. What follows is a "broad brush" survey, and is generally accurate, but by no means could be applied to the individual believer.

Amillennialism

Sadly, much of mainline "Christianity" has rejected the "face value" interpretation of the word of God. Discarding the plain meaning and instead choosing to allegorize the Word of God, they close their eyes to the truth that God presents and so have blinded themselves. In the modern church we see the mishandling of the Word happening with many issues concerning morality and doctrine, but this phenomenon is especially significant when is comes to the prophetic word, perhaps because of the colorful language used in biblical prophecy.

The majority of Old Testament prophecies concerning Christ relate to His literal physical reign over all the earth from Jerusalem. The book of Revelation tells us exactly how long this physical kingdom will last. Those who would deny the reality that Jesus will set up a 1000 year kingdom here on earth as clearly stated in Revelation 20:1-5 have allegorized scripture where the plain text makes common sense. This "allegorizing away" of Christ's prophesied 1000 year reign is commonly called the amillennial view. Most of those who subscribe to this school of thought do not believe that Christ will actually reign in literal Jerusalem, but instead believe that Christ will establish his kingdom in heaven with spiritual implications here on earth for "a long time." Amillennialism gained popularity during the rise of Romanized Christianity during the early church.[10] Early so-called "church fathers" (we will explore the ideas of some of these later), popularized this view and it became widely accepted because the Roman church, led by those faithful to the Roman leadership, did not look kindly on the notion that another king (the Messiah) would eventually reign on a literal throne here on the Earth. The Catholic Church and most old line denominations including Presbyterian, Methodist, the Church of Christ, as well as other churches that adhere to "Reformed Theology" hold to this position. Because studies of the "last things" are rarely taught among churches that hold to the amillennial position, many members of these churches are often unaware of the theological position that their own leadership holds with respect to the end times.

In addition to amillennialism, there is another school of thought that is worth mentioning. Closely related, and often a coincidental viewpoint to amillennialism is the preterist position. Those who hold to the preterist doctrine generally believe that Christ has already returned (in 70 A.D.) and that eventually Christianity will rise up and take over the world and establish a permanent kingdom for Christ. Much of what happened in 70 AD during the fall of Jerusalem was indeed accurately predicted by Christ's Olivet discourse (Matthew 24). Upon reading the accounts recorded by the Jewish historian Josephus,[11] it is easy to see why one would believe that some of the events spoken of in that portion of the scripture have already taken place. A startling example of this is found in Jesus' warning **"Woe to those who are nursing children in those days."** Josephus records a horrifying account of starvation to the point of a mother eating her own child during the Roman siege of Jerusalem circa 70 AD.[12] Josephus even uses language to describe this time such as "nor did any age ever breed a generation more fruitful in wickedness that this was, from the beginning of the world"[13] much like the descriptive language of Jesus as he describes the Great Tribulation in Matthew 24: 21 where Jesus said, **"For then there will be great tribulation, such as has not been since the beginning of the world until this time, no, nor ever shall be."**

As it turns out, this is an excellent example of a "near/far" prophecy. Biblical prophecy often has near/far applications, meaning the prophetic word is applicable twice, once near to the time of the giving of the prophetic word, and another at a remote time. We will prove this concept by pointing out several instances of these as this book progresses. As would be expected among those who allegorize scripture, there are many permutations of the amillennial/preterist theme, including something called the "postmillennial" position. The postmillennial position holds that after Christ's "return" in 70 A.D. there would be a 1000 year "church age" and then the judgment — a proposition that has been discredited for obvious reasons.

By simply taking Revelation 20 at face value, one cannot escape the conclusion that indeed our Messiah will reign for 1000 years.[14] Remarkably, much of the Old Testament also speaks of this wonderful time period. In fact, the Jews were expecting their Messiah to reign over a physical earthly throne, and because of this expectation many missed Christ's first coming. Additionally, one cannot escape this simple point: The Jews had only Old Testament Scriptures available and their understanding of these Scriptures likely far surpassed our own understanding today. If they were looking for a physical king to reign here on earth, isn't it most likely because this is what the Old Testament Scriptures indicate?

In fact, there is much more written in the Old Testament about Jesus' second coming than his first. Here are just a couple of examples:

"For unto us a Child is born, Unto us a Son is given; and the government will be upon His shoulder. And His name will be called Wonderful, Counselor, Mighty God, Everlasting Father, Prince of Peace." Isaiah 9:6

"And it shall come to pass that everyone who is left of all the nations which came against Jerusalem shall go up from year to year to worship the King, the LORD of hosts, and go up to keep the Feast of Tabernacles." Zechariah 14:16.

The preterist doctrine, supposing that Christ had already returned has a huge problem, for one thing seems certain, Jesus *did not return in 70 AD*. Moreover, the sun *did not* darken, the moon *did not* turn blood red, and the stars *did not* fall from heaven. (Matthew 24:29, Joel 2:31 Revelation 6:12-13) Christ did not return in the clouds (Matthew 24:30), He did not begin to rule on a literal throne in Israel, and His kingdom has not been fully established here on the Earth as the Old Testament prophecies predict. Furthermore, it is fairly obvious as we look around and see the decay and moral decline of our society that it doesn't look like true believers are gaining ground when it comes to restoring Christ's Kingdom on Earth. Society as a whole is getting *worse* and not better. In fact, as evidenced by the rise of homosexuality and moral permissiveness in the church today, "Christianity" as a whole is getting worse, not better!

Roots of Replacement Theology

The preterist/amillenialist adherents also believe that the "church" has replaced Israel as the "elect" (This is called Replacement Theology). Supposing that all of God's Promises concerning the Messiah were fulfilled by A.D. 70, they believe that the Kingdom of God is here on earth now. They also believe that all of God's covenant promises have either been fulfilled to completion, or have been taken away from the Jew and given to the "church." It is easy to see how those who look at Matthew 24 as being fulfilled could hold this view. There are, however, a couple of glaring problems with the view that all of Matthew was fulfilled in 70 A.D. First of all, aside from the fact that Christ did not return in the clouds in 70 A.D. as mentioned above, consider the similarities between Matthew 24 and the seven seals mentioned in Revelation 6. These similarities make it evident that these two passages describe the same event.[15] If the seven seals of Revelation were *completely fulfilled* in A.D. 70, then why was John given them as prophecy yet to be accomplished at the giving of John's apocalyptic vision some 25 years later?[16] Furthermore, God's promises to Abraham and his seed – through Isaac and Jacob – were *unconditional* promises.[17] These promises concerning God's people and their land were not dependant upon Israel's obedience (as were the promises of blessings that came by keeping God's instruction), and notably, God's covenant with Abraham is described as "everlasting."[18] To say that the "church" has replace Israel and has taken on all of the promises given to Israel is

nothing short of calling God a liar for not keeping those unconditional promises. History bears witness to the fact that the doctrine of
replacement theology has led to the slaughter of countless Jews by
means of the inquisition, pogroms, and the holocaust.

Graphically, the amellennial view and the preterist looks like
this:

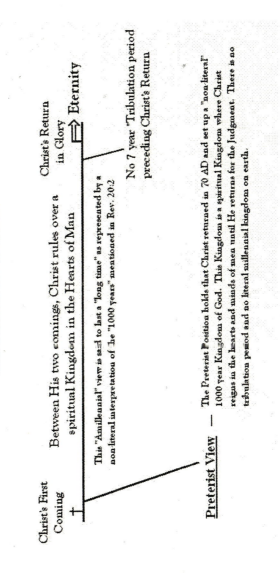

Premillennialism

The most commonly held view among evangelical Christians is based on a face value interpretation of Revelation 20 and is called the "premillennialists" viewpoint. Adherents to this view believe that Messiah will return and literally establish a 1000 year kingdom, and that this will occur sometime in the future. Most "evangelical," Baptist, Charismatic and Pentecostal Churches adhere to this view.

The Premillennialist's view looks like this:

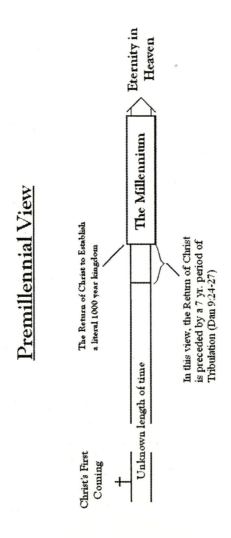

The premillennial view has been made enormously popular by the enormous success of the *fictional* series *Left Behind* written by Timothy LeHay and Jerry Jenkins. I have read these books and found them well written and quite entertaining. While they are fiction books, the authors admit that they are also meant to be a teaching and evangelizing tool. The series has been wildly successful placing the authors on top of the New York Times best seller's list every year since their release. I have often wondered why the "god of this age," Satan,[19] would allow these books to be so successful. While I admit the mere fact of their success does not indicate they contain profound error, it does make me a little hesitant to jump wholeheartedly on the bandwagon.[20]

The timing of the "rapture" is the center of controversy among those who hold to the premillennialist doctrine. The rapture, as defined by mainstream Bible teachers, is the event that occurs when Christ returns to earth and gathers his followers. In further chapters the rapture event will be further explored and defined. For now, when the term rapture is used it generally refers to that time when Christ returns to receive to Himself those who will be resurrected from the dead, and to gather His faithful that are alive at the time of His coming.

In the *Left Behind* series, the "rapture" takes place at least seven years before the return of Christ. This view is called a "pre-tribulation rapture view." Pre-trib adherents believe that Christ will come twice during his second coming — once for His Bride, the church, and then later in power and great glory to bring judgment upon the earth. This belief is unsupported in the plaintext of scripture. In fact, even the proponents of the pre-trib view admit that their position can not be explicitly found in the Bible but is merely implied.[21]

Most premillennial biblical scholars agree that a seven-year time span will precede the coming of Christ and His one thousand year kingdom. This is based on Daniel 9 and will be discussed in detail in the next chapter. As noted above, the major controversy between those of a premillennialist's mindset concerns the question of whether The Messiah will return *before* this seven-year time span (the pre-tribulation view), or *after* the seven-year time span (a view called the post-tribulation and rapture view). Some even believe that Christ's return will be at the midpoint of the seven-year tribulation. Here is a visual presentation of what the commonly held views look like:

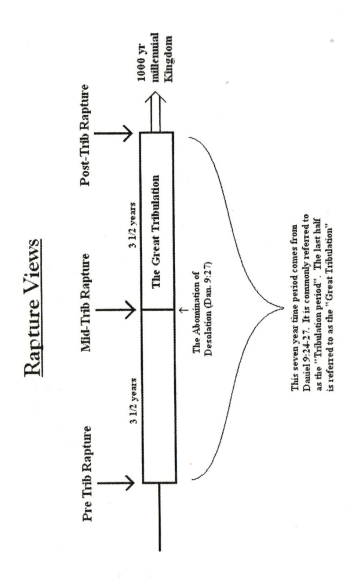

Rapture Views

Pre Trib Rapture

Mid-Trib Rapture

Post-Trib Rapture

1000 yr millennial Kingdom

3 1/2 years

3 1/2 years

The Great Tribulation

The Abomination of Desolation (Dan. 9:27)

This seven year time period comes from Daniel 9:24-27. It is commonly referred to as the "Tribulation period". The last half is referred to as the "Great Tribulation"

The view that I will put forth in what follows is a version of what is called the "prewrath" view, and is none of the above. The prewrath view graphically looks like this:

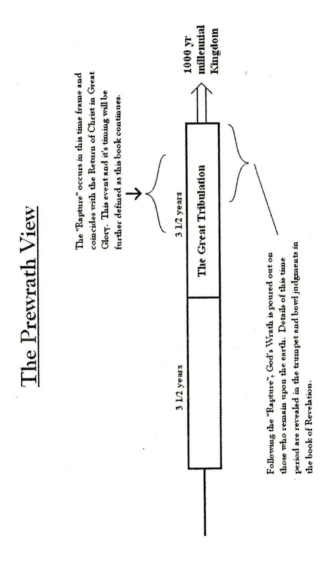

The prewrath view is not a new idea. The term was first used by Robert Van Kampen and can be found in his exhaustive work, *The Sign*. This text is not a rehashing of the ground that has been covered by Van Kampen, Marvin Rosenthal and others, but rather it is an attempt to clear the muddied waters with the addition of some significant new information that will shed light on this position. Additionally, this book will address the *single issue* that seems to determine which view one takes — this issue being that of the *identity* of Gods "elect" spoken of in Matthew chapter 24.

Before we get into a deeper discussion of the prewrath view and the identity of God's elect in Matthew 24, we will lay the groundwork for the discussion in the next couple of chapters.

CHAPTER 2

A Little More Background Information

*B*efore we jump into the details of the prewrath viewpoint it is necessary to go over a little more background information. This chapter is full of some of the "loose end" detail, and a lot of information will be covered, including the seventy weeks of Daniel, the Day of the Lord and the millennial kingdom. We will also briefly touch on the time period known as the Great Tribulation.

The vast majority of those who believe in a Pre-millennial kingdom agree that Christ's 1000 year reign is to be preceded by a seven-year time period. Readers who are not familiar with biblical prophecy will wonder where in the world this belief came from. The seven-year period is commonly called the "70th week of Daniel" and comes from Daniel chapter 9. In this chapter, Daniel, who is reading from the scroll of Jeremiah (Daniel 9: 2), realizes that the time of Babylonian captivity is about to come to an end. It is interesting to note that even though the Scriptures indicated this would be the case, Daniel still prays fervently — asking God to bring it to pass. It is also important to note that Daniel is in fact interpreting the Scripture at *face value*, believing that when Jeremiah said 70 years — 70 years is what he meant. Daniel is reading from Jeremiah chapter 25, and we can still read these words today!

The First 69 of Daniel's 70 weeks

In Daniel chapter 9, after Daniel presents his supplications to God he is approached by the Angel Gabriel who gives him a vision that spans the rest of history as we know it. A good grasp of this chapter is *essential* to understanding biblical prophecy.

In verse 24, Gabriel states that **"70 weeks are determined for your people and for your holy city,"** he then goes on through the remainder of verse 24 to explain what else will be done during the time frame of this prophecy: **"to finish the transgression, to make an end of sins, to make reconciliation for iniquity, to bring in everlasting righteousness, to seal up vision and prophecy, and to anoint the most Holy."** As you can see, not everything on this list has been brought to completion. *The 70 weeks period is not yet complete for all of these things have not fully come to pass.*

The term used for weeks in this text is the Hebrew word shebuwa (Strong's 7620) and means "seven." It's much like the word dozen that we have in English. For example, if I use the word "dozen," I could be referring to 12 days or 12 eggs or a dozen doughnuts. "Seventy shebuwa" is a Hebrew way to say 70 sets of seven years, or 490 years. In verse 9:25 Gabriel tells Daniel when this 490 year period is to begin when he states that from **"the going forth of the command to restore and build Jerusalem..."** (The starting point for the 490 years) until **"Messiah the Prince"** (the endpoint) — will be seven weeks and 62 weeks, or 69 weeks. Gabriel then goes on to point out that after this time —**"Messiah shall be cut off, but not for himself"** (clearly prophetic of Christ's sacrifice). It turns out that by secular history we can identify when the **"going forth of the command to restore and build Jerusalem"** happened and locate the start date of this prophecy. According to work done by Sir Robert Anderson[22] the date of this decree was March 14th 445 B.C.[23]

Anderson also realized that God's prophetic year is 360 days long rather than our 365 day year. This is the case in Revelation chapter 12 where the time period of 1260 days is equated to 42 months and also to 3½ years. It is interesting to note that before 701 B.C. all calendars, including the Jewish calendar had 360 days in a year. This happens to be why we have 360 degrees in a circle.[24]

Now back to Daniel's seventy weeks: Taking the first 69 "weeks" of the prophecy, if we multiply 483 years (seven weeks plus 62 weeks or (7x7) + (62x7) =483) by 360 days per year we end up with 173,880 days. If we add 173,880 days to the date March 14th 445 B.C., and account for the fact that there was no year zero, we come to the date April 6, 32 A.D.

According to Anderson, this turns out to be the very day that Jesus Christ first allowed himself to be worshiped as the Messiah, on "Palm Sunday."[25] According to the Gospel accounts,[26] Jesus actually *made arrangements* for His transportation on this day, a donkey and its colt, and entered Jerusalem just as was prophesied, **"Rejoice greatly, O daughter of Zion! Shout, O daughter of Jerusalem! Behold, your King is coming to you; He is just and having salvation, lowly and riding on a donkey, a colt, the foal of a donkey." Zechariah 9:9** — thus proving that for Jesus this day had special significance as an important fulfillment of prophecy.

Prior to this event Jesus seemed to shy away from the worship of man. In fact, when He was told by His brothers to go into Jerusalem during the Feast of Tabernacles to declare Himself as Messiah, Jesus said, **"My time has not yet come."**[27] On *this* day however, He did allow himself to be worshiped and in fact He even arranged the scene. Those gathered in Jerusalem did not miss the importance of this event and began singing from Psalm 118, indicating that they recognized that Jesus was the Messiah. Psalm 118 is clearly Messianic, and when the Pharisees heard the multitudes singing "Hosanna in the highest" they also understood the implication of what was happening and demanded that Jesus rebuke the multitude. Remember what Jesus told them? He said that if these were to hold their silence even the rocks would cry out. It is so exciting to see how God fulfills His Word down to the very day!

Admittedly, there has been some controversy surrounding the exact calculations and the exact calendar dates. But, **"let God be true and every man a liar."** We must confess that Jesus' first coming was right on schedule on the only calendar that matters — *God's calendar.* I believe that God's word is true down to the *very* day, even if we can't verify it unequivocally on our mixed up secular calendar. I believe that Luke 19: 41 – 44 proves this, as Jesus held those of Jerusalem accountable for not knowing the "time of your visitation."

The 70th week

The prophecy that Gabriel gave Daniel was for "70 weeks," and up until now we have only discussed 69 of these weeks. After the completion of the 69th week there has been a gap between the 69th and the 70th week that has lasted almost 2000 years. It sounds pretty strange that God would stop His time clock and allow an almost 2000 year break in action to occur. Amazingly, this is not the only time that God has dealt with His people in a 490 year span that was not exactly contiguous.[28]

For example, the time span between the birth of Abraham and the exodus of the Israelites to Egypt totaled of 505 years.[29] For 15 years however, Abraham was not walking according to the leading of the Spirit, but was walking according to the flesh. During this time Ishmael was conceived.[30] If you subtract these 15 years from the total of 505 years you find that God dealt with His people from the promise given to Abraham to the birth of the nation over a 490 year time span. This may sound a little contrived, but wait. From the time of the exodus to the completion of the temple was 601 years. Remarkably, if you subtract the years that the entire nation of Israel was in servitude to other nations during the times of the judges — a total of 111 years, then this time period was also 490 years![31] As fantastic as it sounds, for a third time beginning at the time of the temple completion in 1005 B.C. to the decree of Artexerxes in Nehemiah 2: 1 (which happens to be the starting point for Daniel's 70 weeks) is 560 years. If you subtract the 70 years of Babylonian captivity from 560 years, you again have a 490 year time period in which God has dealt with his people! It seems that when Israel is either in apostasy or in captivity out of the land, God's time clock stops, and that God deals with His people in cycles of 70 times 7 years. By the way, this is why Judah was sent into captivity for 70 years. Judah had failed to keep the Sabbath year and let the land lay fallow for 70 Sabbatical cycles.[32] This is very interesting in light of the fact that Jesus said that we should forgive one another not only seven times, but **"seventy times seven"**[33] — the same number of times God had forgiven Judah for her sin before sending her into the Babylonian captivity.

After the crucifixion of Christ, Israel was in a state of apostasy as they had rejected the Messiah. Furthermore, after A.D. 70 they were not only in captivity, but were scattered to the nations.[34] This is the reason it is so exciting to see the nation of Israel back in its biblical land. Could it be that God's time clock is about to resume? If so, exciting times are ahead because apparently once God's time-piece is restarted there is only "one week" (seven years) left until the "end of the age."

In case you still doubt this notion that there has been a gap of time between the 69th and 70th week lets take another look at verse 26. Immediately following the line **"Messiah shall be cut off but not for himself"** we find the phrase **"and the people of the prince who is to come shall destroy the city in the sanctuary."** From history we know that there was at least 38 years between the time of Christ's sacrifice and the destruction of the Temple and the city of Jerusalem in 70 A.D., indicating an obvious time gap. This gap continues through to this day.

Based on the fact that there has been a "timeout" in God's clock, many theologians, mostly those who hold to the premillennial viewpoint, have erroneously postulated that during this "time-out" God has turned His attention away from Israel, and has instead turned His attention to the "church." This belief is called "Dispensationalist Theology" and is the basis for believing that Christ will gather His church before the 70th week of Daniel. Incredibly, there is not a single bit of solid scriptural backing for this line of thinking. Implicit in dispensationalist theology is the notion that God was surprised by the Jew's rejection of the Messiah, and so He turned His back on the Jewish people and His Face toward the gentile church. We will see as this book unfolds, nothing could be further from the truth! In fact, when we realize that there have been other sets of "490 year cycles" (or 70 weeks) during which God dealt with Israel as noted above, and that in none of the other cycles did God turn his back on His chosen people and turn His attention to another people, we realize that dispensational theology is built on a weak foundation of fanciful thinking. As the chapters that follow unfold, a more accurate presentation of the elect of God will be presented, one that is not based on the notion that God has forgotten His promises to Israel.

The Final Seven Years

Verse 27 picks up the action of the 70th week, "**then he shall confirm a covenant with many for one week; but in the middle of the week he shall bring an end to sacrifice and offering. And on the wings of abominations shall be one who makes desolate, even until the consummation which is determined, is poured out on the desolate.**"

During this last seven years, God will finish his dealings with sinful man and will "**bring in ever everlasting righteousness, and seal up vision and prophecy, and anoint the most holy.**" (vs.24) In Revelation 12, a three and a half-year time period is spoken of and correlates with the last half of this seven year time period. This second half of the 70th week correlates with the time period after "**but in the middle of the week he shall bring an end to sacrifice and offering**" in Daniel 9:27 and is commonly referred to as the time of "Great Tribulation." Jesus makes reference to this time of Great Tribulation in Matthew 24:15. "**Therefore when you see the abomination of desolation, spoken of by Daniel the prophet...**"

The "**one who shall confirm a covenant with many**" at the beginning of verse 27 is believed by most scholars to be the Antichrist.

Daniel's 70th Week

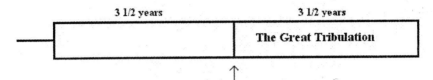

The Abomination of Desolation occurs at
the midpoint of this 7 year time period.

When will this 70th week begin? While no one knows for sure, we do know that certain things must happen before the 70th week can start. First of all, Israel cannot be in captivity. For over 1900 years Israel was scattered among the nations. The regathering of the Jews to Israel in 1948 ushered in exciting times since an Israelite presence in the land is apparently a prerequisite for God's time clock to resume. We notice also in verse 27 that "sacrifice and offerings" are taking place. This indicates the resumption of temple worship by the Jews. Strictly speaking, the temple does not have to be rebuilt *before* the 70th week of Daniel can begin; however, sometime during the 70th week animal sacrifice will be resumed, presumably in a rebuilt temple, although technically it could be in a portable tabernacle as well.

These facts make what is going on in Jerusalem these days of profound interest. The whole world is watching with intense anxiety what happens in Jerusalem. In fact, the low-level war that has been going on between the Israelis and Palestinians over the past few years began when Ariel Sharon visited the Temple Mount. The political tension surrounding Jerusalem is fulfillment of Zechariah 12: 2-3 **"behold, I will make Jerusalem a cup of reeling to all the surrounding peoples, when they lay siege against Judah and Jerusalem. And it shall happen in that day that I will make Jerusalem a very heavy stone for all peoples; all who would heave it away will surely be cut in pieces, though all nations of the earth are gathered against it."**

Daniel 9:27 indicates there will be a covenant that will last for "one week." This *is* the 70th week of Daniel, and so we can look for a seven year covenant sometime in the future that will indicate that God's time clock has once again resumed. This will be the "covenant with death"[35] between the Antichrist and the State of Israel. In light of the present situation in the Middle East, this could occur at any moment. Tensions are very high and the entire world's attention is focused on the Jerusalem problem. Even Muslims are looking for one who would come in and establish peace. The problem is — they are looking for the wrong guy. It is fascinating that the Olso accord was a seven year treaty, setting precedent in the future for another seven year pact. Wouldn't WWIII be a grand opportunity for the Antichrist to burst on the scene, seemingly with all the answers?

The Day of the Lord

Another very important concept pertinent to biblical prophecy is that of the "Day of the Lord." The Day of the Lord is spoken of in the Old and New Testament as a time in which God will pour out His wrath on the "inhabitants of the earth," and will establish His 1000 year kingdom. The term "day" when used in the context of "the Day of the Lord" is not speaking of a single 24-hour day; it is referring to the entire time period of the establishment of the kingdom of the Messiah. As proof that this time period is not a 24-hour day we can look at a few of the "Day of the Lord" passages and see that the events that take place during these passages could not possibly occur in a single 24-hour period. The establishment of the Day of the Lord will be the most awesome event this world has ever seen, and there is no way to overstate its magnitude. Perhaps you have been in a church meeting and have heard the church body cheer with excitement at the announcement that the Lord would be coming back soon. Yes, His return is something to anticipate with great excitement. However, after taking a look at what the Scripture says about this matter, you will agree that we ought to be a little more sober in our approach. This day will be a terrible and dark day for many. Let us see what the Scripture says:

"Woe to you who desire of the day of the LORD! For what good is the day of the LORD to you? It will be darkness, and not light. It will be as though a man fled from a lion and a bear met him! Or as though he went into the house, leaned his hand on the wall, and a serpent bit him. Is not the day of the LORD darkness, and not light? Is it not very dark, with no brightness in it?" Amos 5: 16-20

"Wail, for the day of the LORD is at hand! It will come as destruction from the Almighty. Therefore all hands will be limp, every man's heart will melt, and they will be afraid. Pangs and sorrow will take hold of them; they will be in pain as a woman in childbirth; they will be amazed at one another; their faces will be like flames. Behold, the day of the LORD comes, cruel, with both wrath and fierce anger, to lay the land desolate; and He will destroy its sinners from it. For the stars of heaven and the constellations will not give their light; the sun will be darkened in its going forth, and the moon will not cause its light to shine." Isaiah 13:6-10.

"The great day of the LORD is near; it is near and hastens quickly. The noise of the day of the LORD is bitter; there the mighty men shall cry out. That day is a day of wrath, a day of trouble and distress, a day of devastation and desolation, a day of darkness and gloominess, a day of clouds and thick darkness, a day of trumpet and alarm against the fortified cities and against the high towers. I will bring distress upon man, and they shall walk like blind men, because they have sinned against the LORD; their blood shall be poured out like dust, and their flesh like refuse. Neither their silver nor their gold shall be able to deliver them in the day of the LORD's wrath; but the whole land shall be devoured by the fire of his jealousy, for he will make speedy riddance of all those who dwell in the land." Zephaniah 1: 14-18.

"But the day of the Lord will come as a thief in the night, in which the heavens will pass away with a great noise, and the elements will melt with fervent heat; both the earth and the works that are in it will be burned up." 2 Peter 3:10

"And I will show wonders in the heavens and in the earth; blood and fire and pillars of smoke. The sun shall be turned into darkness, and the moon into blood, before the coming of the great an awesome day of the LORD." Joel 2:30-31.

"Multitudes, multitudes in the valley of decision! For the day of the LORD is near in the valley of decision. The sun and moon will go dark and the stars will diminish their brightness. For the LORD also will roar from Zion, and utter his voice from Jerusalem; the heavens and earth will shake; but the LORD will be a shelter for His people and the strength of the children of Israel." Joel 3: 14-16

There are many other passages in the Old Testament that describe this time that we called the "Day of the Lord," but the above should give the reader a feel for what the Day of the Lord is about.[36] As you can see from the passages above this will be a terrible and awesome time, and my feeble efforts to describe it pale compared to what scripture says. This time is also known as "The last day," and "The day of wrath." From the above passages we can learn a few things: The Day of the Lord will be preceded by signs in heavens. The sun will go dark, the moon will not give its light and will become as blood, and the stars will fall from the heavens. Furthermore, this will be a "Day" of tremendous fear for those who dwell on the earth. To those who dwell on the earth, the day will come as a shock, they will not be expecting what is coming, and it will come as "a thief in the night."

Thankfully, our citizenship is in heaven, and we are not considered as those "who dwell upon the earth." The next few passages will be a great comfort if you know to whom you belong: Speaking of the Day of the Lord... "Seek the LORD, all you meek of the earth, who have upheld His justice. Seek righteousness, seek humility. It may be that you will be hidden in the day of the LORD's anger." Zephaniah 2: 3

"Come, my people, enter your chambers, and shut your doors behind you; hide yourself, as it were, for a little moment, until the indignation is past. For behold, the LORD comes out of his place to punish the inhabitants of the earth for their iniquity; the earth will also disclose her blood, and will no more cover her slain." Isaiah 26:20-21.

"For you yourselves know perfectly that the day of the LORD so comes as a thief in the night. For when they say, "peace and safety!" Then sudden destruction comes upon them, as labor pains upon a pregnant woman. And they shall not escape. **But you, brethren are not in darkness, so that this day should overtake you as a thief. You are all sons of light and sons of the day. We are not of the night nor of darkness…For God did not appoint us to wrath, but to obtain salvation through our LORD Jesus Christ, who died for us, that whether we wake or sleep, we should live together with him." 1Thes 5: 2-10**

Believers are not appointed unto wrath! We do have reason to rejoice, but when we look at what is about to befall the whole Earth, should we not approach this issue with the utmost seriousness? We need to be absolutely sure which side we are on and what it is that places us on the side of the Lord.

The "Day of the Lord" *is* Christ's second coming. It is the time in which God will pour out His wrath on the entire earth. It initiates His kingdom that will last 1000 years.

Let us now take a look at this 1000 year kingdom. First of all, how do we know that this kingdom will last 1000 years? As discussed in chapter 1 of this book, if we take Revelation chapter 20 at face value we cannot escape the conclusion that Christ will reign for 1000 years. The Old Testament does not expressly say that this kingdom will last for 1000 years, but there are some clues. First, we will establish that His kingdom will last for many years. Now, take a look again at the following passage in Zechariah chapter 14:16 **"and it shall come to pass that everyone who is left of all the nations which came against Jerusalem shall go up from year-to-year to worship the King, the LORD of Hosts, and to keep the**

Feast of Tabernacles." Based on the phrase "year to year" we can gather that for years (plural) following the Day of the Lord, a kingdom will be set up with its headquarters in Jerusalem. Interestingly, there will be a requirement that the Feasts of God are kept. A question worth pondering is this: why does God require us to keep the Feast of Tabernacles during the millennial kingdom, but does not require us to keep it during our time? We will attempt to address this question in a later chapter.

We see some indication that the millennial kingdom will last for one thousand years when we take a careful look at the Sabbath day. Have you ever considered the significance of the Sabbath? Why did God create the world in six days, and rest on the 7th? Couldn't the Creator have just spoken everything into existence all at once? God has appointed days and festivals not only to remind us of the past, but to show us the future.

"For whatever things were written before were written for our learning, that we through the patience and comfort of the Scriptures might have hope." Romans 15:4

We see this in the Passover, which began as a celebration of the exodus of the Israelites from Egypt. Jesus perfectly fulfilled the Passover when *on* the Feast of Passover He became the Passover lamb and was slain for all of us. He fulfilled the Feast of the Firstfruits when on that very feast day He became *the* First Fruit upon His resurrection.

The Feast of Weeks some 50 days later was a God ordained festival remembering the occasion that God gave Moses the "Law" (Torah) from Mt. Sinai. Prophetically speaking, the Feast of Weeks (also known as the day of Pentecost) was fulfilled when the Spirit of God descended upon man on that very day, and the Law was written on the hearts of men by the power of the Holy Spirit.[37]

The weekly celebration of Sabbath seems to have an as yet unfulfilled prophetic meaning as well. It seems that God is planning to deal with the redemption of man in seven one-thousand year long "days." Both in Psalms 90:4 and in 2 Peter 3:8 we are told that for God, a single day is as 1000 years.

"For a thousand years in Your sight are like yesterday when it is past" Psalm 90:4

"But, beloved, do not forget this one thing, that with the Lord one day is as a thousand years, and a thousand yeas as one day." 2 Peter 3:8

Incredibly, biblical chronology indicates that we are somewhere near the end of 6000 years since Adam was created. Could it be that as we enter the Sabbath millennium, this will be the millennium Christ establishes Himself as King and reigns upon the Earth?

God's people were instructed in the Ten Commandments to remember the Sabbath and to keep it set apart (the meaning of Holy). The significance of the Sabbath is deeper than that Christ became our Sabbath. Christ is indeed our Sabbath rest! But He will reign again for 1000 years in the millennium of rest. This will be an unparalleled time of peace and prosperity! Isaiah chapter 2, Joel 3:18-21, Zephaniah 3:14-20, Amos 9:11-15, Isaiah 2:1-4, are messianic prophecies in the Old Testament that speak of the Sabbath millennium, when Christ will reign and true peace will be restored to the Earth.

In Hosea 6:1-2, we find a similar concept that seems to confirm this idea: **"After two days he will revive us; on the third day he will raise us up, that we may live in his sight."** Could this be a way of saying that after 2000 years (2 days as seen by God) God will raise up the nation of Israel and they will live in His sight? Astoundingly, two-thousand 360 day years from the time of Jesus' crucifixion brings us somewhere in the neighborhood 2003/2004.

Could the current groundswell of interest among Christians for things "Hebraic" be nothing more that fulfillment of biblical prophecy?

The Great Tribulation

The Great Tribulation is a term that Jesus coined in Matthew 24:21. *Strictly speaking*, the time of the Great Tribulation will begin at the midpoint of the 70th week of Daniel, and last until the "Day of the Lord." We will go into more detail concerning the Great Tribulation in chapter 12. Briefly, this time period will be a time of unprecedented hardship for God's people. It will be a time when family members betray one another, and many people will be put to death for their faith.

CHAPTER 3

"So what difference does it make anyway?"

"My people are destroyed for a lack of knowledge." Hosea 4:6

"Therefore my people have gone into captivity, because they have no knowledge; their honorable men are famished, and their multitude dried up with thirst. Therefore Sheol has enlarged itself and opened its mouth beyond measure; their glory and their multitude and their pomp, and he who is jubilant, shall descend into it. People shall be brought down, each man shall be humbled, and the eyes of the lofty shall be humbled. But the LORD of host shall be exalted in judgment, and God who is holy shall be set apart in righteousness" Isaiah 5:13-16

So far, we have tried to steer clear of most controversial issues as they relate to biblical prophecy. Most biblical scholars who take the Bible seriously and interpret the Word at face value are in agreement concerning the things that were written about in chapter 2. In this chapter we will explore in more detail the differences between rapture viewpoints.

Simply put, differences between one's rapture viewpoints have to do with the timing of the so-called "rapture."

In point of fact, the word rapture is not even in the Bible, it is a word that has been adapted from the Latin Vulgate, which uses the word *Rapere* in I Thessalonians 4:15-17 for "snatched away." I prefer to think of the "rapture" as **"our gathering together to Him"** — a more scriptural designation taken from 2 Thessalonians 2:1.

As stated in chapter one, the pre-tribulation rapture view believes that the "snatching away" of the saints to our Lord Jesus Christ will occur sometime before the 70th week of Daniel begins. Central to their viewpoint is the idea of imminence — the notion that Christ could possibly return at *any moment*. It is for this reason that you will occasionally see bumper stickers that proclaim *"Caution: in case of rapture this car will be unoccupied!"* While I certainly agree that this would be great if it were true, it just cannot be proven *explicitly* from scripture. The pre-trib viewpoint hinges on the notion that Christ could return at any moment, but we will prove in some detail later, that this idea simply is not biblically sound. "Proof texts" for the pretribulation rapture position include:

"Much more then, having now been justified by His blood, we shall be saved from wrath through Him." Romans 5:9

"And to wait for His Son from heaven, whom He raised from the dead, even Jesus who delivers us from the wrath to come." I Thessalonians 1:10

"For God did not appoint us to wrath, but to obtain salvation through our Lord Jesus Christ." I Thessalonians 5:9

Notice that the main point of these verses is that we are to be kept from *God's Wrath*. Notice also what these verses don't say... they *don't say* that we will be kept from persecution or from tribulation. To the contrary, many places in the scripture seem to indicate that those alive at the end of the age will have to endure some very difficult times.

"Then they will deliver you up to tribulation and kill you, and you will be hated by all nations for My name's sake." Matthew 24:9

"And you will be hated by all for My name's sake But he who endures to the end shall be saved." Mark 13:13

"It was granted to him to make war with the saints and to overcome them." Revelation 13:7

Throughout the Bible it has never been God's style to keep His people from hardship, but instead we often see that God tests His people through various trials just as He did during the wilderness wanderings under the leadership of Moses.

Post-tribulationists believe that Christ will return at the end of the 70th week of Daniel. There are problems with this view. Namely, the above verses indicate that God will spare us from his wrath. A careful look back at Daniel 9:25-27 shows us in vs. 27 that sometime after the halfway point of the 7 years **"even until the consummation, which is determined is poured out on the desolate"** (a reference to the Day of the Lord, the time of God's wrath). If God's wrath happens *during* the 70th week (as implied in the above verse), and we are to be *spared* from Gods wrath, then the "rapture" cannot take place *after* the 70th week.

Despite this point, post-tribulationists will mention the following verses as proof texts of their position. For the sake of clarity the key portions of the verses have been underlined:

**"For then there will be <u>great tribulation</u>, such as has not been since the beginning of the world until this time, no, nor ever shall be. And unless those days were shortened, no flesh would be saved, but for the elect's sake those days will be shortened. Then if anyone says to you 'Look, there is the Christ!' or 'There!' do not believe it. <u>For false christs and false prophets will arise and show great signs and wonders to deceive, if possible, even the elect.</u>" Matthew 24:21-24. And following...
"Immediately after the tribulation of those days the sun will be darkened, and the moon will not give its light; the stars will fall from heaven and the powers of the heavens will be shaken. Then the sign of the Son of Man will appear in heaven, and then all the tribes of the Earth will mourn, and they will see the Son**

of Man coming on the clouds of heaven with power and great glory. And he will send his angels with a great sound of a trumpet, and they will gather together his elect from the four winds, from one end of the heaven to the other." Matthew 24: 29-31

"Now brethren, concerning the coming of our Lord Jesus Christ and our gathering together to him, we ask you, not to be soon shaken in mind or troubled, either by spirit or by word or by letter, as if from us, as though the day of Christ had come. <u>Let no one deceive you by any means; for that Day will not come unless the falling away comes first, and the man of sin is revealed, the son of perdition, who opposes and exalts himself above all that is called God, or that is worshiped, so that he sits as God in the temple of God, showing himself that he is God</u>." 2 Thessalonians 2:1-4.

"So they worshiped the dragon who gave authority to the beast; and they worshiped the beast, saying, 'Who is like the beast? Who is able to make War with him?' And he was given a mouth speaking great things and blasphemies, and he was given authority to continue for 42 months. He then opened his mouth in blasphemy against God, to blaspheme his name, his tabernacles, and those who dwell in heaven. <u>It was granted to him to make War with the Saints and to overcome them.</u> And authority was given him over every tribe, tongue, and nation. All who dwell on the earth will worship him, whose names have not been written in the Book of Life of the Lamb slain from the foundation of the world." Revelation 13: 4-8

These verses, and others, certainly do indicate that there will be "saints" or the "elect" present during the last days, and so they argue against a pre-trib rapture, and contradict the notion that the church will be "out of here" when the trouble starts. Notice though, that these post-trib proof texts do not mention Saints or the elect being present during *God's Wrath*. The post-tribulation view is very similar to the prewrath view in that both have God's elect going through a measure of Great Tribulation. We will take a closer look

at what distinguishes the post-trib position from the prewr
in chapter 12.

Pre-tribulationists try to skirt the issues raised by the above verses
by claiming that the term "elect" in these verses refer to the Jewish
converts who have come to know Christ *after* the rapture. They do
this by applying faulty Dispensationalist theology mentioned earlier.
The fact is, every time the "elect" are spoken of in the New Testament, it is referring to the believer in Christ, the true church, and so it
makes no sense to call the elect in certain portions of scripture (the
portions they don't like) the "Jews after the rapture," and then turn
around and claim that the elect in the rest of the New Testament
represents the "church." Actually, there is more to this matter, much
more, and it happens to be one of the main issues addressed in this
book. But that will have to wait for later.

The Restrainer

Pre-tribulationists also will point to 2 Thessalonians 2:6-8 in
support of the view that they will not be here on the Earth after the
Antichrist is revealed, **"And now you know what is restraining,
that he may be revealed in his own time. For the mystery of
lawlessness is already at work; only he who now restrains will
do so until he is taken out of the way. And then the lawless one
will be revealed, whom the Lord will consume with the breath
of his mouth and destroy with the brightness of his coming."**

Pretribulationists believe that the Holy Spirit is the **"one who
restrains,"** and the "lawless one" is the Antichrist. They claim that
at the time of the rapture, the Holy Spirit is removed from the earth
with the saints (at the time of the rapture), and thus the son of perdition (another name for the Antichrist) will be able to reveal himself.
Thoughtful consideration of this view reveals a couple of problems.
First, if the Holy Spirit has been removed from the earth, how can
anyone left be converted? We know that it is the Holy Spirit that
draws us to the Lord. So how do the post rapture Jewish converts
come to know their Messiah? Secondly, since when has it been the
work of the Holy Spirit to restrain evil? There is simply no other
evidence of this in Scripture.

Who then is the restrainer? We will take a look at this question in some detail, because it relates to the pretribulation argument. In Daniel 12:1, we are given prophecy concerning the end times. **"At that time Michael shall stand up, the great prince who stands watch over the sons of your people; and then there shall be a time of trouble, such as never was since there was a nation,[38] even to that time. And at that time your people shall be delivered, every one who is found written in the book."**

The Hebrew word translated stand up in this verse is Amad.[39] Amad can also be translated *arise* or *stand still*. In this context, we understand then that Michael will "stand still" in his work on earth (as the restrainer) and will "arise" from earth and go into heaven where he will battle in heaven with other angels and will cast Satan out of heaven once and for all just as described by John in the book of Revelation: **"And war broke out in heaven: Michael and his angels fought with the dragon; and the dragon and his angels fought, but did not prevail, nor was a place found for them in heaven any longer. So the great dragon was cast out, that serpent of old, called the devil and Satan, who deceives the whole world; he was cast to the earth, and his angels were cast out with him." Revelation 12: 7-9** For further confirmation that Michael is the restrainer, take a look at Daniel 11:21, **"But I will tell you what is noted in the Scripture of Truth. No one upholds me against these, except Michael your prince."**

Why it Matters

So why does it matter? *What is the big deal?* Well, here is the problem, look carefully again at the above verses cited as proof texts for the post-tribulation position. They indicate that Satan will be given power to *overcome* the saints. This is evident in other verses as well.[40] It is bad enough that the Word of God is indicating that some of the elect will be physically overcome by the powers of darkness, but it is much worse when one considers that the scriptures indicate that a "falling away" or an "apostasy" will occur.

As pointed out in the introduction, Matthew 24:12 indicates that the *Agape* of many will grow cold! *This should alarm you!* If it doesn't it is because you do not understand the implications. Love is at the center of God's two greatest commandments — To Love the Lord your God with all your heart and to Love your neighbor as yourself. If the God imparted Love within us grows cold, then we are lost!

"Beloved, let us love one another, for love is of God; and everyone who loves is born of God and know God. He who does not love does not know God, for God is love." 1 John 4:7-8

Scripture explicitly says: "the *Agape* of *many* will grow cold." It is an act of sheer denial to think this couldn't happen to you. As much as we would like to ignore the facts, an honest appraisal of the word of God reveals that *we are all at risk!*

Those who believe that they will be raptured away before the 70th week of Daniel simply do not believe they will be around during that terrible time and so they make themselves vulnerable. In fact, I have on several occasions heard pre-trib preachers say "We don't need to worry about who the Antichrist is because we will not be here when he is revealed." This is in spite of Revelation 3:18 that says, **"Here is wisdom, Let him who has understanding calculate the number of the beast, for it is the number of a man: His number is 666."** Why would God give us this information, pointing out that it is wisdom, if we were not going to be here?

As pointed out earlier, pre-tribulationists argue this verse was meant for the remnant Jewish believer converted *after* the rapture and does not apply to the New Testament Christian. Can you see the folly of that kind of logic? If one believes that they are "safe," they may fall for anything and indeed, some already have. We must sound the alarm in this area because the Word of God makes it plain..."*the Agape of many will grow cold.*" The Gospel of Mark elaborates on this same time period, **"Brother will betray brother to death, and a father his child: and children will rise up against parents and cause them to be put to death. And you will be hated by all for My name's sake. But he who endures to the end shall be saved." Mark 13:12-13**

Heads up!

In sports, you will occasionally hear players or bystanders shout "Heads up!" to alert others of a wayward ball. In Luke 21:28, Jesus tells us **"Now when these things begin to happen, look up and lift up you heads, because your redemption draws near."** What follows is most definitely a "heads up." It is with the *utmost love and compassion* that I write these next few thoughts.

If you are an amillenialist or a preterist, you have allegorized away the word of God, and you risk being caught unaware, you are apparently oblivious to the explicit warnings of scripture. If you believe in a pre-tribulation "rapture," you could be lulled asleep by the notion that we will all be "beamed up" before the Antichrist appears and begins to prevail over the Saints.

God's Word clearly indicates that Satan will overcome many[41] in the last days and that the agape of many will grow cold. Consider this, what is Satan *really* after? He knows the difference between the physical and the spiritual. He doesn't want to kill us physically only to have us live forever in heaven — *Satan would rather see us dead spiritually* — eternally separated from the One who loves us so much that He gave us His only begotten Son.[42]

Most of the church today is asleep at the wheel. Since we are told that we don't have to worry about the future, the Antichrist, and the apostasy — we worry about earthly things! We worry about the payment on our new car, our house, the economy, and our kid's soccer game. We self righteously talk about politics, oblivious to the bigger picture. We are appalled that the Ten Commandments are taken out of our schools and government buildings, yet we have taken them out of our churches! We glibly say, "He that is in me is greater than he who is in the world." Listen, my brother! If we can't even resist the Devil and avoid looking upon a woman with eyes filled with lust, how in the world do you think we will be able to withstand the evil one in the day of great deception? And my dear sister! If you can't resist the Devil today in your sin of gossip and if you can't respect your husband as the word of God instructs but instead hold your husband in contempt, what makes you think that you will be able to stand firm in that day? Teenagers! If the minute you are away from your parent's watchful eyes you are scheming all kinds of lawlessness, you are weak and will not be able to resist the wiles of the Devil!

Indeed, He that is in you is greater than he who is in the world — the question becomes then, is He in you? Or are you "in the world?"

"Because you say 'I am rich, I have become wealthy, and have need of nothing' — and do not know that you are wretched, miserable, poor, blind, and naked." Revelation 3:17

We are a lawless generation; many of us are simply not mature enough to resist the falling away.[43] Corporately the church is *not* spiritually prepared for what is about to happen to the whole world.[44]

Today's typical New Testament Christians are *carnally minded* with minds that are set upon things of this world. We want earthly blessings, and ministries that cater to those who are carnally minded *abound*.

"For those who live according to the flesh set their minds on the things of the flesh, but those who live according to the spirit, the things of the spirit. For to be carnally minded is death, but to be spiritually minded is life and peace. Because the carnal mind is enmity against God; for it is not subject to the laws of God, nor indeed can it be. So then, those who are in the flesh cannot please God. But you are not in the flesh but in the Spirit, if indeed the Spirit of God dwells in you. Now if anyone does not have the Spirit of Christ, he is not His." Romans 8:5-9

It is quite possible that the "falling away" has already begun. In chapter 8 we will take a hard look at the state of the church today. For now, we need to continue to build the case for the prewrath rapture of the church, the topic of the next chapter.

CHAPTER 4

The Prewrath "gathering together"

*L*et us now take a look at the prewrath viewpoint. This chapter is by no means intended to be an exhaustive analysis of the prewrath rapture view. Rather, this is a simple presentation of scripture that will allow the reader to understand this position that is not widely known among the body of Christ today. We will use Matthew chapter 24, Jesus' so called 'Olivet Discourse' as our primary text. We will compare scripture with scripture and let the word speak for itself.

In Matthew 24:1-2, the disciples were walking with Jesus at the temple and marveling at its magnificence. Jesus informed his disciples that **"Not one stone shall be left here upon another that shall not be thrown down."** The disciples then approached Him privately and asked Him **"When will these things be? And what will be the sign of Your coming, and the end of the age?"** Notice that the disciples assumed that the events they were inquiring of occurred simultaneously. The amazing answer than Jesus gives therefore had to be what we will refer to as a near/far prophecy. Some of the elements of this prophecy were indeed fulfilled in A.D. 70 as mentioned briefly in chapter One. This was an answer to the first part of the disciple's question, the question concerning the destruction of the Temple. Interestingly, when it burned in 70 A.D., gold from the Temple melted and ran down into the cracks between the stones. Roman soldiers literally fulfilled Christ's words exactly when they dismantled the Temple stone by stone, throwing each stone down in an effort to get at the gold. As already discussed, however, much of what Jesus foretold has not yet happened, thus the "far" application of Christ's prophecy unquestionably refers to the time of His second coming.

In order to rightly understand this portion of scripture, it is helpful at this time to compare Matthew chapter 24 with its parallel passage found in Revelation chapter 6. Here the Lamb of God (Christ) has been given a scroll that only He is able to open. The scroll has seven seals that must be opened. You can picture this scroll as a long document that has been rolled up with a line of seven individual seals (like the wax seals one would put their 'seal' or stamp their ring into) spaced across the visible end of the rolled up document:

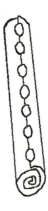

As the Lamb opens each of the seals, certain judgments are allowed to come forth upon the earth. While it does appear that some of the events in the seal judgments, namely the first four seals, have been happening since time immemorial, it seems from the details of Revelation 6 that there will be a major crescendo in the intensity of the judgments just before the Day of the Lord.

Let's take a look at these seals one by one and see how they relate to Matthew chapter 24. The following table will be helpful in comparing the two different accounts. In order to understand the prewrath viewpoint it is essential to understand the information presented below and I cannot overstate the importance of understanding the parallel between these two sections of scripture. Notice how Matthew 24 *precisely* corresponds to Revelation 6.

Comparison between Matthew 24 and the Seals of Revelation 6

The Seals	Some commentary-(read the outside columns first)	Matthew's account
The first seal – Rev. 6:1-2 **"Now I saw when the Lamb opened one of the seals; and I heard one of the four living creatures saying with a voice like thunder, "Come and see." And I looked, and behold, a white horse. He who sat on it had a bow; and a crown was given to him, and he went out conquering and to conquer."**	Don't make the mistake of confusing the rider of the white horse for Christ... he is the antichrist. His bow without arrows probably indicates that he will conquer by political intrigue and by threats. It is interesting that he is given a crown – he is given his authority for a season.	Matt. 24:4-5 – **"Take heed that no one deceives you. For many will come in My name, saying, 'I am the Christ,' and will deceive many."**
The Second Seal – Rev. 6:3-4 **"When He opened the second seal, I heard the second living creature saying, "Come and see." Another horse, fiery red, went out. And it was granted to the one who sat on it to take peace from the earth, and that people should kill one another; and there was given to him a great sword."**	The false sense of peace brought by the antichrist will not last very long. With the opening of the 2nd seal, war breaks out. This will likely be an obvious World War.	Matt 24:6-7a **"And you will hear of wars and rumors of wars. See that you are not troubled; for all these things must come to pass, but the end is not yet. For nation will rise against nation, and kingdom against kingdom."**
The Third Seal – Rev 6:5-6 **"When He opened the third seal, I heard the third living creature say, "Come and see." So I looked, and behold, a black horse, and he who sat on it had a pair of scales in his hand. And I heard a voice in the midst of the four living creatures saying, "A quart of wheat for a denarius, and three**	A Denarius can be thought of as one days pay for a 'working man'. So this implies that because of the scarcity of food, a man will have to labor all day long for just enough food to feed his family. This is already happening in some parts of the world today.	Matt 24:7b **"and famine"**

quarts of barley for a denarius; and do not harm the oil and the wine."		
The Fourth Seal – Rev. 7-8 "When He opened the fourth seal, I heard the voice of the fourth living creature saying, "Come and see." So I looked, and behold, a pale horse. And the name of him who sat on it was Death, and Hades followed with him. And power was given to them over a fourth of the earth, to kill with sword, with hunger, with death, and by the beasts of the earth."	Disease is common in the aftermath of war.	Matt 24:7c-8 "**pestilences, and earthquakes in various places. All these are the beginnings of sorrows.**"
The Fifth Seal – Rev 6:9-11 "**When He opened the fifth seal, I saw under the altar the souls of those who had been slain for the word of God and for the testimony which they held. And they cried with a loud voice, saying, "How long, O Lord, holy and true, until You judge and avenge our blood on those who dwell on the earth?" Then a white robe was given to each of them; and it was said to them that they should rest a little while longer, until both the number of their fellow servants and their brethren, who would be killed as they were, was completed.**"	Notice, this happens before our gathering together to Him, (which occurs between the sixth and seventh seal). -Jesus points out in Matt. That the Agape of many will grow cold. -This could be the "falling away spoken of by Paul in 2 Thes. 2:3. We need to be grounded in the truth in order to avoid deception -This is the Great Tribulation. If we are alive during this time, we will undoubtedly see horrendous atrocities, as this time will be worse than any time…ever. (This includes the holocaust!) -Satan will try to deceive even the elect "if possible" – here is why we need to make our election sure! It is no wonder Paul admonished us to "work out our salvation with fear and trembling"	Matt 24:9-13 "**Then they will deliver you up to tribulation and kill you, and you will be hated by all nations for My name's sake. And then many will be offended, will betray one another, and will hate one another. Then many false prophets will rise up and deceive many. And because lawlessness will abound, the love of many will grow cold. But he who endures to the end shall be saved.**"…"**For then there will be a time of Tribulation, such as has not been since the beginning of the world until this time, no, nor ever shall be**" vs. 21…"**For false christs and false prophets will**"

		rise and show great signs and wonders to deceive, if possible even the elect."
The Sixth Seal – Rev 6:12-17 **"I looked when He opened the sixth seal, and behold, there was a great earthquake; and the sun became black as sackcloth of hair, and the moon became like blood. And the stars of heaven fell to the earth, as a fig tree drops its late figs when it is shaken by a mighty wind. Then the sky receded as a scroll when it is rolled up, and every mountain and island was moved out of its place. And the kings of the earth, the great men, the rich men and commanders, the mighty men, every slave and every free man, hid themselves in the caves and the rocks of the mountains, and said to the mountains and rocks "Fall on us and hide us from the face of Him who sits on the throne and from the wrath of the Lamb! For the great day of His wrath has come, and who is able to stand?"**	Compare this to the Day of the Lord passages in Joel2:31,**"The sun shall be turned into darkness, and the moon into blood, Before the coming of the great and awesome day of the Lord."** – notice how the signs in the heavens immediately precede the day of the Lord – which is also know as the day of God's Wrath – and remember... we are **"not appointed unto wrath"** as noted in 1 Thes 1:10. If the "Day of Wrath is the very next thing on the agenda, then we should see the "rapture" as the very next event!	Matt 24:29-30 **"Immediately after the tribulation of those days the sun will be darkened, and the moon will not give its light; the stars will fall from heaven, and the powers of the heavens will be shaken. Then the sign of the Son of Man will appear in heaven, and then all the tribes of the earth will mourn and they will see the Son of Man coming on the clouds of heaven with power and great glory."**
*** The appearance of a great multitude in heaven! Rev7:9-10, 13-14 **"After these things I looked, and behold, a great multitude which no one could number, of all nations,**	Here it is, the gathering of the saints, the elect, to Christ. Right on time – just before the Wrath of God is poured out on the whole earth.	Matt 24:31 **"And He will send His angels with a great sound of a trumpet, and they will gather together His elect from the four winds, from one end of heaven to the**

tribes, peoples, and tongues, standing before the throne and before the Lamb, clothed with white robes, with palm branches in their hands, and crying out with a loud voice, saying, "Salvation belongs to our God who sits on the throne, and to the Lamb!"		other."
The Seventh Seal – Rev. 8 – Silence in Heaven for one half an hour, and the beginning of the trumpet judgments.	The wrath of God is so severe, that there is a collective gasp in heaven that lasts for half an hour.	

A Jigsaw Puzzle

Have you ever sat down a put a puzzle together? I am talking about the cardboard kind with about a thousand pieces. I can remember as a child putting these kinds of jigsaw puzzles together with my grandmother. Usually we would first look for the edge pieces and put these together so that the rest of the puzzle pieces could be positioned in their proper context. Putting together the prophetic word of God is not unlike assembling a jigsaw puzzle. If we are able to align certain portions of scripture and understand that these sections are discussing the same event, we can begin to build a framework for understanding other sections that also "fit" into this picture.

In this way, by realizing that Matthew 24 "fits" together with Revelation 6, and taking note that Jesus also aligns the prophecies of Daniel with the events spoken of in Matthew 24 (Matt24:15), we too can begin to "see" what the end times picture will look like. As this book progresses, we will put the puzzle together, piece by piece.

By comparing Matthew 24 with the seven seals of Revelation, we see that Christ will return for His elect just before the seventh seal, when the scroll will then be opened and God's Wrath will fall upon the world. Christ explains explicitly to us in Matthew 24 that we will be going through a time of Great Tribulation! Graphically, here is how these pieces of the puzzle come together:

Correlating Daniel's 70th Week with Revelation and Matthew 24

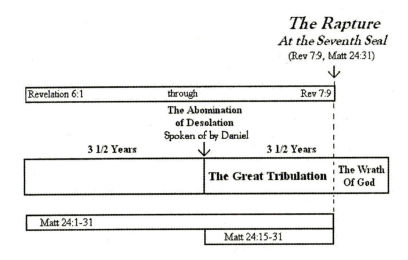

The Rapture
At the Seventh Seal
(Rev 7:9, Matt 24:31)

Simply put, Christ does not "rapture" His bride before the trouble starts, but instead He rescues her from the throws of tribulation and then with His Great wrath judges those who "dwell upon the earth." The only way to construct an end time scenario that removes the "church" from the Great Tribulation is to say that the "church" is not the "elect" mentioned in Matthew chapter 24. Unfortunately, by doing this, Bible teachers exclude themselves from those who are gathered together to Christ! Incredibly, this is exactly what pretribulationalists argue. The definition of the "elect" in Matthew 24 is of profound importance to this matter and will be discussed in much detail in chapters six and seven.

When I took a careful look at these verses for the first time and saw the correlation, I was compelled to give up my pre-tribulation beliefs. With this understanding came an important realization. I desperately wanted there to be a pre-trib rapture... but ultimately it is not what we want that matters, it is what God ordains that counts.

Graphically, here again is what the prewrath view looks like:

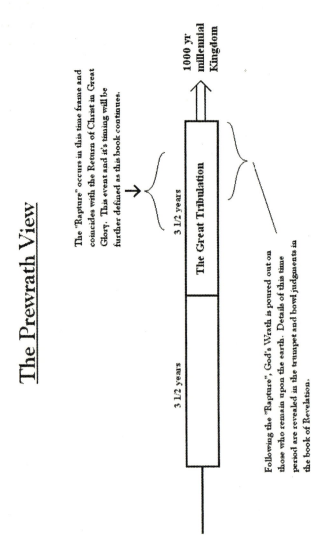

The Prewrath View

The "Rapture" occurs in this time frame and coincides with the Return of Christ in Great Glory. This event and it's timing will be further defined as this book continues.

1000 yr. millennial Kingdom

3 1/2 years

The Great Tribulation

3 1/2 years

Following the "Rapture", God's Wrath is poured out on those who remain upon the earth. Details of this time period are revealed in the trumpet and bowl judgments in the book of Revelation.

There are many details of the last days that have not yet been addressed, and have to do mainly with some of the events and characters that will show up in the last days. These include the Antichrist, the two witnesses, the 144,000 sealed from the nation Israel, the false prophet, and the woman riding the beast as well as "mystery, Babylon." A *complete* discussion of all of these important figures is beyond the scope of this book. However, in the next chapter we will touch briefly on some of these and later we will look with much interest at the identity of the Woman riding the Beast.

CHAPTER 5

More Prewrath Detail

*L*et's take a look at a few more passages from the Bible to make sure this prewrath theory is true. My favorite Old Testament passage dealing with this issue is a passage that clearly points to a prewrath position and is found in Isaiah 26:19-21:

> **"Your dead shall live; Together with my dead body they shall arise. Awake and sing, you who dwell in dust; For your dew is like the dew of herbs, and the earth shall cast out the dead. Come, My people, enter you chambers and shut your doors behind you; for a little moment, until the indignation is past. For behold, the LORD comes out of His place to punish the inhabitants of the earth for their iniquity; The earth will also disclose her blood, and will no more cover her slain."**

From this we can infer that God's Wrath will immediately follow the resurrection and the rapture — a prewrath view!

We can also infer that the resurrection will precede the rapture. Paul confirms this for us in 1 Thessalonians 4:15, **"For this we say to you by the Word of the Lord, that we who are alive and remain until the coming of the Lord will by no means precede those who are asleep."** Also, take a look at the phrase, **"enter your chambers and shut your doors behind you"** — considering the context, this reminds us of Christ's words **"My Father's house has many mansions"** in John 14:2.

Notice also what else the Prophet Isaiah has to say about the events that will occur around the time of the "Day of the Lord": **"Behold, the day of the LORD comes, cruel, with both wrath and fierce anger, to lay the land desolate; and He will destroy its sinners from it. For the stars of heaven and the constellations will not give their light; the sun will be darkened in its going forth, and the moon will not cause its light to shine." Isaiah 13:6-10.** Particularly, notice that the "stars will not give their light, the sun will be darkened, and the moon will not cause its light to shine." This is exactly in line with the accounts given by both Matthew and Joel:

"Immediately after the tribulation of those days the sun will be darkened, and the moon will not give it's light; the stars will fall from heaven and the powers of the heavens will be shaken" Matthew 24:29

"The sun shall be turned into darkness, and the moon into blood, before the coming of the great and awesome day of the LORD" Joel 2:31.

"Multitudes, multitudes in the valley of decision! For the day of the LORD is near in the valley of decision. The sun and moon will grow dark, and the stars will diminish their brightness. The LORD will roar from Zion, and utter His voice from Jerusalem; the heavens and earth will shake: but the LORD will be a shelter for His people, and the strength of the children of Israel." Joel 3:14-16

Notice how the prophecies are consistent. There will be a signs in heavens with the darkening of celestial bodies, and then the Day of the Lord will come, **"but the LORD will be a shelter for His people, and the strength of the children of Israel"** dovetailing perfectly with the prewrath position.

Shadows of God's Wrath

Throughout the Bible, we find occasions where God teaches us by examples.[45] Theologians call the study of this phenomenon "typeology." Indeed there are countless examples of "types" in scripture where events or people in Biblical history foreshadow future events or people. There are two obvious examples or types of God's wrath in the book of Genesis, the account of the Flood and the destruction of Sodom and Gomorrah.

In the Flood account, God poured out His wrath on the entire Earth saving only the "elect" — Noah and his family. Notice that Noah was invited by God to "Come" into the ark. This is very similar language to the passage in Isaiah 26 mentioned above, **"Come, my people, enter your chambers..."** The fact that God caused Noah to enter the ark seven days before the rain began to fall[46] is intriguing but does not indicate a pre-trib "gathering together" rather it confirms a prewrath event. The obvious type is this, God gathered His chosen to a safe place, and then shortly after this gathering, His wrath began to be poured out upon the earth. In the story of the destruction of Sodom and Gomorrah we see God's angels taking "righteous Lot" out of Sodom immediately prior to the pouring out of God's wrath. Again, this clearly fits the pattern of a prewrath "gathering together."

Imminent Return?

Let's consider now the notion of imminence — the belief that Jesus Christ could return at *any* moment. This notion is a cornerstone of pre-tribulation doctrine. Paul addresses this very issue in writing to the Thessalonians in 2nd Thessalonians 2:1-4. Let's take a look at this once again:

"Now brethren, concerning the coming of our Lord Jesus Christ and our gathering together to Him, we ask you, not to be soon shaken in mind or troubled, either by spirit or by word or by letter, as if from us, as though the day of Christ had come. Let no one deceive you by any means; <u>for that Day will not</u>

71

come unless the falling away comes first and the man of sin is revealed, the son of perdition, who opposes and exalts himself above all that is called God or that is worshipped, so that he sits as God in the Temple of God, showing himself that he is God."

In order to skirt around these verses, pre-tributionists believe that when Christ returns, He will return *twice*. The first time will be "in secret" for the church, and the second time will be openly. They believe that the second part of Christ's second coming is what is spoken of in Matthew 24, and here in 2 Thessalonians.

The problem with this view is that it is *simply not supported in scripture*. Jesus Christ will return *once* at the time of His second coming. To those who are in darkness, it will be a surprise. But to those who are "children of the light," His second coming will be no surprise, and it will be met with eager anticipation. First Thessalonians 5:1-11 is a section of biblical text that pre-tribulation-ists will point to as a section that purportedly demonstrates "two second comings of Christ." A careful look at this passage actually proves the opposite to be true, however. Paul is writing of a single event, *not two parts of the second coming*. This single event is seen from *two different* viewpoints: **"But concerning the times and the seasons, brethren, you have no need that I should write to you. For you yourselves know perfectly that the day of the Lord so comes as a thief in the night. For when they say, 'peace and safety!' then sudden destruction comes upon them as labor pains upon a pregnant woman. And they shall not escape. But you, brethren, are not in darkness, so that this day should overtake you as a thief. You are all sons of light and sons of the day. We are not of the night nor of darkness. Therefore let us not sleep, as others do, but let us watch and be sober. For those who sleep, sleep at night, and those who get drunk are drunk at night. But let us who are of the day be sober, putting on the breastplate of faith and love, and as a helmet the hope of salvation. For God did not appoint us to wrath, but to obtain salvation through our Lord Jesus Christ, Who died for us, that whether we wake or sleep, we should live together with Him. Therefore comfort each other and edify one another, just as you also are doing."**

In his classic work <u>The Coming Prince</u>, Sir Robert Anderson, *writing in the late 1800's*, explained that the Lord would not return until the Jew is restored to the land of "Palestine." At the time of his writing, the prospect of a Jewish nation in that land was inconceivable. The Turks were firmly rooted in the land of "Palestine" and there was no serious movement among Jews to reestablish their own country in their own land. Who would have imagined what would happen in two world wars that would entice the Jewish people to move en masse during the twentieth century to their historic homeland? Anderson believed the scriptures, which history has proven true. In the same way, we can see that the notion of imminence — the thought that Christ could return *at any moment* — is just not scripturally valid. Before the coming of the Lord we have shown with scripture that the following must happen *first*:

- The 70th week of Daniel must begin. It will likely begin with the signing of a 7 year treaty between the nation of Israel and a rising world leader.[47]
- Since the rapture occurs between the sixth and seventh seals, the events described in the first four scrolls in Revelation must take place. Look for a powerful world leader, world war, worldwide famine, and pestilence.
- The abomination of desolation must take place, which means temple worship must be resumed and there must be a temple in place.[48]
- Massive persecution of the elect will take place, many will die. Many will fall away.[49]
- Signs in the heavens will occur, the sun will grow dark, the moon will turn dark red, and the "stars will fall from heaven." The nations will mourn, and then, the Lord will return, and the Angels will gather the elect.[50]

The Abomination of Desolation

The major event that will mark the beginning of the Great Tribulation is the abomination of desolation. It will be an incredible occurrence when the Antichrist will actually defile the Temple of

God and set himself up to be worshipped as God. As was shown above in 2 Thessalonians 2, this is an event that must happen before the coming of the Day of the Lord.

Jesus speaks of this event in Matthew 24:15 and following, **"Therefore when you see the 'abomination of desolation,' spoken of by Daniel the prophet, standing in the holy place"** (Let the reader understand) **"then let those who are in Judea flee to the mountains...For then there will be great tribulation, such as has not been since the beginning of the world until this time, no, nor ever shall be."** Here, Jesus is directing our attention to the book of Daniel, where the prophet speaks of an event called the abomination of desolation in two different passages.

In Daniel 9:27 we find out that this event will occur at the midpoint of Daniel's 70th week when the Antichrist breaks a seven year covenant in the middle of the week of years: **"Then he shall confirm a covenant with many for one week; but in the middle of the week he shall bring an end to sacrifice and offering. And on the wing of abominations shall be one who makes desolate."**

Daniel also spoke of this event in Daniel 11:31, **"And forces shall be mustered by him, and they shall defile the sanctuary fortress; then they shall take away the daily sacrifices, and place there the abomination of desolation."**

In these passages Daniel gives us a fascinating prophecy with both "near" and "far" applications. The first fulfillment of this came about 200 years before Christ, during the time of the Maccabees. At that time, Antiochus Epiphanes — as a precursor (or type) of the Antichrist — took over Jerusalem and defiled the temple by sacrificing a sow on the altar and erecting a statue of Zeus in the Holy of Holies. Historians tell of the Maccabean revolt that followed leading to the ousting of Antiochus Epiphanes and the cleansing and rededication of the Temple.

Since all of these events took place a couple of hundred years *before* the time of Christ, and since Jesus pointed to these events as yet being in the future from His time period, we can deduce that Daniel's prophecy has both "near" and "far" applications. The events of the first fulfillment offer us some indication of what will happen the second time around.

It becomes clear that at the mid point of the 70th week of Daniel there will be a temple and a sacrificial system in place. The Antichrist will enter into the temple and defile it by setting himself up to be worshipped. As says 2 Thessalonians 2:3-4, **"Let no one deceive you by any means; for that Day will not come unless the falling away comes first and the man of sin is revealed, the son of perdition, who opposes and exalts himself above all that is called God or that is worshipped, <u>so that he sits as God in the temple of God,</u> showing himself that he is God."**

Now let's take a look at Revelation 13 in this light. After a prophetic description of the Antichrist and his origins in the first part of the chapter, we learn about some of this evil character's activities in verses 5-7: **"And he was given a mouth speaking great things and blasphemies, and he was given authority to continue for forty-two months. Then he opened his mouth in blasphemy against God, to blaspheme His name, His tabernacle, and those who dwell in heaven. It was granted to him to make war with the saints and to overcome them. And authority was given him over every tribe, tongue, and nation."** The dragon (Satan) gives power to the "beast," the Antichrist, who is given authority for 42 months (the last 3 _ years of Daniel 70th week, the time of the Great Tribulation). The Antichrist blasphemes the temple immediately after he is given this authority. A false prophet then arises (the second beast) who **"deceives those who dwell on the earth by those signs which he was granted to do in the sight of the beast, telling those who dwell on the earth to make an image to the beast** (the Antichrist) **who was wounded by the sword and lived."** In the latter half of Revelation 13, we see that severe tribulation will come upon the earth after the temple is blasphemed (the abomination of desolation) — even to the point that the second beast will **"cause as many as would not worship the image of the beast** (first beast) **to be killed."** Those who do not pledge allegiance to the beast with the acceptance of his mark will be unable to buy or sell. When we consider the severity of these events, we begin to understand why Jesus warned those in Judea in Matthew Chapter 24 to "flee to the mountains" when the abomination of desolation takes place.

Overview of the Book of Revelation

The book of Revelation is the only book in the Bible that opens with a promise of a blessing to the reader[51] — and so it should be approached with great enthusiasm. Unfortunately, because of the prophetic and controversial nature of this book, it is rarely discussed in churches today. What follows below is this author's understanding of the book of Revelation. It will be best understood if this section is taken slowly, reading parallel the Book of Revelation along with this outline of events. This is by no means meant to be an in depth analysis, but rather a framework to aid in comprehending this amazing book.

chapter one is an introductory chapter, here we learn of the scope of the book "the things which you have seen, and the things which are, and the things which will take place after this." Chapters 2 and 3 are the wonderful letters to the seven churches. There are those who believe that these letters spell out church history in advance. While this may seem a little far fetched, there are some valid reasons this may be true. A full discussion of the seven letters to the seven churches is beyond the scope of this book. However, I have found a study of these to be quite fruitful, and recommend it highly.

Because John was writing in the "Lord's Day" (Revelation 1:10, the Day of the Lord?), one can rightly assume that the seven letters to the seven churches also speak of the state of the church at the end of the age. Notice also that each of these letters seems to be addressed also to the individual believer with the statement **"He who has an ear let him hear what the Spirit says to the churches."** Since all of us have physical ears, and since we all ought to have spiritual ears, these letters were written also *to us*.

Chapters 4 and 5 shift the scene to occurrences in Heaven. We have a description of the throne room of God. Here we are introduced to the Lamb of God, the Lion of the Tribe of Judah who alone is able to take the scroll, the title deed to all of creation, and open it.

In Chapters 4 and 5 we catch a glimpse of the majesty of the scene in heaven and the adulation that all creation has for the true and Living God Lamb (who is also God as he is seen in the *midst* of the throne). Once the Lamb of God begins opening the scroll in Revelation 6, we enter into the realm of "the things that will take place after this." A continuous narrative follows that is occasionally interrupted for explanation and elaboration. It is useful to understand how all of this unfolds:

4 "After these things I looked, and behold, a door standing open in heaven. And the first voice I heard was like a trumpet speaking with me, saying, "Come up here, and I will show you things which must take place after this. Immediately I was in the Spirit; and behold, a throne set in heaven, and One sat on the throne. And He who sat there was like a jasper and a sardius stone in appearance; and there was a rainbow around the throne, in appearance like an emerald. Around the throne were twenty four thrones, and on the thrones I saw twenty four elders sitting, clothed in white robes; and they had crowns of gold on their heads. And from the throne proceeded lightnings, thunderings, and voices. Seven lamps of fire were burning before the throne, which are the seven Spirits of God. Before the throne there was a sea of glass, like crystal. And in the midst of the throne, and around the throne, were four living creatures full of eyes in front and in back. The first living creature was like a lion, the second living creature like a calf, the third living creature had a face like a man, and the fourth living creature was like a flying eagle. The four living creatures, each having six wings, were full of eyes around and within. And they do not rest day or night, saying:

'Holy, Holy, Holy, Lord God Almighty, Who was and is and is to come!'

Whenever the living creatures give glory and honor and

thanks to Him who sits on the throne, who lives forever and ever, the twenty-four elders fall down before Him who sits on the throne and worship Him who lives forever and ever, and cast their crowns before the throne, saying:

'You are worthy, O Lord, To receive glory and honor and power; For You created all things, And by Your will they exist and were created.'"

5 "And I saw in the right hand of Him who sat on the throne a scroll written inside and on the back, sealed with seven seals. Then I saw a strong angel proclaiming with a loud voice, 'Who is worthy to open the scroll and to loose its seals?' And no one in heaven or on the earth or under the earth was able to open the scroll, or to look at it. So I wept much, because no one was found worthy to open and read the scroll, or to look at it. But one of the elders said to me, 'Do not weep. Behold, the Lion of the tribe of Judah, the Root of David, has prevailed to open the scroll and to loose its seven seals.' And I looked, and behold, in the midst of the throne and of the four living creatures, and in the midst of the elders, stood a Lamb as though it had been slain, having seven horns and seven eyes, which are the seven Spirits of God sent out into all the earth. Then He came and took the scroll out of the right hand of Him who sat on the throne. Now when He had taken the scroll, the four living creatures and the twenty-four elders fell down before the Lamb, each having a harp, and golden bowls full of incense, which are the prayers of the saints. And they sang a new song, saying:

'You are worthy to take the scroll, and to open its seals; for You were slain, and have redeemed us to God by Your blood out of every tribe and tongue and people and nation, and have made us kings and priests to our God; and we shall reign on the earth.'

Then I looked, and I heard the voice of many angels around

the throne, and living creatures, and the elders; and the number of them was ten thousand times ten thousand, and thousands of thousands, saying with a loud voice:

'Worthy is the Lamb who was slain to receive power and riches and wisdom, and strength and honor and glory and blessing!'

And every creature which is in heaven and on the earth and under the earth and such as are in the sea, and all that are in them, I heard saying:

'Blessing and honor and glory and power be to Him who sits on the throne, and to the Lamb, forever and ever!'

Then the four living creatures said, 'Amen!' And the twenty four elders fell down and worshiped Him who lives forever and ever.

Revelation 6 — Revelation 10

This section presents a continuous narrative beginning with the opening of the first four seals (which likely coincides with the beginning of the 70th week of Daniel and the "beginning of sorrows" of Matthew chapter 24. This section proceeds through the "Great Tribulation" events of the fifth seal and the "Signs in the Heavens" that occur with the opening of the sixth seal. This is followed by the sealing of the 144,000 from Israel, which is followed by the "rapture" in Revelation 7:9.

Following along the continuous narrative we then come to the opening of the seventh seal which begins the "Day of the Lord" and is the starting point for the "Wrath of God" that begins with the trumpet judgments. The continuous narrative in the section of scripture below ends with the first woe and the sixth trumpet. To better understand this, take a look at the graphic correlating Matthew 24, the seventieth week of Daniel, and this section of scripture. Revelation 6 through Revelation 10 is printed for your convenience below.

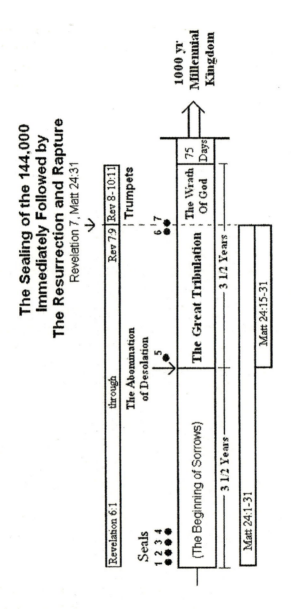

6 "Now I saw when the Lamb opened one of the seals; and I heard one of the four living creatures saying wit a voice like thunder, 'Come and see.' And I looked, and behold, a white horse. He who sat on it had a bow; and a crown was given to him, and he went out conquering and to conquer."

"When He opened the second seal, I heard the second living creature saying, 'Come and see.' Another horse, fiery red, went out. And it was granted to the one who sat on it to take peace from the earth, and that people should kill one another; and there was given to him a great sword.'"

"When He opened the third seal, I heard the third living creature say, 'Come and see.' So I looked, and behold, a black horse, and he who sat on it had a pair of scales in his hand. And I heard a voice in the midst of the four living creatures saying, 'A quart of wheat for a denarius, and three quarts of barley for a denarius; and do not harm the oil and the wine.'"

"When He opened the fourth seal, I heard the voice of the fourth living creature saying, 'Come and see.' So I looked, and behold, a pale horse. And the name of him who sat on it was Death, and Hades followed with him. And power was given to them over a fourth of the earth, to kill with sword, with hunger, with death, and by the beasts of the earth.'"

"When He opened the fifth seal, I saw under the altar the souls of those who had been slain for the word of God and for the testimony which they held. And they cried with a loud voice, saying, 'How long, O Lord, holy and true, until You judge and avenge our blood on those who dwell on the earth?' Then a white robe was given to each of them; and it was said to them that they should rest a little while longer, until both the number of their fellow servants and their brethren, who would be killed as they were, was completed.'"

"I looked when He opened the sixth seal, and behold, there was a great earthquake; and the sun became black as sackcloth of hair, and the moon became like blood. And the stars of heaven fell to the earth, as a fig tree drops its late figs when it is shaken by a mighty wind. Then the sky receded as a scroll when it is rolled up, and every mountain and island was moved out of its place. And the kings of the earth, the great men, the rich men, the commanders, the mighty men, every slave and every free man, hid themselves in the caves and in the rocks of the mountains, and said to the mountains and rocks, 'Fall on us and hide us from the face of Him who sits on the throne and from the wrath of the Lamb! For the great day of His wrath has come, and who is able to stand?' "

7 "After these things I saw four angels standing at the four corners of the earth, holding the four winds of the earth, that the wind should not blow on the earth, on the sea, or on any tree. Then I saw another angel ascending from the east, having the seal of the living God. And he cried with a loud voice to the four angels to whom it was granted to harm the earth and the sea, saying, 'Do not harm the earth, the sea, or the trees till we have sealed the servants of our God on their foreheads.' And I heard the number of those who were sealed. One hundred and forty-four thousand of all the tribes of the children of Israel were sealed;

> Of the tribe of Judah twelve thousand were sealed;
> Of the tribe of Reuben twelve thousand were sealed;
> Of the tribe of Gad twelve thousand were sealed;
> Of the tribe of Asher twelve thousand were sealed;
> Of the tribe of Nathalie twelve thousand were sealed;
> Of the tribe of Manasseh twelve thousand were sealed;
> Of the tribe of Simeon twelve thousand were sealed;
> Of the tribe of Levi twelve thousand were sealed;
> Of the tribe of Issachar twelve thousand were sealed;
> Of the tribe of Zebulun twelve thousand were sealed;
> Of the tribe of Joseph twelve thousand were sealed;
> Of the tribe of Benjamin twelve thousand were sealed."

7:9 "After these things I looked, and behold, a great multitude which no one could number, of all nations, tribes, peoples, and tongues, standing before the throne and before the Lamb, clothed with white robes, with palm branches in their hands, and crying out with a loud voice, saying, 'Salvation belongs to our God who sits on the throne, and to the Lamb!'

All the angels stood around the throne and the elders and the four living creatures, and fell on their faces before the throne and worshiped God, saying:

'Amen! Blessing and glory and wisdom, thanksgiving and honor and power and might, be to our God forever and ever. Amen.'

Then one of the elders answered, saying to me, 'Who are these arrayed in white robes, and where did they come from?' And I said to him, 'Sir, you know.'

So he said to me, 'These are the ones who come out of the great tribulation, and washed their robes and made them with in the blood of the Lamb. Therefore they are before the throne of God, and serve Him day and night in His temple. And He who sits on the throne will dwell among them. They shall neither hunger anymore nor thirst anymore; the sun shall not strike them, nor any heat; for the Lamb who is in the midst of the throne will shepherd them and lead them to living fountains of waters. And God will wipe away every tear form their eyes.' "

8 "When He opened the seventh seal, there was silence in heaven for about half an hour. And I saw the seven angels who stand before God, and to them were given seven trumpets. Then another angel, having a golden censer, came and stood at the altar. He was given much incense, that he should offer it with the prayers of all the saints upon the golden altar which was before the throne. And the smoke of the incense, with the prayers of the saints, ascended before God from the angel's hand. Then the angel took the censer, filled it with fire from the altar, and threw it to the earth. And there were noises, thunderings, lightings, and an earthquake. So the seven angels who had the seven trumpets prepared themselves to sound."

"The first angel sounded: And hail and fire followed, mingled with blood, and they were thrown to the earth. And a third of the trees were burned up, and all green grass was burned up."

"Then the second angel sounded: and something like a great mountain burning with fire was thrown into the sea, and a third of the sea became blood. And a third of the living creatures in the sea died, and a third of the ships were destroyed."

"Then the third angel sounded: And a great star fell from heaven, burning like a torch, and it fell on a third of the rivers and on the springs of water. The name of the star is Wormwood. A third of the waters became wormwood, and many men died from the water, because it was made bitter."

Then the fourth angel sounded: And a third of the sun was struck, a third of the moon, and a third of the stars, so that a third of them were darkened. A third of the day did not shine, and likewise the night. And I looked, and I heard an angel flying through the midst of heaven, saying with a loud voice, 'Woe, woe, woe to the inhabitants of the earth, because of the remaining blasts of the trumpet of the three angels who are about to sound!' "

9 "Then the fifth angel sounded: And I saw a star fallen from heaven to the earth. To him was given the key to the bottomless pit. And he opened the bottomless pit, and smoke arose out of the pit like the smoke of a great furnace. So the sun and the air were darkened because of the smoke of the pit. Then out of the smoke locusts came upon the earth. And to them was given power, as the scorpions of the earth have power. They were commanded not to harm the grass of the earth, or any green thing, or any tree, but only those men who do not have the seal of God on their foreheads. And they were not given authority to kill them, but to torment them for five months. Their torment was like the torment of a scorpion when it strikes a man. In those days men will seek death and will not find it; they will desire to die, and death will flee from them.

The shape of the locusts was like horses prepared for battle. On their heads were crowns of something like gold, and their faces were like the faces of men. They had hair like women's hair, and their teeth were like lions' teeth. And they had breast-plates like breastplates of iron, and the sound of their wings was like the sound of chariots with many horses running into battle. They had tails like scorpions, and there were stings in their tails. Their power was to hurt men five months. And they had a king over them, the angel of the bottomless pit, whose name in Hebrew is Abaddon, but in Greek his has the name Apollyon. One woe is past. Behold, still two more woes are coming after these things."[52]

Then the sixth angel sounded: And I heard a voice from the four horns of the golden altar which is before God, saying to the sixth angel who had the trumpet, 'Release the four angels who are bound at the great river Euphrates.' So the four angels, who had been prepared for the hour and the day and month and year, were released to kill a third of mankind.

Now the number of the army of the horsemen was two hundred million; I heard the number of them. And thus I saw the horses in the vision: Those who sat on them had breast-plates of fiery red, hyacinth blue, and sulfur yellow; and the heads of the horses were like the heads of lions; and out of their mouths came fire, smoke and brimstone. By these three plagues a third of mankind was killed — by the fire and the smoke and the brimstone which came out of their mouths. For their power is in their mouth and in their tails; for their tails are like serpents, having heads, and with them they do harm. But the rest of mankind, who were not killed by these plagues, did not repent of the works of their hands, that they should not worship demons, and idols of gold, silver, brass, stone, and wood, which can neither see not hear nor walk. And they did not repent of their murders or their sorceries or their sexual immorality or their thefts."

10 "I saw still another mighty angel coming down from

heaven, clothed with a cloud. And a rainbow was on his head, his face was like the sun, and his feet like pillars of fire. Te had a little book open in his hand. And he set his right foot on the sea and his left foot on the land, and cried with a loud voice, as when a lion roars. When he cried out, seven thunders uttered their voices. Now when the seven thunders uttered their voices, I was bout to write; but I heard a voice from heaven saying to me, 'Seal up the things which the seven thunders uttered, and do not write them.'"

"The angel whom I saw standing on the sea and on the land raised up his hand to heaven and swore by Him who lives forever and ever, who created heaven and the things that are in it, the earth and the things that are in it, and the sea and the things that are in it, that there should be delay no longer, but in the days of the sounding of the seventh angel, when he is about to sound, the mystery of God would be finished, as He declared to His servants the prophets."

Then the voice which I heard from heaven spoke to me again and said, 'Go, take the little book which is open in the hand of the angel who stands on the sea and on the earth.' So I went to the angel and said to him, 'Give me the little book.' And he said to me, 'Take and eat it; and it will make your stomach bitter, but it will be as sweet as honey in your mouth.'"

"Then I took the little book out of the angel's hand and ate it, and it was as sweet as honey in my mouth. But when I had eaten it, my stomach became bitter. And he said to me, 'You must prophesy again about many peoples, nations, tongues, and kings.'"

Revelation 11:1 — 11:14

This section describes events of the Great Tribulation as it pertains to the two witnesses. It begins at the midpoint of the 70th week of Daniel and ends with the death and resurrection of the two witnesses — the second woe. We are told that the activity of the two witnesses lasts for $3\frac{1}{2}$ years, indicating that the two witnesses die at the end of the last half of the 70th week of Daniel. By understanding the time framework we are able to see that this is an overview section that goes back to fill in some of the details and occurrences of the Great Tribulation which likely begin at approximately the 5th seal and for the elect continue until sometime between the sixth and seventh seals.

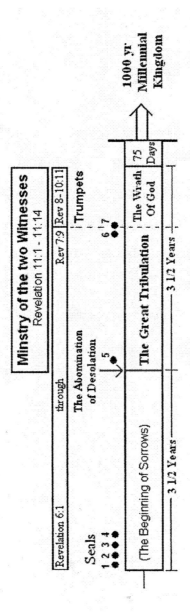

11:1 – 11:14 "Then I was given a reed like a measuring rod. And the angel stood, saying, 'Rise and measure the temple of God, the altar, and those who worship there. But leave out the court which is outside the temple, and do not measure it, for it has been given to the Gentiles. And they will tread the holy city underfoot for forty-two months. And I will give power to my two witnesses, and they will prophesy one thousand two hundred and sixty days, clothed in sackcloth.' These are the two olive trees and the two lampstands standing before the God of the earth. And if anyone wants to harm them, fire proceeds from their mouth and devours their enemies. And if anyone wants to harm them, he must be killed in this manner. These have power to shut heaven, so that no rain falls in the days of their prophecy; and they have power over waters to turn them to blood, and to strike the earth with all plagues, as often as they desire.

When they finish their testimony, the beast that ascends out of the bottomless pit will make war against them, overcome them, and kill them. And their dead bodies will lie in the street of the great city which spiritually is called Sodom and Egypt, where also our Lord was Crucified. Then those from the peoples, tribes, tongues, and nations will see their dead bodies three and a half days, and not allow their dead bodies to be put into graves. And those who dwell on the earth will rejoice over them, make merry, and send gifts to one another, because these two prophets tormented those who dwell on the earth."

Revelation 11:15 — 11:19

Here the continuous narrative is picked back up again and carries on where both of the above two sections left off, at the end of the 3½ years. So you may understand the timeline, notice that this section refers to the seventh trumpet, and it ends with a scene in Heaven and the opening of the Temple of God in Heaven with the Ark of the Covenant being seen:

11:15 — 11:19 "Then the seventh angel sounded: And there were loud voices in heaven, saying, 'The kingdoms of this world have become the kingdoms of our Lord and of His Christ, and He shall reign forever and ever!'
And the twenty-four elders who sat before God on their thrones fell on their faces and worshiped God, saying:

'We give You thanks, O Lord God Almighty, the One who is and who was and who is to come, because You have take Your great power and reigned. The nations were angry, and Your wrath has come, and the time of the dead, that they should be judged, and that You should reward Your servants the prophets and the saints, and those who fear Your name, small and great, and should destroy those who destroy the earth.' "

11:19 "Then the temple of God was opened in heaven, and the ark of His covenant was seen in His temple and there were lightnings, noises, thunderings, an earthquake, and great hail."

Revelation 12:1 – 15:4

This section begins as a broad historical overview spanning all creation. It describes Israel bringing forth a "Male Child" (The Messiah), and the dragon's attempt to devour the child who "Was to rule all nations with a rod of iron."

The Woman (Israel, specifically the 144,000 from each tribe) is described as fleeing into the wilderness for the last 3½ years of this age. This exile of the Israel begins right at the time of Satan's banishment from Heaven. This occurs at the midpoint of the 70th week of Daniel and relates to Daniel chapter 12 as well.

The Serpent, having great wrath, begins to persecute the "offspring" of the woman, those who "Keep the commandments of God and have the testimony of Jesus Christ"

Beginning in Revelation 12:13, the narrative describes the events of the Great Tribulation from a different perspective than Revelation 6:1 - Revelation 11:19.

Notice in reading below that the order of events is consistent with what we have already learned. The Great Tribulation begins when Satan is kicked out of heaven and then the abomination of desolation occurs at the midpoint of Daniel's 70th week. Notice that the time period of the Great Tribulation is defined explicitly three different ways as being 3½ years. It is hard to imagine that even though God makes this definite time period so obvious, there are still those who want to allegorize it to mean something else. The events in this section begin at the midpoint of Daniel's 70th Week and can be summarized as follows:

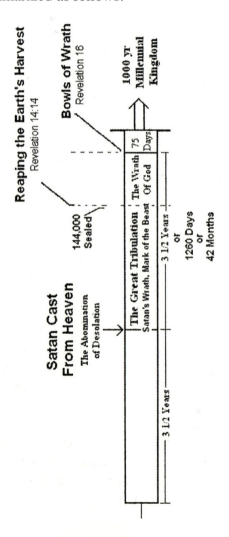

The text is presented with few interruptions below:

12 "Now a great sign appeared in heaven: A woman clothed with the sun, with the moon under her feet, and on her head a garland of twelve stars. Then being with child, she cried out in labor and in pain to give birth. And another sign appeared in heaven: Behold, a great, fiery red dragon having seven heads and ten horns, and seven diadems on his heads. His tail drew a third of the stars of heaven and threw them to the earth. And the dragon stood before the woman who was ready to give birth, to devour her Child as soon as it was born. She bore a male Child who was to rule all nations with a rod of iron. And her Child was caught up to God and His throne. Then the woman fled into the wilderness where she had a place prepared by God, that they should feed her there one thousand two hundred and sixty days.

And war broke out in heaven: Michael and his angels fought with the dragon; and the dragon and his angels fought, but they did not prevail, nor was a place found for them in heaven any longer. So the great dragon was cast out, that serpent of old, called the Devil and Satan, who deceives the whole world; he was cast to the earth, and his angels were cast out with him. Then I heard a loud voice saying in heaven, 'Now salvation, and strength, and the kingdom of our God, and the power of His Christ have come, for the accuser of our brethren, who accused them before our God day and night, has been cast down. And they overcame him by the blood of the Lamb and by the word of their testimony, and they did not love their lives to the death. Therefore rejoice, O heavens, and you who dwell in them! Woe to the inhabitants of the earth and the sea! For the devil has come down to you having great wrath, because he knows that he has a short time.' "

The Great Tribulation begins as does the persecution of the saints, vs. 12:13 - 13:18. This is the passage of scripture that describes in some detail the exploits of the Antichrist and his false prophet. Namely, the famous description of the "mark of the beast" is found in Revelation Chapter 13.

12:13 **"Now when the dragon saw that he had been cast to the earth, he persecuted the woman who gave birth to the male Child. But the woman was given two wings of a great eagle, that she might fly into the wilderness to her place, where she is nourished for a time and times and half a time, from the presence of the serpent. So the serpent spewed water out of his mouth like a flood after the woman, that he might cause her to be carried away by the flood. But the earth helped the woman and the earth opened its mouth and swallowed up the flood which the dragon had spewed out of his mouth. And the dragon was enraged with the woman, and he went to make war with the rest of her offspring, who keep the commandments of God and have the testimony of Jesus Christ."**

13 **"Then I stood on the sand of the sea. And I saw a beast rising up out of the sea, having seven heads and ten horns, and on his horns ten crowns, and on his heads a blasphemous name. Now the beast which I saw was like a leopard, his feet were like the feet of a bear, and his mouth like the mouth of a lion. The dragon gave him his power, his throne, and great authority. And I saw one of his heads as of it had been mortally wounded, and his deadly wound was healed. And all the world marveled and followed the beast. So they worshiped the dragon who gave authority to the beast; and they worshiped the beast saying 'Who is like the beast? Who is able to make war with him?' And he was given a mouth speaking great things and blasphemies, and he was given authority to continue for forty-two months. Then he opened his mouth in blasphemy against God, to blaspheme His name, His tabernacle, and those who dwell in heaven. It was granted to him to make war with the saints and to overcome them. And authority was given him over every tribe, tongue, and nation. All who dwell on the earth will worship him, whose names have not been written in the Book of Life of the Lamb slain from the foundation of the world. If anyone has an ear, let him hear. He who leads into captivity shall go onto captivity; he who kills with the sword must be killed with the**

sword. Here is the patience and faith of the saints.

Then I saw another beast coming up out of the earth, and he had two horns like a lamb and spoke like a dragon. And he exercises all the authority of the first beast in his presence, and causes the earth and those who dwell in it to worship the first beast, whose deadly wound was healed. He performs great signs, so that he even makes fire come down from heaven on the earth in the sight of men. And he deceives those who dwell on the earth by those signs which he was granted to do in the sight of the beast, telling those who dwell on the earth to make an image to the beast who was wounded by the sword and lived. He was granted power to give breath to the image of the beast, that the image of the beast should both speak and cause as many as would not worship the image of the beast to be killed. He causes all, both small and great, rich and poor, free and slave, to receive a mark on their right hand or on their foreheads, and that no one may buy or sell except one who has the mark or the mane of the beast, or the number of his name. Here is wisdom. Let him who has understanding calculate the number of the beast, for it is the number of a man: His number is 666."

In Revelation Chapter 14, we again see the 144,000 who are sealed with the Father's name. This proves again that this section is a retelling of the events that take place during the Great Tribulation. What should follow a description of the 144,000 is an account of the "Rapture" or the harvest of the earth:

14 "Then I looked, and behold, a Lamb standing on Mount Zion, and with Him one hundred and forty-four thousand, having His Father's name written on their foreheads. And I heard a voice from heaven, like the voice of many waters, and like the voice of loud thunder. And I heard the sound of harpists playing their harps. They sang as it were a new song before the throne, before the four living creatures, and the elder; and no one could learn that song except the hundred and forty-four thousand who were redeemed from the earth. These are the ones who were not defiled with women, for they are virgins.

These are the ones who follow the Lamb wherever He goes. These were redeemed from among men, being Firstfruits to God and to the Lamb. And in their mouth was found no deceit, for they are without fault before the throne of God.

In Revelation 14:6-13, the gospel is preached to "all the world" by the proclamation of the three angels. It is fascinating to realize that this is what is described by Christ in Matthew 24:14, "And this gospel of the kingdom will be preached in all the world as a witness to all the nations, an then the end will come." It will not be our feeble efforts to evangelize the earth that will cause the return of Christ as some believe and teach.

Understanding this point helps to prove that this section, Revelation 12:13-14:20, presents an overview of the "Great Tribulation" since Jesus connected this event with the Great Tribulation in Matthew 24:14.

14:6 The I saw another angel flying in the midst of heaven, having the everlasting gospel to preach to those who dwell on the earth — to every nation, tribe, tongue, and people — saying with a loud voice, 'Fear God and give glory to Him, for the hour of His judgment has come; and worship Him who made heaven and earth, and the sea and springs of water.' And another angel followed, saying, 'Babylon is fallen, is fallen, that great city, because she has made all nations drink of the wine of the wrath of her fornication.' Then a third angel followed them, saying with a loud voice, 'If anyone worships the beast and his image, and receives his mark on his forehead or on his had, he himself shall also drink of the wine of the wrath of God, which is poured out full strength into the cup of His indignation. He shall be tormented with fire and brimstone in the presence of the holy angels and in the presence of the Lamb. And the smoke of their torment ascends forever and ever; and they have no rest day or night, who worship the beast and his image, and whoever receives the mark of his name.'

Here is the patience of the saints; here are those who keep the commandments of God and the faith of Jesus. Then I heard

a voice from heaven saying to me, Write: 'Blessed are the dead who die in the Lord from now on' 'Yes,' says the Spirit, 'That they may rest from their labors, and their works follow them'"

Revelation 14:14-20 The "harvest of the earth" — this is the separation of the Tares and the Wheat spoken of by Jesus in Matthew 13. This section of Revelation describes the general event of the earth's harvest.

14:14 "Then I looked, and behold, a white cloud, and on the cloud sat One like the Lon of Man, having on His head a golden crown, and in His hand a sharp sickle. And another angel came out of the temple, crying with a loud voice to Him who sat on the cloud, 'Thrust in Your sickle and reap, for the time has come fro You to reap, for the harvest of the earth is ripe.' So He who sat on the cloud thrust in His sickle on the earth, and the earth was reaped.

As we have already shown, the "wrath of God" follows the "harvest." Here in Revelation 14:17 - 15:5 we see an account of God's Wrath that follows the rapture. (Notice that in 15:2 the over-coming saints are already in Heaven — indicating that the gathering together has already taken place). The specific events that occur during this time period are described in the "trumpet judgment section" of Revelation 8:1 - 9:21 and 11:15-19.

14:17 "Then another angel came out of the temple which is in heaven, he also having a sharp sickle. And another angel came out from the altar, who had power over fire, and he cried with a loud cry to him who had the sharp sickle, saying, 'Thrust in your sharp sickle and gather the clusters of the vine of the earth, for her grapes are fully ripe.' So the angel thrust his sickle into the earth and gathered the vine of the earth, and threw it into the great winepress of the wrath of God. And the winepress was trampled outside the city, and blood came out of the winepress, up to the horses' bridles, for one thousand six hundred furlongs

15 "Then I saw another sign in heaven, great and marvelous: seven angels having the seven last plagues, for in them the wrath of God is complete. And I saw something like a sea of glass mingled with fire, and those who have the victory over the beast, over his image and over his mark and over the number of his name, standing on the sea of glass having harps of God. They sing the song of Moses, the servant of God, and the song of the Lamb, saying:

'Great and marvelous are Your works, Lord God Almighty! Just and true are Your ways, O King of the saints! Who shall not fear You, O Lord, and glorify Your name? For You alone are holy. For all nations shall come and worship before You, for Your judgments have been manifested.'"

15:5 "After these things I looked, and behold, the temple of the tabernacle of the testimony in heaven was opened."

Revelation 15:5 — 16:21

This picks up again with a description of the opening of the Temple in Heaven right where the continuous narrative left off in verse 11:19, again placing this section right at the end of the 3½ years. Notice that the bowl judgments begin with the opening of the Temple with the Ark of the Testimony being seen. What is inside the Ark? The two tablets of stone on which the Ten Commandments are written — God's Law! This indicates that those who remain upon the earth will be held accountable and suffer judgment based upon failure to follow God's Commandments.

The bowl judgments are the completion of the Wrath of God[53] and take place immediately after the completion of the 70th week of Daniel. Notice also that the seven bowl judgments are actually the 7th trumpet judgment. In other words, the seventh trumpet causes the seven bowls to be brought forth. (Just as the seventh seal unleashed the seven trumpet judgments) The seventh trumpet is the "3rd Woe," which we are told will begin shortly after the conclusion of the 2nd Woe in Revelation 11:14. We know that the 2nd Woe occurs at the end of the 3½ years and so by this we can also conclude that the bowl judgments begin at the end of the 70th week of Daniel.

The seven bowl judgments are what happens during the extra days found in Daniel 12:11 **"And from the time that the daily sacrifice is taken away, and the abomination of desolation is set up, there shall be one thousand two hundred and ninety days."** We can conclude from this verse in Daniel that the bowl judgments will unfold in rapid succession taking only thirty days to complete. Since we are picking up form the continuous narrative in Revelation 11:19, where there is an earthquake and great hail (these events occur with the pouring out of the seventh bowl), we can conclude that the bowls judgments must happen one right after the other at the sounding of the seventh trumpet. Indeed, this will be the final woe pronounced upon the earth!

15:5 "After these things I looked, and behold, the temple of the tabernacle of the testimony in heaven was opened." And out of the temple came the seven angels having the seven plagues, clothed in pure bright linen, and having their chests girded with golden bands. Then one of the four living creatures gave to the seven angels seven golden bowls full of the wrath of God who lives forever and ever. The temple was filled with smoke from the glory of God and from His power, and no one was able to enter the temple till the seven plagues of the seven angels were completed."

16 "Then I heard a loud voice from the temple saying to the seven angels, 'Go and pour out the owls of the wrath of God on the earth.'"

"So the first went and poured out his bowl upon the earth, and a foul and loathsome sore came upon the men who had the mark of the beast and those who worshiped his image."

Then the second angel poured out his bowl on the sea, and it

became blood as of a dead man; and every living creature in the sea died."

"Then the third angel poured out his bowl on the rivers and springs of water, and they became blood. And I heard the angel of the waters saying: 'You are righteous, O Lord, the One who is and ho was and how is to be, Because You have judged these things. For they have shed the blood of saints and prophets, and You have given them blood to drink. For it is their just due.' And I heard another from the altar saying, 'Even so, Lord God Almighty, true and righteous are Your judgments.'"

"Then the fourth angel poured out his bowl on the sun, and power was given to him to scorch men with fire. And men were scorched with great heat, and they blasphemed the name of God who has power over these plagues; and they did not repent and give Him glory."

"Then the fifth angel poured out his bowl on the throne of the beast, and his kingdom became full of darkness; and they gnawed their tongues because of the pain. They blasphemed the God of heaven because of their pains and their sores, and did not repent of their deeds."

"Then the sixth angel poured out his bowl on the great river Euphrates, and its water was dried up, so that the way of the kings from the east might be prepared. And I saw three unclean spirits like frogs coming out of the mouth of the dragon, out of the mouth of the beast, and out of the mouth of the false prophet. For they are spirits of demons, performing signs, which go out to the kings of the earth and of the whole world, to gather them to the battle of that great day of God Almighty."

Here, in the middle of the description of the sixth bowl judgment, the Lord interjects this pointed warning:

"Behold, I am coming as a thief. Blessed is he who watches,

and keeps his garments, lest he walk naked and they see his shame."

Now the description of the sixth bowl continues:

"And they gathered them together to the place called in Hebrew, Armageddon."

"Then the seventh angel poured out his bowl into the air, and a loud voice came out of the temple of heaven, from the throne, saying, 'It is done!' And there were noises and thunderings and lightnings; and there was a great earthquake, such a mighty and great earthquake as had not occurred since men were on the earth. Now the great city was divided into three parts, and the cities of the nations fell. And great Babylon was remembered before God, to give her the cup of the wine of the fierceness of His wrath. Then every island fled away, and the mountains were not found. And great hail from heaven fell upon men, each hailstone about the weight of a talent. Men blasphemed God because for the plague of the hail, since that plague was exceedingly great."

Revelation 17 — 19:4

Again, the action reverts to an "overview" section. Here is where we find the woman riding the beast and "Mystery Babylon," the Harlot. In chapter 8, this book will examine this section more closely as we take shocking look at the identity of these characters.

Revelation 19:5 — 19:10

This section describes the marriage supper of the Lamb. This is not part of the continuous narrative but is a continuation of the description of Babylon the Harlot. Here the true bride of Christ is contrasted with Babylon.

Revelation 19:11 through the end of the Revelation

The continuous narrative again picks up where it left off at the end of Revelation Chapter 16, and is carried through the battle of Armageddon, the casting of Antichrist and the False prophet into the lake of fire, the binding of Satan for 1000 years, the millennial kingdom, the loosening of Satan, the final deception, the rebellion crushed (the Great white throne judgment and then the bringing in of the New Jerusalem).

The key to understanding the book of Revelation is to realize that it is basically presented in chronological order, but certain events are retold to bring out more detail. Presented graphically and overlaid on Daniel's 70th week, the book of Revelation looks like this:

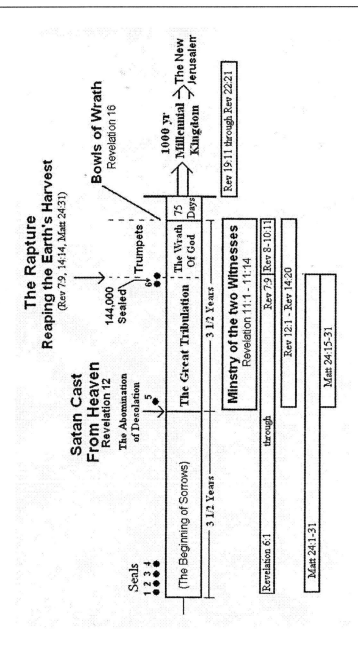

This overview of Revelation will hopefully shed some light on this difficult book; it was composed by comparing scripture with itself, and by placing Revelation in the context of the rest of the Bible. While I believe the above to be true, I do not wish to be dogmatic. I have heard it said that in the book of Revelation alone, there are over 800 allusions to the Old Testament. I have to believe that our illiteracy with the Old Testament is the reason for so much confusion with the Book of Revelation.

CHAPTER 6

The Missing Puzzle Piece — the Identity of "the Elect"

Shortly after I came to understand the prewrath viewpoint, I enthusiastically began trying to share what I believed the Word of God was indicating. Much to my dismay, however, this teaching was not met with much acceptance. At first, I wondered how this could be since the prewrath position seemed so plain and biblically sound, and since the implications of a prewrath rapture were staggering. Even with good scriptural support, I couldn't seem to make people understand the importance of the matter, nor could I convince them of this point of view. Thinking that there may be some sort of deception going on, I sought the Lord's guidance. *Why*, I remember earnestly praying, did people hang on to the false notion of a pre-tribulation rapture so desperately? If Satan is behind this deception, then there *must* be a reason. What occurred to me initially was the realization that both the pre-tribulation rapture position and amillennialism left the church *totally unprepared* for the Great Tribulation and thus vulnerable to the wiles of the evil one. This was discussed in chapter 3. What didn't occur to me initially though was Satan's *deeper* deception.

"Iron sharpens iron" — and besides that, I enjoy a lively debate about the rapture question. For this reason, and because I *thought* I understood the reason behind the deception, the rapture question would often come up in my conversations with fellow believers. In almost every discussion on this topic, we would end up at the same sticking point — *the identity of the elect in Matthew 24*. I distinctly remember having a wonderful night of fellowship with a couple who attended church where I was involved as the praise and worship leader. Just as in other similar conversations, all debate on the pre-trib/ prewrath issue eventually became circular because we disagreed on the identity of the "Elect" in Matthew 24. Driving home that night I remember crying out, *"Lord! Who are the 'Elect' spoken of in Matthew 24?"* Our Heavenly Father is indeed faithful to reveal such matters to us when we ask!

Often times when there is a disagreement about a matter of interpretation in the Bible what seems to be the "issue" isn't the real issue at all, and often neither side is totally right in their position. To demonstrate this, allow me to use the following illustration: Suppose the two of us are walking through the forest on the same hiking trail. This trail has several places where there are "forks" in the path that each lead to a different destination.

On our hike, we are headed in the same direction and have the same "goal" or endpoint in mind, the desired destination is the truth. Because we are traveling at different speeds, however, we end up getting separated. It is easy to walk along not paying careful attention, haphazardly assuming that we are on the right path but eventually we find ourselves on two separate trails, and these trails happen to be going in different directions!

So that we can "hike" together, in this illustration you would call over to me, and I would answer back, each of us trying to convince the other that *our* trail is the correct trail. We both have a map (the Bible), but because we have walked too far from the fork in the trail, we can't settle on who is right and who is wrong. After all, we can't *both* be right! (Although, we could both be wrong). The only way to sort this out is to go back to the fork in the road, then look at the map, and then we can come to agreement on the right trail.

In the case of the pre-trib vs. prewrath argument, we both had missed the *first* fork in the trail (by making some wrong assumptions) and we took a wrong turn together. Later we became separated from each other at a subsequent fork in the trail, but the truth was — both of us were equally lost.

The Fork in the Trail — Where Did We Go Wrong?

In this case, the fork in the road of the rapture argument boils down to the *identity* of the elect in Matthew 24. Pre-tribulationist and preterist believe that the elect spoken of here are the Jews, while those of the prewrath and post-tribulation camps maintain that this refers to the "church." In my "discussions" I would reason the "elect" were the church, but had no good way of proving my point. Here, the argument would become circular, and neither side could be convinced.

Please allow a brief explanation as to why this issue is the "fork in the trail." First, let's look at the verses in question:

"And unless those days were shortened, no flesh would be saved; but for the <u>elect's</u> sake those days will be shortened." Matthew 24:22

"For false christs and false prophets will rise and show great signs and wonders to deceive, if possible, even the <u>elect</u>." Matthew 24:24

"Then the sign of the Son of Man will appear in heaven, and then all the tribes of the earth will mourn, and they will see the Son of Man coming on the clouds of heaven with power and great glory. And He will send His angels with a great sound of a trumpet, and they will gather together His <u>elect</u> from the four winds, from one end of heaven to the other." Matthew 24:31

If one believes the "elect" here in Matthew 24 are the Jewish people, either past or present, then in order to maintain that view, one has to fashion an entire interpretation of other end-times scriptures to fit this belief.

Consider the argument — if the "elect" are the saved Jews, since there is no mention of another group called the "church" in the remainder of Matthew 24, the "church" must have already been "taken up." Similarly, if one believes the "elect" in Matthew 24 are the "church," then one necessarily has to interpret the rest of the end-times passages in that context. My experience again and again is that this is the place where different camps get separated and where diverse theological positions are birthed.

Those who hold to dispensationalist theology argue that the so-called Olivet discourse (the discussion taking place in Matthew 24) was written chiefly to the Jew. They contend the elect in this passage refers to "Jewish Christians" who are saved after the rapture. The Gospel of Mark also records the Olivet discourse, but in Mark's account, immediately after His explanation of the end times, Jesus says, **"And what I say to you, I say to all; Watch!" Mark13:37.** This verse alone is irrefutable proof that the Olivet discourse was not written only "for the Jewish remnant" left on the Earth after the rapture, but to *everyone* — just as Jesus proclaimed.

It is likely that there are those who determine the identity of the elect based on a theological position that they already hold. This seems to be the case for those who hold to dispensationalist theology and also true of those who hold the preterist position and believe that the church has *replaced* Israel. In any case, a scriptural look at the identity of the elect should bring some clarity to this issue.

Who is it then? Are the "elect" in Matthew 24 the "Saved Jewish remnant" or the "church?" Wait a minute though, are we even asking the *right question*? To sort this out, let's take a step back to the first fork in the trail and look at this question more closely. Rather than asking "Jews or church" perhaps we ought to simply ask — who are God's chosen people? *Who are the elect*?

God's Chosen People

In both the New Testament and the Old, the term "elect" refers to God's chosen ones. In the Old Testament, the Hebrew word for elect is bachiyr,[54] which comes from the word bachar[55] which means chosen. We use the words chosen and elect interchangeably even today. For example, in the United States, if we as a nation *choose* a president, we do this by the process of an *election*. Below are a few examples of verses that include the elect or the chosen. As we take a look at these, let's try to keep in mind that we ought to use God's definition of the 'elect' instead of our own. (Our labels might include, for example, "Christian, or "Catholic," or insert denominational name here "_____").

"**For you are a holy people to the LORD your God; the LORD your God has <u>chosen</u> you to be a people for Himself, a special treasure above all the peoples on the face of the earth." Deuteronomy 7:6, 14:2**

"**But you Israel, are My servant, Jacob whom I have <u>chosen</u>, the descendants of Abraham my friend. You whom I have taken from the ends of the earth, and called from its farthest regions, and said to you, 'you are My servant, I have <u>chosen</u> you and have not cast you away.'" Isaiah 41:8-9**

"**And He will send His angels with a great sound of a trumpet, and they will gather together His elect from the four winds, from one end of heaven to the other." Matthew 24:31**

"**'You are my witnesses,' says the LORD, and my servant whom I have <u>chosen</u>, that you may know and believe Me, and understand that I am He. Before Me there was no God formed, nor shall there be after Me." Isaiah 43:10**

"**I will bring forth descendants from Jacob, and from Judah an heir of My mountains; My <u>elect</u> shall inherit it, and My servants shall dwell there." Isaiah 65:9**

"**O seed of Abraham His servant, you children of Jacob, His <u>chosen</u> ones!" Psalms 105:6**

"**Therefore, as the <u>elect</u> of God, holy and beloved, put on tender mercies, kindness, humility, meekness, longsuffering; bearing with one another and forgiving one another, if anyone has a complaint against another; even as Christ forgave you , so**

you also must do." Colossians 3:12-13

"But you are a <u>chosen</u> generation, a royal priesthood, a holy nation, His own special people, that you may proclaim the praises of Him who called you out of darkness into His marvelous light; who once were not a people but are now the people of God, who had not obtained mercy but now have obtained mercy." 1 Peter 2:9-10 (1 Peter 1:2 addresses this letter to the "elect").

There are many other verses in the Bible that speak about God's chosen ones. Let's take a look at the verses above and see if we can draw some conclusions about this special group. What follows here can be thought of as pieces to a puzzle. When we put these pieces together, we ought to have a picture of who the "elect" really are.

- They are a holy people (a set apart people). Deuteronomy 7:6
- God chose them as a special people. Deuteronomy 14:2
- They are descendants of Abraham through Jacob. Psalms. 105:6, Isaiah 65:9
- They will be gathered from the farthest ends of the earth. Isaiah 41:8-9, Matthew 24:31
- They will be witnesses that God is God. Isaiah 43:10
- They have traits such as tender mercies, kindness, humility, meekness, and forgiveness. Colossians 3:12-13
- They were once "not a people," but are now the people of God. 1 Peter 2:9-10
- They once did not have mercy, but now have obtained mercy. 1 Peter 2:9-10
- They will inherit the land as God has promised. Isaiah 65:9
- Christ has forgiven them. Colossians 3:12-13
- They are of both Judah *and* Israel. Isaiah 65:9 (see next section below.)
- *Most importantly, there is no where in the Bible any reference to God changing who His elect people are!*

Putting it Together — the Prophet Hosea

In assembling the pieces of our prophecy puzzle, the "missing piece" that once found brings clarity to the picture is this issue of the identity of the elect. An understanding of God's prophecies given in the book of Hosea is vital to understanding this critical issue. Hosea records the strange story of God ordering Hosea to take of wife of harlotry. This marriage then served as a picture of Israel's harlotry against God. Hosea fathered children with the harlot Gomer and the names of their children were prophetic, in that their Hebrew names described God's judgment upon Israel. God, however, promised that this judgment would not last forever, and that He would restore Israel and Judah (the Northern and Southern Kingdoms). **"And she conceived again and bore a daughter. Then God said to him; 'Call her name Lo-Ruhamah, for I will <u>no longer have mercy on the house of Israel</u>, but I will utterly take them away. Yet I will have mercy on the house of Judah, will save them by the LORD their God, and will not save them by bow, nor by sword or battle, by horses or horsemen.' Now when she had weaned Lo-Ruhamah, she conceived and bore a son. Then God said; 'Call his name Lo-Ammi, for <u>you are not my people and I will not be your God</u>.' 'Yet the number of the Children of Israel shall be as the sand of the sea, which cannot be measured or numbered. <u>And it shall come to pass in the place where it was said to them, 'you are not My people,' there it shall be said to them, 'you are sons of the living God</u>.'"** Hosea **1:6-10.**[56] (underlined for emphasis)

Notice that in this section of Hosea, the prophet spoke concerning the *House of Israel*, the Northern Kingdom. If we take a look now at some New Testament writings we are able to come to some amazing conclusions:

"But you are a chosen generation, a royal priesthood, a holy nation, His own special people, that you may proclaim the praises of Him who called you out of darkness into His marvelous light; who once were not a people but are now the people of God, who had not obtained mercy but now have

obtained mercy." 1 Peter 2:9-10

By comparing these two passages, we can deduce that the elect included the "House of Israel," who were once **not a people, but now are called the people of God.**" This is consistent with the identity of the elect throughout the entire Bible.

Perhaps we missed the first "fork in the trail" when we assumed that God had somehow given up on the "elect" of the Old Testament and found a new kind of "elect" people in the New Testament (as in dispensationalist theology).

If the "House of Israel" continues to be God's elect people however, what then about the church? Is the church elect? Or... have we tried to define the "elect" by using *our* labels instead of the designations that God gave? This important question will be addressed in part in chapter 8.

Importantly, the elect in Matthew 24 is spoken of in the context of the Great Tribulation. During this time many of our man made institutions and labels will be shaken up and may not even exist as we presently know them. Many will turn to the Lord in that Day, and many will also turn away. Considering this fact, we realize that it is far better to use God's terminology as found in His word and not attempt to redefine His definitions to fit our theology. Such is the case when we say that the "church" (the man made institution) is the elect.

Hosea offers us another clue that further clarifies the issue of the identity of the elect while speaking specifically about the time of the Great Tribulation:

"For I will be like a lion to Ephraim (Israel)**, and like a young lion to the house of Judah. I, even I, will tear them and go away; I will take them away, and no one shall rescue. I will return again to My place till they acknowledge their offense. Then they will seek My face; in their affliction they will earnestly seek Me. Come, and let us return to the LORD; for He has torn, but He will heal us; He has stricken but He will bind us up. After two days He will revive us, on the third day He will raise us up, that we may live in His sight." Hosea 5:14-6:2**

The original nation of Israel split into the Northern Kingdom of Israel (often called Ephraim) and Southern Kingdom of Judah. The above section of scripture clearly is speaking to *both* Ephraim and Judah — the *whole house of Israel* — as God's chosen. From this verse it becomes apparent that the "elect" (or chosen) are from the *whole* nation of Israel, both the Northern (Israel) and Southern kingdoms (Judah),[57] and that both Houses will have to endure the Great Tribulation.

Again, the elect have always been from "all Israel" throughout the Old Testament, but now we see through 1 Peter 2:9-10 shown above that the elect *continue* to be Israel, even in the New Testament scriptures.

It is essential to realize also that the context of Hosea 5:14-6:2 is the Great Tribulation, and that they (Israel) will be "torn," confirming that many will perish during the Great Tribulation.

The Great Tribulation is sometimes referred to as the time of "Jacobs Trouble;"[58] **"Alas! For that day is great, so that none is like it; and it is the time of Jacob's trouble, but he shall be saved out of it." Jeremiah 30:7**. It is worthwhile to point out that this time period is called the time of "*Jacob's* trouble" and not just the time of "Judah's Trouble."[59]

From Hosea 5, we also note that something is required from each of these two Houses of Israel *before* the Lord returns, **"I** (Jesus) **will return again to My place** (heaven, at the right hand of God) **till they** (plural – both Ephraim and Judah) **acknowledge their offense."** It is easy to pick on Judah and to point out their offense. Judah, for the most part, does not know the identity of the Messiah. But who is Ephraim? And what is his offense? For that matter, the really important question becomes, "Who is Israel?" If Judah (the Jewish people) is spoken of separately from Ephraim, does Ephraim exist today separately from those that we call the Jews? Does the "church" fit into all of this? And if so, where?

The next few chapters of this book will address these exciting questions. The answers will shock and amaze you — and if you will receive the Word of God, *your identity* in the Messiah will be changed forever!

CHAPTER 7

Who then is Israel?

*I*n the previous chapter, we discussed the "Fork in the trail," the apparent place where one's theology leads him to either a pre-tribulation viewpoint, a post-tribulation/prewrath interpretation, or for that matter, an amillenialist/preterist position. Using the word of God to interpret itself, and linking Old Testament passages with New Testament scripture (compare Hosea 1:9-10 with 1 Peter 2:10) we have shown that the identity of the elect is none other than *Israel*. We will now explore the identity of the people of Israel today.[60]

In this chapter, we will present some ideas that are presently outside of "mainstream" Christian theology. Indeed, in the book, *Rapture: under attack*, Timothy LaHaye on p.223 states, "We must understand that Israel and the church are distinct!" Mr. LaHaye spends a significant amount of time in the appendix portion of the book to explain that understanding Israel and the church as separate entities is a "key" to understanding biblical prophecy.

I contend that understanding the *true identity* of "Israel" is the key to understanding the end times and will prove this position using the word of God.

This chapter and the previous chapter will challenge the widely held "separate entity" notion as being unscriptural. It is for this reason that I ask you the reader to approach these topics prayerfully. I ask that you would allow the words of God that are quoted here, and the Holy Spirit to speak — and do not put this book aside because of preconceived ideas, rather, be like those in Berea who **"Received the Word with all readiness, and searched the scriptures daily to find out whether these things were so."** Let us rely on the Word of God, and not put all of our faith in those who have gone before us and who have established traditions and church dogma. Listen to the words of the prophet Jeremiah who plainly tells us that in the "day of affliction"[61] the gentiles will realize that we have been misled by the traditions of men all along the way:

"O LORD, my strength and my fortress, my refuge in the day of affliction, the gentiles shall come to You from the ends of the earth and say, 'Surely our fathers have inherited lies, worthlessness, and unprofitable things.'" Jeremiah 16:19

At this extraordinary point in history, there is a country in the Middle East that claims the title of Israel — and rightly so. It is fascinating to note that there was some disagreement as to what the name of this newly reestablished country should be. Many wanted the name to be Zion, some wanted Judea — but in the end David Ben Gurion, citing Ezekiel as his authority, declared the name to be Israel![62] Was this an accident of History? What does the Bible say about this matter? Since the people of all *Israel* are the elect, this is a very important question indeed.

To understand Israel, we must first take a look at Abraham and the promises that God gave to him. In Genesis 12:1-3, 15: 1-6 and 17:1-6, God promised Abraham that he would be the father of many nations. Abraham believed God's promise, and it was accounted to him as righteousness.[63] Although Abraham became the "Father of many nations" in his own right, through both Isaac and Ishmael, as well as through later sons born after the death of Sarah, the specific birthright blessing of being the "father of many nations" as well as the lineage through which the "whole earth will be blessed" was passed on to only one of his sons. We see in Genesis 26:4 that this birthright blessing was given by God to Abraham's son Isaac.

This birthright blessing was then given by Isaac to Jacob in Genesis 28:3-4, **"May God Almighty bless you, and make you fruitful and multiply you, that you may be an assembly of** peoples; and give you the blessing of Abraham to you and your descendants with you that you may inherit the land in which you are a stranger, which God gave to Abraham." The specific blessing of becoming the father of many nations was then passed from Jacob through Joseph to Ephraim by Jacob's adoption of Joseph's sons in Genesis 48:5, then Jacob's blessing of Joseph's younger son Ephraim in Genesis 48:16, "Let my name be named upon them, and the name of my fathers Abraham and Isaac; and let them grow into a multitude in the midst of the earth." And in 48:19, Jacob blesses Ephraim specifically, "his descendants shall become a multitude of nations."

We should now ask ourselves, do we believe what Abraham believed? Do we believe that through this lineage (Abraham — Isaac — Jacob — Joseph — Ephraim) a multitude of nations would come forth? Remember, Abraham believed God, and it was accounted to him as righteousness. Do we *really* believe that Ephraim became many nations? What does the Bible say about what happened to Ephraim anyway?

What the History Books Don't Tell...

After Jacob died, his sons lived in Egypt and were led by Joseph. Of course Jacob eventually died, but the entire clan (who were already quite diverse considering the fact that Joseph had twelve children from four different women) stayed and dwelt in land of Goshen, the best land in Egypt. Over two hundred and fifty years passed. The clan grew into an enormous nation — a nation without a home. Considering the change that has taken place in North America over the last 250 years, one is able to easily see that quite a bit can happen over this length of time. The Bible records that a new pharaoh then came to power, one that was different and did not know Joseph.[64] This Pharaoh oppressed and enslaved the Israelites. Through Moses, God miraculously freed the fledgling nation and returned them to the land of their fathers—the Promised Land.

After forty years of wilderness wanderings, God restored the Israelites to their land through the conquests of Joshua. For a period of time, the nation existed without an earthly king, and Judges were placed over them to settle disputes. Eventually the nation of Israel wanted to be like the other nations of the world and they asked God for a King. During the eighty year time period of the reigns of King David and King Solomon, the nation of Israel grew to worldwide prominence. It would be difficult to overstate the magnificence of the Israelite empire during this time period approximately 1000 years before the birth of Christ.

After the death of Solomon, the entire nation was divided into two Kingdoms. The Southern half, consisting primarily of the Tribes of Judah, Benjamin, and some of Levi, became known as Judah (or the House of Judah). The Northern half, consisting of the remaining 10 tribes kept the name Israel (the House of Israel). In the Scriptures, the House of Israel is often referred to as "Ephraim." It is *extremely important* to note that the division of the kingdom was by the hand of God. It was *His* design to fulfill *His* purpose.[65] The books of 1 and 2 Kings and 1 and 2 Chronicles document the histories of these two separate Kingdoms.

Eventually, both the House of Israel, and the House of Judah fell into idolatry and were judged by God, just as He promised He would in Deuteronomy 28:58-68.[66] Judah went into captivity by the hand of the Babylonians almost 600 years before the time of Christ, and was kept in captivity for 70 years, just as God had decreed they would through the prophet Jeremiah.[67]

After their return from Babylon, and for the next 2500 years, the house of Judah kept their national identity preserved despite great hardship and persecution. The House of Judah became the "Jews" of Jesus' time, and to this day they have miraculously been able to maintain a sense of identity through the careful preservation of God's Laws. Today, the House of Judah is back in the Land of Israel, and they have claimed the title of Israel. Indeed, they are of the seed of the man Israel (Jacob), and are deserving of the title, but are they the *Whole* House of Israel? What happened to Ephraim?

Scattered Seed

Remember, Ephraim was the heir of the promise to become *many nations*. The house of Israel is often referred to as Ephraim in the Bible, because indeed Ephraim was the most prominent tribe of the Northern Kingdom. In Hosea 1:10, we see that Israel, or Ephraim became **"not my people."** (Just as was discussed in the last chapter) We find out in the New Testament that they became "my people" once again.

Speaking of gentiles, let's take a look at what Paul says to the Romans while writing about the "Gentiles." Speaking of the gentiles, Paul says, **"As He says in Hosea: "I will call them my people, who were not my people, and her beloved, who was not beloved. And it shall come to pass in the place where it was said to them, 'You are not My people,' there they shall be called sons of the living God.""** **Romans 9:25-26.** By this we get a hint that Paul knew that the scattered Northern Kingdom of Israel could be found among the "gentiles."

Let us also take a look at 1 Peter. To whom was Peter writing? His letter is addressed **"To the sojourners of the Dispersion in Pontus, Galatia, Cappadocia, Asia, and Bithynia,"** (1 Pet 1:1) A cursory glance of this might give one the impression that Peter is writing to the "Jews" who were dispersed to Gentile cities after 70 A.D. However, Bible scholars generally agree that 1 Peter was written in the early 60's A.D., *before* the dispersion of the Jews, therefore Peter *must be writing to the dispersed Israelites*. Notice then *what* he writes to these (whom Peter also refers to as the "elect" in vs. 1:2): **"But you are a chosen generation, a royal priesthood, a holy nation, His own special people, that you may proclaim the praises of Him who called you out of darkness into His marvelous light; who once were not a people but are now the people of God, who had not obtained mercy but now have obtained mercy." 1 Peter 2:9-10.** Here again is a New Testament reference to Hosea's prophecy, thus "connecting the dots" and allowing us to follow the nation Israel across generations till we come to an "elect" people who have put their faith in the Messiah of Israel — Yeshua, Jesus of Nazareth.

More New Testament Proof of the Identity of Israel

In Acts 2, Luke records the events surrounding the day of

Pentecost. Notice verse 5 **"and there were dwelling in Jerusalem Jews, devout men, from every nation under heaven."** And later note verses 9-11 **"Parthians and Medes and Elamites, those dwelling in Mesopotamia, Judah and Cappadocia, Pontus and Asia, Phrygia and Pamphylia, Egypt and the parts of Libya adjoining Cyrene, visitors from Rome, both Jews and proselytes, Cretans and Arabs – we heard them speaking in our own tongues the wonderful words of God."** What were these people from all over the world doing in Jerusalem? In Deuteronomy 16:16 we find that God commands every male to travel to **"the place which He chooses"** three times per year to celebrate the Feasts of God. These sojourners were faithful and so were not considered "Gentiles" by the Jews, but instead were considered 'Proselytes' or Gentile converts to Judaism. But who would God consider these? I would submit that these people by the proof of their infilling by the Holy Spirit, and by their having been added to the congregation (vs. 2:41) are among the "elect" of God.

Ephraim was given the promise that he would become "many nations." Here we see representatives from *many nations*. If we simply believe what Abraham believed, and believe the Bible — by faith we begin to realize that these faithful sojourners are most likely of Ephraim, and rightly are part of Israel!

Let's now take a look at the epistle written by James, the brother of Jesus. The book of James is addressed to **"the twelve tribes which are scattered abroad."** This is a clear indication that in the first century there was awareness that remnants of the original Kingdom of Israel, *the whole house*, were an identifiable people that had been scattered abroad.

In Matthew 15:21-28, Jesus is approached by a Canaanite woman who repeatedly asks our Savior to heal her daughter. He eventually gives in to her persistence, but not before proclaiming in verse 24 that **"I was not sent except to the lost sheep of the house of Israel."** This is an amazing confirmation that the identity of the elect is Israel. *Israel is the group to whom Christ was sent!*

The Ancient Fate of the House of Israel

The Scripture records that there were many from the Northern tribe of Israel taken into captivity by the Assyrians. In order to maintain the stability of the Assyrian Empire, the Assyrians had a practice of taking the prominent people from a conquered nation and resettling them so as to decrease the likelihood of an uprising due to nationalistic identity. The Northern House of Israel was quite populous and there is speculation that the small number of recorded captives does not fully represent the entire surviving nation.

The Bible records that there was a famine in the land caused by Elijah's closing of the heavens for 3½ years. Famines typically cause mass emigration out of an area. Where could they have gone? Some think they went to Judah, but there is no biblical or extra biblical record of a large influx of those from the Northern Kingdom into Judah. In fact, the books of Kings were written just before the Babylonian captivity of Judah about 550 years before Christ, a good 175 years *after* the Assyrian conquest of the Northern Kingdom of Israel. Second Kings 17:23-41 states, **"Israel was carried away from their own land to the land of Assyria, as it is to this day,"** and proves that no such influx happened.

It is a bit speculative, but compelling, to note that the populous state of Israel had historical (and biblically documented[68]) alliances with the Phoenicians, who were renowned sea travelers. If fleeing Israelites found passage on Phoenician ships, they could have wound up literally anywhere on the Earth. Amazing proof of this possibility is an ancient site near Los Lunas, NM that dates to about 1000 B.C. Incredibly, at this site archeologists have discovered the Ten Commandments written in ancient paleo-Hebrew! Further proof includes another "Decalogue Tablet" unearthed in Ohio in 1860 that is inscribed with the Ten Commandments in ancient Hebrew.[69]

There are many interesting theories and conjectures as to the whereabouts of the "lost tribes" today. Indeed, there is some good evidence that lends credibility to the notion that Israel became many nations. However, after reviewing some available information carefully, it is my opinion that there is much out there that is quite speculative. While some of these accounts may be true, much is based on myth and legend and sorting the truth from the fiction is difficult, if not impossible. The concept of "British Israelism" comes from this sort of work. We will discuss the notion of British Israelism, which is heretical and perhaps even racist, in chapter 13 in the context of some interesting speculation about the identity of the Antichrist.

Because we are interested in the truth about the identity of Israel, we will stick to what the scripture says about this matter. By doing this we see that God has indeed shown us his plan to make the seed of Abraham as numerous as the sands of the sea through Abraham's grandson, Israel.

The Foreigner — Brought near by the Blood!

At this juncture, you may be asking, "But what about non-Israelites? Can they also be 'elect?'" This is certainly a pertinent question since practically no person these days can definitely prove his or her heritage. Even Jews, who have preserved their beliefs and their way of life for millennia, cannot prove their biological lineage with certainty.

Consider the fact that the scriptural way of determining ones heritage was through the father and that for several hundred years, Jews have determined ones "Jewishness" based on the heritage of the *mother*. Consider this also, if a Proselyte was to have children — wouldn't his offspring after several generations be considered fully Jewish despite the reality of their genetics? Additionally, what about cases of marital infidelity and non-paternity? Wouldn't these offspring be mistakenly called Jewish? Since the Jew cannot prove their heritage, and since true Israelites have lost their identity and become "not My people," there is simply no way to prove who is and who isn't a descendant of the man Jacob.

Thankfully, the Creator of the Universe knows who is of Israel, **"For I will command, and will sift the house of Israel among all nations, as grain is sifted in a sieve; yet not the smallest grain shall fall to the ground."** Amos 9:9 [70] Notice **"Not the smallest grain will fall to the ground"** in verse 9. This indicates that our Heavenly Father (who is also Yeshua), the Good Shepherd, is aware of who and where His sheep are. We see the same concept in John 10:27-29: **"My sheep hear My voice, and I know them, and they follow Me. And I give them eternal life, and they shall never perish; neither shall anyone snatch them out of My hand. My Father, who has given them to Me is greater than all; and no one is able to snatch them out of My Father's hand. I and My Father are one."** [71]

Still, we have asked a valid question and have not answered it. What about the non-Israelite? Paul address this very issue in his letter to the Ephesians: **"Therefore remember that you, once Gentiles in the flesh — who are called uncircumcision by what is called circumcision made in the flesh by hands — that at that time you were without Christ, being aliens from the commonwealth of Israel and strangers from the covenants of promise, having no hope and without God in the world. But now in Christ Jesus you who once were far off have been brought near by the blood of Christ...now therefore you are no longer strangers and foreigners, but fellow citizens with the saints and members of the household of God." Ephesians 2:11-13, 19**

This passage is very enlightening. I have to admit that I personally must have read this dozens of times, but never understood the implications until the veil was removed from my eyes. Paul is clearly saying here that through Christ, those who were once "Gentiles in the flesh" are now part of the *commonwealth of Israel* (the elect).

In the Old Testament we find provisions for those who are non-Israelite who desire to become a part of the nation. (Leviticus 19:34; Numbers 9:14, 15:15-16; Is.56:6-8, Ezekiel 47:23) In short, foreigners were allowed to join Israel by observing the commandments, becoming circumcised, keeping Passover, sojourning (going up to Jerusalem for mandatory feasts), and thereafter were considered as natives of the land. After the foreigner accomplished all of these things, he was *by all rights* an Israelite.

Thus, we begin to understand the heart of the Father of all creation. He desires than none should perish, and all are invited to join His elect and become part of the "commonwealth of Israel." Blood heritage just does not matter in the end!

Does this mean that we have to become "Jewish" in order to become one of the elect? Of course not! This was the very thing that Paul was addressing in his letter to the Galatians.

When we look at the Old Testament requirements for foreigners who wished to become part of Israel and compare them to requirements under the renewed covenant we do see some parallels. Instead of becoming circumcised in the flesh, we are to become circumcised of the heart. With respect to keeping the commands of God, Jesus said **"If you love me you will keep my commands"** and 1 John mentions the importance of keeping his commands several times as in the following passage:

"By this we know that we love the children of God, when we love God and keep His commandments. For this is the love of God, that we keep His commandments. And His commandments are not burdensome." 1 John 5:2-3

Much more will be discussed regarding the keeping of the commandments in chapters 9 and 10.

The concept that we need to understand is this: We do not need to become "Jewish" per se to be part of God's people, because when we accepted the Israelite Messiah (Jesus Christ) as both our Savior *and* our Lord — we were then grafted into the commonwealth of Israel![72] This concept of being grafted into Israel is very important. Paul actually uses this very illustration in the Book of Romans.

The Olive Tree

In Romans 9-11, Paul spends three chapters discussing the fate of "Israel" and the role of the "Gentiles" to provoke jealousy. We can glean some interesting tidbits through these chapters. Notice first, in Romans 9:6, Paul indicates, **"They are not all Israel who are of Israel."** This is a strange verse, until we realize this is a word play. Israel is a synonym for "elect" when it is used the first time in this phrase, and "of Israel" as it is used the second time refers to the natural physical seed of Jacob. More clearly stated Paul is saying,

"They are not all *the elect* who are of the seed of Jacob." Clearly, this indicates there is more to salvation then one's pedigree. We learn throughout the Bible, specifically in Romans 10:9-10, that salvation is of *faith.*

When Paul is speaking of the *Gentiles* in this section of Scripture, he is not only referring to those who are non-Jews, but he is also referring to those who "were not my people." This is proven by Paul's explicit quote of the prophet Hosea in Romans 9:25,[73] thus linking those referred to as the "House of Israel" in the book of Hosea with those called "Gentiles" in this section of Scripture. Therefore, according to the apostle Paul, if you call yourself a "Son of the Living God," then you are saying by virtue of Hosea 1:10 that you are a returning Israelite![74]

In Romans 11, Paul uses the analogy of the Olive Tree that we may understand how God is gathering a people for Himself. When Paul describes the grafting of the wild olive branches into the Olive tree, the Gentiles are represented as "wild" branches, and those who have kept their identity are referred to as "natural" branches. It is worth pointing out that the Gentiles are indeed *olive* branches, and not branches from some other kind of tree.

Consider what happens to a "cultivated" variety of plant if it is allowed to grow on its own and is not tended or pruned and actively kept "domesticated." (Interestingly, this occupation of tending to crops in this way is sometimes referred to as plant <u>husband</u>ry). If a cultivated variety of plant is not actively tended, in several generations it will revert to the "wild type." In Hosea, Israel became "**not my people.**" This happened when Israel lost her husband because of her unfaithfulness, and after a few generations she became "wild" and lost her identity.

The important point of this metaphor used by Paul is that the Olive Tree is *still an Olive Tree!* It did not turn into a different kind of tree (for example, into the "church" tree—as dispensationalist doctrine implies), nor was the tree replaced with a different kind of tree (as replacement theology implies). The "Natural branches" were branches that retained their identity as Israel, so why wouldn't the grafted in "wild olive" branches also identify with the tree, and thus with the nation of Israel? After all, it is the root that makes holy, **"...and if the root is holy, so are the branches." Romans 12:16** The "wild branches" do not make the whole tree "wild," but rather the root makes the wild branches holy!

What Does This Mean?

Let us now put the case together, if the following statements are true, then the conclusion will be inescapable:

- The elect, throughout biblical history, are Israel.
- Ephraim, *like Judah*, is of Israel.
- Ephraim became "not my people," lost their sense of identity, and were scattered among the nations.
- Ephraim, through the birthright blessing *became many nations.*
- God kept track of who Ephraim/Israel became.
- Israel became "my people" once again, and "obtained mercy" through the work of the Messiah.
- Through Christ, believers have become part of the commonwealth of Israel, regardless of their genetic heritage.
- The wild branches are made holy by the root, and are grafted in to the identity of "Israel"

What does this mean? It means that our *identity* as the "church" is terribly wrong! We call ourselves the "church" and proclaim that there are two dispensations and that our omnipotent, all-knowing God has had to deal with the Jews and the "church" separately, because he didn't foresee the Jew's rejection of Jesus. This is despite Jesus' clear proclamation in John 10:16 that there will be *one* flock, and one shepherd. What we must see is the fact that the "one flock" is *still* Israel, made up of faithful believers from both the House of Judah and the House of Israel (Ephraim), and of those foreigners who would join the commonwealth of Israel through the Messiah.

We can now see that just as His word proclaims, God's plan all along was to reveal Himself through His witness, His chosen people Israel. God did not put the nation of Israel on "hold" as the dispensationalist doctrine purports. We have shown above that God is working to redeem all of mankind through his people Israel, even today.

We think that we are the "elect" because we call ourselves the church, but now we find that the "elect" are Israel! If we want to be counted as part of the "elect" then we must identify with *Israel*, not the man made "church" that has discarded God's ordinances and has adopted her own set of laws and religious doctrines. In doing this, we have tried to make that which is holy into something that is "wild." Instead of identifying with Israel, we have separated ourselves from Israel and our brother Judah. Worse yet, not realizing that Judah is our brother, we as Christians have been guilty of intense persecution of the Jews in times past. Not understanding our identity, we have considered His Word in the Old Testament as being somehow less important than the New Testament Scriptures.

Just as Judah has become blinded in part to the reality of her Messiah, *Ephraim has been blinded to his identity*. Foolishly, we argued that the "church" is the elect in Matthew 24, or conversely, we argued that the "Jews" are the elect.

So we see that the "elect" includes believers in Messiah from *both* of the Houses of Israel *as well as* the foreigner who would join to Israel. This is despite the fact that *not one of us*, whether we are Jew, or Israelite, or Gentile, can prove our biological heritage. Nevertheless, since God promised Abraham that he would be the father of many nations, and since that promise was passed down through Isaac, then to Jacob, then Joseph, and then was given to Ephraim, and since Ephraim was the predominant tribe in the Northern Kingdom that was scattered among the nations, we see that God caused the offspring of the man Israel (Jacob) to be scattered among the nations! If we simply believe what Abraham believed, so that it was accounted to him for righteousness, then we must agree that *many nations today are of Ephraim*. We are faced with the inescapable conclusion that we who have heard the call of God, and who are believers in the Messiah—*could very well be the physical offspring of Israel!*

Has the "church" then replaced Israel? Heavens no! This teaching is not about the "church" replacing Israel — it is about Ephraim coming *alongside* of Judah, as an *equal* partaker in the commonwealth of Israel and thus fulfilling Ezekiel chapter 37:15-28. **"Thus says the LORD God: 'Surely I will take the stick of Joseph,**

which is in the hand of Ephraim, and the tribes of Israel, his companions; and I will join them with it, with the stick of Judah, and make them one stick, and they will be one in My hand." Ezekiel 37:19

The "church" is a *man made* institution that has abandoned her Israelite roots. To say that God is dealing with the church and Israel separately and that the church will be exempt from tribulation while the Jew suffers...this is the *real* "Replacement Theology."

Ecclesia, the Greek word that means the "called out ones" has been translated into the word "church." This word "church" has in turn taken on a whole new meaning. It is impossible to describe the "elect" of God using our own terms and definitions. We must use God's terminology, and so our only response to the question "Who is the 'elect'?" is the simple response: "The 'elect' are those of both houses of Israel, as well as foreigners, who have received Messiah, and who are faithful to Him." We see then that there is no distinction or superiority between those who are of the House of Israel, and those who are of the House of Judah. We are all truly "one new man" in the Messiah.[75] As for the term "church," which comes from the Greek word "ecclesia" (meaning the called out ones), let us remember the words of Jesus:

"many are called, but few are chosen." Matthew 22:14

Hear, O Israel!

Do you find yourself watching news from the Middle East and Israel with intense interest? Do you feel drawn to the Biblical feasts? Does you heart quicken when you hear a Messianic praise song? Perhaps God is calling you to identify with His elect! The startling revelation of your identity as God's elect will forever change the way that you look at the scriptures. The Word will come alive as you realize that the words spoken in the Old Testament are about *your* forefathers, and the prophecies pertain to *you*. Read carefully these words spoken of the house of Israel (Ephraim) by the prophet Jeremiah many generations ago. Let God speak to your heart, and open your eyes to the fact that He has declared His truth down through the ages, and that this truth has been preserved for this very day, when He is bringing His Word to pass:

The LORD has appeared from afar to me, saying: "Yes, I have loved you with an everlasting love; Therefore with lovingkindness I have drawn you. Again I will build you, and you shall be rebuilt, O virgin of Israel! You shall again be adorned with your tambourines, and shall go forth in the dances of those who rejoice. You shall yet plant vines on the mountains of Samaria; The planters shall plant and eat them as ordinary food. For there shall be a day when the watchmen will cry on Mount Ephraim, 'Arise, and let us go up to Zion, to the LORD our God.'"

For thus says the LORD:

"Sing with gladness for Jacob, and shout among the chief of the nations; Proclaim, give praise, and say, 'O LORD, save Your people, The remnant of Israel!' Behold, I will bring them from the north country, and gather them from the ends of the earth, Among them the blind and the lame, the woman with child and the one who labors with child, together; A great throng shall return there. They shall come with weeping, and with supplications I will lead them. I will cause them to walk by the rivers of water, in a straight way in which they shall not stumble; For I am a Father to Israel, and Ephraim is My first-born. Hear the word of the LORD, O nations, and declare it in the isles afar off and say, 'He who scattered Israel will gather him, and keep him as a shepherd does his flock.' For the LORD has redeemed Jacob, and ransomed him from the hand of one stronger than he. Therefore they shall come and sing in the height of Zion, Streaming to the goodness of the LORD – For wheat and new wine and oil, for the young of the flock and the herd; their souls shall be like a well-watered garden, and they shall sorrow no more at all. Then shall the virgin rejoice in the dance, and the young men and the old, together; for I will turn their mourning to joy, will comfort them, and make them

rejoice rather than sorrow. I will satiate the soul of the priests with abundance, and My people shall be satisfied with My goodness, says the LORD."

Thus says the LORD:

"A voice was heard in Ramah, Lamentation and bitter weeping, Rachel weeping for her children, refusing to be comforted for her children, because they are no more."

Thus says the LORD:

"Refrain your voice from weeping, and your eyes from tears; for your work shall be rewarded, says the LORD, and they shall come back from the land of the enemy. There is hope in your future, says the LORD, that your children shall come back to their own border. I have surely heard Ephraim bemoaning himself: 'You have chastised me, and I was chastised, like an untrained bull; Restore me, and I will return, for You are the LORD my God. Surely, after my turning, I repented; and after I was instructed, I struck myself on the thigh; I was ashamed, yes, even humiliated, because I bore the reproach of my youth.' "

"Is Ephraim my dear son? Is he a pleasant child? For though I spoke against him, I earnestly remember him still; Therefore My heart yearns for him; I will surely have mercy on him, says the LORD." Jeremiah 31:3-20

CHAPTER 8

What about the Church?

"Ephraim is oppressed and broken in judgment, because he willingly walked by Human precept" Hosea 5:11

*I*n the last two chapters, we have looked at scripture to prove that the elect of God are none other than Israel. We have shown also that as we have been grafted into the olive tree (Israel), we should assume our identity as Israel, and not continue as wild branches. Whether we are former Israelites that have become "My people" once again or true foreigners who have been grafted in, we must realize that this tree is still an Olive tree, and it has not become another kind of tree just because we have been grafted (back) into the tree. In other words, it is up to us to identify with the "tree," and not vice versa. The commonly held "dispensationalist doctrine" says that God is dealing with Israel and the "church" separately and espouses such a view.

This notion that the church is something separate from the congregation of Israel has led to our cutting ourselves off from our heritage and our birthright, and it has led to many false doctrines. We, as the church, have removed ourselves from the root and so have become "wild" once again. Let us consider the words of Yeshua,[76] **"I am the vine, you are the branches. He who abides in Me, and I in him, bears much fruit; for without Me you can do nothing." John 15:5**

So what about the church? As Bible believing Christians, where do we fit into all of this? To answer this question, let's first look at this word "church." As mentioned earlier, this word comes from the Greek word "ecclesia," which means "called out ones." Indeed, we have been called out of the world, and by the blood of the Messiah we have been brought into the Commonwealth of Israel.[77] Interestingly, when the word ecclesia is used in the Septuagint (the Greek translation of the Old Testament) it is used often in relation to *the congregation of Israel* as in the following verse:

"Now you shall keep it until the fourteenth day of the same month. Then the whole assembly (here the word for 'assembly' is *ecclesia*) **of the congregation of Israel shall kill it at twilight." Exodus 12:6**

Thus a biblical understanding of the terms ecclesia or "church" reinforces the fact that we as believers in the True and Living God ought to identify with His people Israel.

Amazingly, there is good reason for Israel's blindness about their identity. We have seen that as a nation, part of God's judgment on Israel was that Israel would become "not My people," but we also know that corporately, the nation of Israel will one day become My people again. If we simply believe what the prophets of God have said, we agree that Israel will awaken to her identity from all over the world, and we will join our brother Judah, just as predicted in Ezekiel 37, as well as other places in the Old Testament.

The fact of the matter is this, even if we have been unaware of our citizenship, and have been kept blinded to our identity, God has not lost track of His people Israel: **"I know Ephraim, and Israel is not hidden from Me." Hosea 5:3** The specifics of what will happen during this exciting time of the regathering of God's people will be discussed in the following chapters.

But Why Now?

The astute Bible student may ask the question, why are we finding this out now? If this is a foundational truth, why is it just recently coming to light? Surely many who have gone on before us as leaders of the church were indeed men of God, led by the Holy Spirit. Why didn't they know about their identity? The answer is both astounding and encouraging.

In Ezekiel chapter four, we are given a strange prophecy. Ezekiel is told by God to build a clay model of Jerusalem. He is told then to lie on his side "against" this model for a certain number of days; each day is to represent the number of years of judgment first against the House of Israel, and then he is told to lie on his other side a second time for a set number of days again representing years of judgment, this time against the House of Judah (thus showing that the judgments are separate). Ezekiel lies on his left side for 390 days "against" the house of Israel, each day representing a year of judgment. Israel, however, did not repent from her idolatry. Because of this, her punishment was multiplied by seven; just as God promised in Leviticus 26:18 **"And after this, if you do not obey Me, then I will punish you seven times more for your sins."**

Remember Sir Robert Anderson's calculations? He used 360-day years to prove that Daniel's prophecy was accurate to the very day. If we apply the same method of calculation in this situation, we come up with the following:

390 years of judgment (not my people) X seven
(because of lack of repentance)
= 2730 years

2730 years (360 day years) adjusted to 365.25 day years
= 2690.75 years

If we add this number to the year 722 B.C.E.,[78] when the last city of Israel, Samaria, fell to the Assyrians — we end up at 1967.[79] Amazingly, this seems to be about the time that what is often called "Messianic Judaism" (often fueled by 'Gentiles' yearning for the things of God[80]) really got off the ground. Interestingly, it was also the year that the Temple Mount became the sovereign property of the nation of Israel for the first time in over 2000 years. Incidentally, using the same method of counting years we find that tory was accurately prophesied by Ezekiel as well.[81]

Judah has been blinded to their Messiah, Ephraim (Israel) has been blinded to the reality of her identity. Finally, *just as prophesied*, in our present time the veil is being removed — and at last we are able to see just who we are in the Messiah. Now, knowing this truth, we look in horror at the sins of our youth, we **"smote our thigh"** [82] and we repent.

Does this sound unbelievable? It is not the first time that God has done something that seems astounding. Let us consider the words of the prophets,

"Look among the nations and watch—be utterly astounded!
For I will work a work in your days
which you would not believe,
Though it were told you." Habakkuk 1:5

So then…What about the Church?

What is the present state of the church? More precisely stated with the understanding of our identity, "What is the offense of Ephraim?" To answer that, we are going to take a look at the "church."

For the sake of this discussion, we will define the "church" as those who know who the identity of the Messiah, but have forgotten *their* identity as Israel.

Throughout the New Testament we are confronted with warnings about false teachers and false doctrine. Paul's passionate plea to the Ephesians in the book of Acts is an example. **"Therefore take heed to yourselves and to all the flock, among which the Holy Spirit has made you overseers, to shepherd the church of God which He purchased with His own blood. For I know this, that after my departure savage wolves will come in among you, not sparing the flock. Also from among yourselves men will rise up, speaking perverse things to draw away the disciples after themselves" Acts 20:28-30.**

In Timothy, Paul also admonishes, **"But know this, that in the last days perilous times will come: for men will be lovers of** themselves, lovers of money, boasters, proud, blasphemers, disobedient to parents, unthankful, unholy, unloving, unforgiving, slanderers, without self-control, brutal, despisers of good, traitors, headstrong, haughty, lovers of pleasure rather than lovers of God, having a form of godliness but denying it's power. And from such people turn away!"** 2 Timothy 3:1-5

And, **"For the time will come when they will not endure sound doctrine, but according to their own desires, because they have itching ears, they will heap up for themselves teachers; and they will turn their ears away from the truth, and be turned aside to fables."** 2 Timothy 4:3-4

Could Paul have been warning us about the church today? Indeed, when we look around, we see a splintered, contentious "body" that would be unrecognizable to the first century believer. This problem, however, is not unique to our times. As we look down through church history, there is much that should embarrass us. What follows, is a painful, honest look at the institution that we have called the "church." But first, carefully consider Paul's warning also to the Corinthians, **"But I fear, lest somehow, as the serpent deceived Eve by his craftiness, so your minds may be corrupted from the simplicity that is in Christ. For if he who comes preaches <u>another Jesus</u> whom we have not preached, or if you receive <u>a different spirit</u> which you have not received, or a <u>different gospel</u> which you have not accepted – you may well put up with it!"** 2 Corinthians 11:3-4 What? Is Paul saying that there is another Jesus? A different Spirit? A different Gospel? Indeed he is! Paul is clearly saying here that false teachers will invoke the name of Jesus. Clearly this is a warning that not everything that claims to be of "Jesus" is of the true and Living God. This is frightening when we consider that the church today has abandoned her heritage! Has the foundation for the great apostasy already been laid? Let us take a brief look at the *"fruit"* of the church both historically and presently — and let the reader decide.

Offenses of Ephraim

I suppose that volumes could be written examining the sins of the church over the last two millennia. Our checkered history is well documented and it is not the intent of this book to rehash all of church history.

What we will try to do, however, is to take a look back at our history in light of our blindness to our true identity. What follows may seem harsh. The church at times has been guilty and we ought to acknowledge the facts. On the other hand, let us temper our anger and condemnation on the church with the realization that Ephraim, who has manifested himself as the "church" over the past centuries, *has been entrusted with the knowledge that Yeshua was the Messiah* (but being under the judgment of God was blinded to her identity). This is in contrast to our brother Judah, who was **"entrusted with the oracles of God" (Romans 3:2b)** but has been for the most part blinded to the identity of the Messiah.

If one were to rank the sins of the church in ages past, surely at the top of the list would be the church's woeful treatment of our Jewish brothers. Throughout the centuries we have called it various things; the inquisition, the crusades, the pogroms, and even the holocaust.[83] The church, having lost her identity, and not realizing that Judah was her brother, caused or allowed immeasurable death and suffering. Literally *millions* of Jews have been slaughtered *in the name of Christianity*. It is no wonder that the Jews today are suspicious of Christians when we approach them about *their* Messiah.

Let us examine the words of some of our "church fathers" as they spewed forth hatred for our Jewish brethren:[84]

Augustine declared:"The true image of the Hebrew is Judas Iscariot, who sells the Lord for silver. The Jew can never understand the Scriptures and forever will bear the guilt for the death of Jesus."

Justin Martyr in his dialogue with Trypho the Jew, stated that the Jews should "rightly suffer," for they had "slain the Just One."

John Chrysostom, known as the "golden mouthed" due to his eloquence in speech, unleashed a series of Homilies against the Jews: *"They sacrificed their sons and daughters to devils; they outraged nature and overthrew their foundations of the laws of relationship. They are become worse than the wild beasts, and for no reason at all, with their own hands, they murder their offspring, to worship the avenging devils who are foes of our life... They know only one thing, to satisfy their gullets, get drunk, to kill and maim one another... The Jews are the most worthless of all men. They are lecherous, greedy, rapacious. They are perfidious murderers of Christ. The Jews are the odious assassins of Christ and for killing God there is no expiation possible, no indulgence or pardon. Christians may never cease vengeance, and the Jews must live in servitude forever. God always hated the Jews. It is incumbent upon all Christians to hate the Jews."*

St. Jerome, who had studied with Jewish scholars in Palestine and translated the Bible into Latin wrote about the synagogue: *"If you call it a brothel, a den of vice, the Devil's refuge, Satan's fortress, a place to deprave the soul, an abyss of every conceivable disaster or whatever you will, you are still saying less than it deserves."*

Peter the Venerable, Abbot of Cluny, declared to the faithful: *"Truly I doubt whether a Jew can be really human... I lead out from its den a monstrous animal and show it as a laughing stock in the amphitheatre of the world. I bring thee forward, thou Jew, thou brute beast, in the sight of all men."*

Pope Innocent III condemned the Jews to eternal slavery by decreeing: *"The Jews, against whom the blood of Jesus Christ calls out, although they ought not to be killed, lest the Christian people forget the Divine Law, yet as wanderers ought they remain upon the earth, until their countenance be filled with shame."*

Lest one presume that this persecution was only a Catholic or medieval phenomenon, Martin Luther himself proposed that the homes of Jews should be burned and that their tongues should be cut out if they do not convert.[85] Martin Luther also wrote, *"Therefore know, my dear Christian, that next to the devil you have no more bitter, more poisonous, more vehement an enemy than a real Jew who earnestly desires to be a Jew... Now what are we going to do with these rejected, condemned, Jewish people? You must refuse to let them own houses among us... You must take away from them all their prayer books and Talmuds wherein such lying, cursing and blasphemy is taught... You must prohibit their Rabbis to teach... You shall not tolerate them but expel them."* And he also

135

wrote, "...*verily a hopeless wicked venomous and devilish thing is the existence of these Jews, who for 1400 years have been and still are our pest, torment and misfortune. They are just devils and nothing more.*"

In our day, Christians who adhere to "Replacement Theology" believe also that the church has *replaced* Israel, and as a result, they often despise today's Jewish people, not realizing that the Jews are also heirs to the promise through Yeshua the Messiah. The "Christians" of this leaning demand that the Jewish convert and give up their Jewishness – while at the same time wallowing in a "Christianity" that has been contaminated with customs and traditions of man, simply because the church lacks appreciation for her true identity as Israel.

History tells us that the church has also been guilty of killing *each other* in the name of doctrinal differences. Sadly, many hundreds of thousands of "saints" were martyred at the hands of supposed fellow believers who, although misguided, thought they were defending the faith.

During the reformation, *hundreds of thousands* of believers were killed simply because they clung to the doctrine of salvation by grace. So called "heretics" were burned at the stakes because they dared to translate the Word of God from the Catholic Latin into their native tongue.

Why has this happened? It happened because the church, at certain times has not only lost her identity as Israel, but has completely removed itself from the root of the olive tree, who is Yeshua. Yeshua said, **"Without Me, you can do nothing."**

Today, the church is still a mess. There are hundreds, perhaps thousands of denominations, each proclaiming to have the "truth." Meanwhile, Jude 19 explains that divisions are caused by men *not having the Spirit of God*. When we realize that Paul tells us in Romans 8:9 that if we do not have the Spirit of God we are *not* His, we see that the *church is in big trouble!*

In our day, we have many "evangelists" throughout the church who preach a message of temporal prosperity. Focusing on the here and now, they preach a carnal message, leading gullible people with broken lives down the primrose path to destruction – the only ones getting rich are the preachers. They fleece the flock because they have tricked them into setting their minds on earthly blessings.

"By covetousness they will exploit you with deceptive words." 2 Peter 2:3 "For when they speak great swelling works of emptiness, they allure through the lusts of the flesh...While they promise them liberty, they themselves are slaves of corruption; for by whom a person is overcome, by him also he is brought into bondage." 2 Peter 2:18-19

The sinful emphasis on money and worldly possessions by some in the "church" is *nothing short of idolatry*.

As we take a hard look at some of the faults of the church, both past and present, we get the feeling that all of these things have taken place as the church has strayed from her roots. Considering God's judgment upon Israel, that she would become **"not My people,"** however, none of this is really all that surprising.

To really answer the question *why* all of this has happened requires digging a little deeper. We need to look at the question — *Why did God judge Israel in the first place?* We find that it was because of a specific particular sin that Israel repeatedly fell into, and as you will see, this error persists today. It is the *"offense of Ephraim."*

Holi-days Of Ephraim

In the light of our identity as Israel, let's take a brief look at some of our "Christian traditions." This is by no means meant to be condemning; rather this is an honest look at the true roots of our traditions.

Sunday Worship

As incredible as it may sound, history shows that many of the traditions of the church today were adaptations of ancient idolatrous religions, particularly the worship of the sun. The foremost example of this that comes to mind is the "Sunday Sabbath." While this will be a point of some controversy, let us examine the facts. Since it seems clear that the first century church met on the Sabbath,[86] where did Sunday worship come from? What follows is a brief paraphrasing of well documented history.

In about 320 A.D., Constantine, then a Roman General in the Region of present day France made a shrewd political maneuver in order to consolidate his power and take over the Roman Empire. Seeing that he needed allies to support his cause, Constantine befriended the Christians, who had already at this time begun to separate themselves from their Hebraic roots, and agreed to adopt their religion as a recognized state religion. Until this time, the Christians had been intensely persecuted, and were essentially cut off from the rest of society because of their beliefs. They had been crucified, burned, and fed to the lions for entertainment. These early believers lived in constant fear and were forced to meet secretly in catacombs and caves. They had been ostracized by early rabbinic Judaism and so they were more than happy to support Constantine and his friendlier policies.

Constantine had a problem, however. He had been a devotee of Sun worship, and he did not want to give up his religion, nor did he want to alienate the majority of the Empire, who also were involved in pagan Sun worship.

Constantine is said to have adopted "Christianity," but he certainly did not bear the fruit of the Spirit in his life after his supposed conversion. Among the notorious acts of Constantine was the giving of the order to have his wife murdered. Additionally, he made and upheld decrees that preserved Sun worship in a disguised form by continuing the ancient festivals and religious rites.

The venerated day of the week for Constantine was Sun-day, and by decree Constantine ordered that the holy day for Christians would no longer be the Sabbath (from Friday night to Saturday night), but would be Sunday!

In light of our identity as Israel, let us revisit the Ten Commandments, the instruction of God to His chosen people throughout "all generations":

"Remember the Sabbath day, to keep it holy. Six days you

shall labor and do all your work, but the seventh day is the Sabbath of the LORD your God. In it you shall do no work: you, nor your son, nor your daughter, nor your male servant, nor your female servant, nor your cattle, nor your stranger who is within you gates." Ex 20:8-10

Keeping in mind our identity as Israel, what shall we make of this? A careful look at the New Testament shows that Paul worshipped on the Sabbath, and taught in the Synagogues as is the Jewish tradition.[87] Believers in the "Sunday Sabbath" use the supposed Sunday resurrection of Christ as the excuse for Sunday Worship. A careful study of the events of Passion Week show that the Messiah was crucified on Wednesday, died in the afternoon, and was placed in the tomb before dark. Just as He had prophesied He was in the "belly of the earth for three days and three nights"[88] and arose after sundown the evening of the Sabbath — Saturday evening by our calendar, just as the "Feast of Firstfruits" began.

As a part of "Christian tradition" we celebrate and worship God in the way of *our* choosing, rather than keeping the Biblical feasts and the Sabbath that God appointed as an *everlasting sign* "throughout all your generations." When we take an honest look at many of these traditions, we are forced to admit they are firmly rooted in the idolatrous worship of false gods.

As Israelites, the chosen people of God, we ought to abhor idolatry. Because we love and respect our heavenly Father, should we not honor Him by remembering and keeping Holy the Sabbath? *To make Sunday our holy day is nothing short of continuing in the idolatrous practices handed to us by our "Fathers."*[89] What we will begin to see as we examine the history of Ephraim of old (the house of Israel) and modern day Ephraim (found in the church), is that idolatry is the *offense of Ephraim.*

Christmas

It is with much anguish that this next subject is introduced. Again, this is not meant to be judgmental, but rather it is a loving admonition concerning the roots of our traditions. Christmas, the supposed birthday of Jesus is without a doubt the most popular holiday of the year. While most informed Bible students realize that Yeshua could not really have been born during the winter, most Christians today *choose to ignore* the true roots of this winter festival. Sadly, Christmas is an adaptation of Sun worship with roots in ancient Babylon.

On ancient calendars the winter solstice occurred on Dec. 25. This shortest day of the year was thought to be the time that marked the death and resurrection of the Babylonian messiah, Tammuz, who was believed to be the Sun incarnate. Tammuz was the supposed son of Nimrod (and in a way *was* Nimrod — *just as Christ is God*), and was said to be conceived by his mother Simmiramus posthumously by Nimrod by the means of the sun's rays (since Nimrod was thought to have become the sun after his death).

The shortening days of winter were thought to be a sign that the sun god was dying. On the eve of the winter solstice, a "Yule" log, depicting the dead sun god would be brought into the house and burned. The next day, a young tree would be brought into the house, trimmed out and decorated. This signified the resurrection of the Sun, and thus the days would become longer.[90]

Much more could be written about the roots of Christmas, but I do not wish to belabor the point. Alexander Hislop said it best, *"There can be no doubt, then, that the Pagan festival at the winter solstice — in other words Christmas — was held in honor of the birth of the Babylonian Messiah."*[91]

But…I like Christmas!

"But wait!" You may object. "We don't worship the Christmas tree!" Realizing that our traditions have become "sacred," let us take a careful look at what has become of this festival called Christmas. It has become so secularized that even the public schools allow it! With Christmas trees, Santa Clause, and jingle bells, the fables that accompany Christmas are so nostalgic that it is indeed hard to break away from. Worse yet, our pride will not allow us to admit that we have been participating in something that is so grossly idolatrous.

When we consider the Christmas tree, and the gifts that magically appear at its feet for our children, we must ask ourselves if we are fostering a kind of worship of the tree in our children. Moreover, given the Babylonian roots of this holiday, can we really participate in it with a clean conscience?

The fact of the matter is this: We participate in Christmas because we *like* it. **"For the time will come when they will not endure sound doctrine, but according to their own desires, because they have itching ears, they will heap up for themselves teachers; and they will turn their ears away from the truth, and be turned aside to fables." 2 Timothy 4:3-4.**

Aware of the problems associated with this holiday, many of us have tried to make it right by reading "the Christmas story" of Christ's birth after we open our presents. But sadly, it is still a mixture of the holy with the profane.

I pray that you, the reader, will understand my heart with respect to Christmas. I am not without empathy when it comes to this matter. My wife and I have both struggled with *our own desires* when we first came to the knowledge of the roots of Christmas. I desire so much that the reader could get a sense of my compassion about this subject. This is not a matter to be harsh about, rather, we ought to realize that our beloved traditions die hard, and that growth happens over time.

As we come to understand the truth about Christmas, we also must realize that among the brethren, we are all in a different place. If we handle this situation with love, our brothers and sisters will become aware of their true identity. Once they come to this knowledge, "the truth will set them free" from the traditions of men.

Let us consider the very words of the Bible as it describes the folly of those following this ancient tradition that has been around long before the first advent. The words of the Bible penned *centuries before the birth of the Messiah* speak for themselves:

Hear the word which the LORD speaks to you, O house of Israel, Thus says the LORD: **"Do not learn the way of the Gentiles; do not be dismayed at the signs of heaven, for the Gentiles are dismayed at them. For the customs of the peoples**

are futile; for one cuts a tree from the forest, the work of the hands of the workman, with the ax. They decorate it with silver and gold; they fasten it with nails and hammers so that it will not topple." Jeremiah 10:1-4

Easter...Ishtar

Sadly, even the very word "Easter" is rooted in pagan idolatry. Easter, as pronounced today is in fact the correct pronunciation of the Babylonian goddess Ishtar.[92] Like other so called "Christian" traditions, the Easter celebration is derived from ancient Babylonian Sun worship. The date for Easter is attached to the Solar cycle rather than the timing of the crucifixion, which is linked to the Jewish Calendar and the celebration of the Passover.

Ishtar, also known as Astarte, was thought to be a reincarnation of Nimrod's wife Simmiramus (the mother of the Babylonian messiah Tammuz). Ishtar was the goddess of fertility, and fertility symbols such as the egg and the rabbit were often employed in the worship rituals because Simmiramus is said to have returned to Earth as the goddess "Easter" riding in a giant egg that descended on the Euphrates River. She is said to have turned a bird into an egg laying rabbit, thus giving us the symbols used for Easter even to this day.

Tammuz, the son of Ishtar was said to have died at the age of 40 after being gored by a wild boar. In ancient Babylon, a forty day fast was held in honor of this first false messiah, one day for each of the years of his life. This forty day fast ended with the "Easter" celebration. This practice was known as "weeping for Tammuz" and is spoken of explicitly in Ezekiel 8:14. Today's church, particularly the Catholic, continue a similar tradition with the fast of "Lent." To further honor Tammuz, ancient Babylonians would eat ham on Easter Sunday, thus exacting revenge on the wild boar that took the life of their most revered god.

Early Christians did not celebrate Easter, but rather they kept the *Passover*[93] — and thus honored the true and living God just as he commanded in the Old Testament. The Passover Feast is a wonderful memorial to the fact that our Messiah Yeshua was indeed our Passover, having been slain as our Passover Lamb on the day of

Passover. As noted previously, a careful study of the week of the crucifixion will reveal that our Savior died on a Wednesday afternoon, and was put in the tomb just before sundown. He then arose just after the passing of the Sabbath — which would be Saturday night on our calendar, and at the beginning of the Feast of Firstfruits on a Biblically accurate calendar. The "church" has forgotten these facts and has allowed idolatrous traditions of men to creep in and replace true God ordained worship. Sadly, we realize that the "sunrise" service held on Easter morning by churches all over the world, often facing east to witness the rising of the Sun, is *rooted* in pure sun worship. *Not to be confused with true Son worship!*

In the Old Testament, we see again and again that idolatry is the offense of Ephraim. It seems that truly there is "nothing new under the sun."

The Golden Calf Example

Still, you might be of the opinion that God is really only concerned with matters of the heart and that He "knows our heart" and excuses our lack of understanding. While I agree that we must acknowledge God's amazing grace, let us look at the example of scripture to prove a specific point. In Exodus chapter 32, we have the story of the "Golden Calf" recorded for our learning. Even Paul points out the fact that we are to learn from the mistakes of our Israelite forefathers, **"Now all these things happened to them as examples, and they were written for our admonition, upon whom the end of the ages have come."** 1 Cor10:11

A careful look at this story is quite enlightening. The Bible records that while Moses had gone up to the mountain to receive the tablets, the Israelites became restless and said, **"Come, let us make gods that shall go before us; for as for this Moses, the man who brought us up out of the land of Egypt, we do not know what has become of him."** **Ex 32:1** Notably, the word translated "gods" in the above translation (NKJV) should rightly be translated as "God." Here the Hebrew word for "gods" is Elohim, which is a plural word and depending on the context could be translated as either "God" or "gods." Proof showing that in this case it should rightly be translated as "God" is found in verse 5 when Aaron helps us to understand the situation and the context:

So when Aaron saw it (the golden calf), **he built an altar before it. And Aaron made a proclamation and said, "Tomorrow is a feast to the LORD." Ex 32:5**

The Hebrew word that is translated "LORD" in this case is YHWH, the great "I AM" name of the God of Abraham, Isaac, and Jacob. By this we see that the *intent* of these ancient Israelites was to worship the true and living God!

For centuries Christians have read this account and shook their heads in disbelief. *"How in world could the Israelites of that day have been so stupid? God had just miraculously brought them out of Egypt, and here they are already worshipping idols!"* When we understand the correct translation, we see that the Israelites *wanted* to worship the true and living God, but they tried to worship Him in a familiar and comfortable way, and not in the approved manner. Instead of waiting for God's instruction, they tried to worship God in the same way that Pagans were known to worship their gods. Since they couldn't see God, they wanted something tangible to worship that represented Him. In the time of Moses, all of the Children of Israel were "babes" in the Lord and did not have the benefit of God's written word. In our day *we have* God's instructions, yet we bring our own golden calves into our houses every year in the form of Christmas Trees and Easter Eggs. "But we are celebrating Christ!" you say. The Israelites also said the same thing as evidenced by Aaron's declaration, **"Tomorrow is a feast to YHWH."** In spite of their good intentions, their actions greatly angered God. *All* of the three thousand Israelites who sacrificed to the golden calf were killed, and if had not been for the intercession of Moses, God likely would have destroyed all of Israel.

There are many, many other traditions kept by the church today — both Catholic and Protestants (charismatics and evangelicals included) that are steeped in Pagan customs and traditions of man. This is despite God's clear instruction in Deuteronomy 12:31, **"You shall not worship the Lord your God in that way..."** (in the way the Pagans worshiped their gods).

We who are of Ephraim have been blinded to our heritage and have fallen into idolatry. As our eyes are opened to the reality of our identity, we are able to see this truth. It ought to be our prayer daily that the veil would be further removed, so that we may see our ways, and repent.

Babylon — the Roots of Idolatry

The point that I am trying to make in discussing the roots of traditional Christian holidays is much deeper than might first appear. Again, these topics were not intended to bring condemnation. The main reason for even bringing up this potentially divisive topic is to establish a link between a major end times figure, Mystery Babylon, and the "church" and to contrast "Mystery Babylon" with the "elect."

It has been shown by many scholars that most of paganism is rooted in ancient Babylon. Babylon arose from the ancient city of Babel. The term babel, from which the word Babylon comes, means "to confuse, or to mix up."[94]

Let us now recall the story of the tower of Babel in Genesis chapter 11. The inhabitants of Shinar wanted to build a tower "whose top is in the heavens." Interestingly, Satan's false religious system is an attempt to deceive us into doing the same thing today. It has been said that, "Religion is man's attempt to *reach up to God*, but Yeshua is God's attempt to reach down to man." Even today, we are easily deceived into trying to elevate ourselves *to righteousness* and *unto salvation* by our own works. Satan's method over the millennia has been to tempt us into building a tower of our own laws, so that we can keep them and thus reach up to heaven by our own efforts.

Part of Satan's plan in accomplishing his will has been to further "mix" his perverted Babylonian religion system with what God truly intended. This mixing of the profane with the Holy is part of what Yeshua was speaking of in Matthew 13 with the parable of the tares and the wheat.

It is very interesting to note that almost all ancient religions have certain similarities. The gods and their roles are often the same, but the names are changed with different languages.[95] Is it any wonder that this is the case when one considers the confusing of languages and the scattering of peoples at the tower of Babel after God saw that, **"nothing that they propose to do would be withheld from them"**[96] because they all spoke the same language.

It is fascinating to note that the chief figures in Babylonian paganism are Simmirammus (who is called the Queen of Heaven), and her son Tammuz, who also became her husband. It is well known that this arrangement of a Queen of Heaven and her son who is also her husband is repeated across many cultures in their ancient religions.

The Catholic Church's veneration of Mary as the "Queen of Heaven" is startling in this light, since this is undoubtedly a Babylonian concept. There is much to learn about all of this, but it is not the main thrust of this book, and so I will make a couple of reading recommendations and leave it up to the reader to explore these details if so inclined. Alexander Hislop's *The Two Babylons* is a thorough look at The Babylonian roots of the Catholic Church. It was written around 100 years ago. The language is a little out of date, but it is quite interesting. What the Protestant reader should keep in mind is that the Catholic Church was the "mother" of the Protestant church — and the reader must realize that the present day Protestant church has not yet dealt with all of the problems of the Catholic Church. Dave Hunt's *A Woman Rides the Beast* is a more modern account that is an exhaustive commentary. In this book, Hunt presents page after page of Catholic history that is nothing less that shocking. Hunt's book is so thorough that it is almost overwhelming to read.

Because the Catholic Church is so blatantly modeled after ancient Babylonian religion, Hunt draws the conclusion that the Catholic Church is the Woman riding the Beast in Revelation 17 and 18. As will be explained below I do not fully agree with this conclusion.

The Protestant church was birthed out of the Roman Catholic Church, and no one can deny that truth. In fact, the term

"Protestant" actually means "protesting Catholic." While the fathers of the Reformation did work to bring in much truth, they simply did not go far enough. As we noted above, the Protestant church also stands guilty of idolatry, as she has held onto the traditions of men when it comes to both our festivals and our holy days. We have turned a blind eye to the Old Testament Commandments — even those that were said by God to be part of His *everlasting* covenant and were to be kept throughout *all generations.* (Exodus 31:13, Leviticus 23:14, 31). It is for this reason that I think it is unfair to point a finger at the Catholic Church, saying they are the "Woman Riding the Beast." In many ways, the Protestant church is not much better.

The Woman Who Rides the Beast

So who is the Woman who rides the Beast, and why is this important? This becomes a pertinent question in light of what we have discussed in this chapter, and in light of our identity as Israel. Let's take a look at Revelation 17, and again take up our discussion of the end times. Let us see if we can draw some conclusions about the identity of the Woman who rides the Beast.

"Then one of the seven angels who had the seven bowls came and talked with me, saying to me, "Come, I will show you the judgment of the great harlot who sits on many waters, with whom the kings of the earth committed fornication, and the inhabitants of the earth were made drunk with the wine of her fornication." So he carried me away in the Spirit into the wilderness. And I saw a woman sitting on a scarlet beast which was full of names of blasphemy, having seven heads and ten horns. The woman was arrayed in purple and scarlet, and adorned with gold and precious stones and pearls, having in her hand a golden cup full of abominations and the filthiness of her fornication, and on her forehead a name was written:

MYSTERY,
BABYLON THE GREAT,
THE MOTHER OF HARLOTS
AND OF THE
ABOMINATIONS OF THE EARTH

I saw the woman, drunk with the blood of the saints and with the blood of the martyrs of Jesus. And when I saw her, I marveled with great amazement." Revelation 17:1-6

Looking carefully at the above verse, we can infer the following. Clearly, figurative language is being used here. This woman "sits on many waters" — an indication that her geographic influence is widespread (Revelation 17:15). The woman is richly adorned, indicating great worldly wealth. In her hand is a gold cup full of **"abominations and the filthiness of her fornication."**

Consider if you will, what is fornication in the spiritual sense? In the Old Testament Israel and Judah alike are often found guilty of "playing the harlot" — and this is always in reference to *idolatry.* As shown above, many of the traditions of the church are rooted in Babylonian idolatry!

We learn that this woman has a name, and that name reveals her identity! She is the false religious system of Babylonian worship! Lest there be any doubt about this fact, the angel in verse 7 promises to explain her identity: **"Why did you marvel? I will tell you the mystery of the woman and of the beast that carries her, which has the seven heads and the ten horns."** The angel goes on to explain: **"The woman that you saw is that great city which reigns over the kings of the earth." Revelation 7:18** This is a clear reference to the city of Babylon that does indeed reign over the kings of the earth, not by a physical kingdom, but by means of the Babylonian religious system that permeates every major religious system today, including "Christianity."

Just in case there is any doubt who or what this woman refers to, another angel appears in chapter 18, verse 1. This angel cries out mightily with a great voice, saying **"Babylon the great is fallen, is fallen and has become a dwelling place of demons, a** prison for every foul spirit, and a cage for every unclean and hated bird! For all the nations have drunk of the wine of the wrath of her fornication, the kings of the earth have committed fornication with her, and the merchants of the earth have become rich through the abundance of her luxury." Revelation 18:2-3

Notice that the same language used of the Woman riding the Beast is used here of Babylon. With both the "Woman riding the Beast" in chapter 17, and "Babylon" in chapter 18, the inhabitants of the earth have drunk the wine of her fornication (idolatry), and the kings of the earth have committed fornication with her.

Notice now, the thing that happens to the woman. In Revelation 17:16, we learn that the beast will *turn on the woman.* **"And the ten horns which you saw on the beast, these will hate the harlot, make her desolate and naked, eat her flesh and burn her with fire."** In Revelation 13:1, we learn a little more about this beast with seven heads and ten horns. This beast is the Antichrist himself, Satan incarnate.

We have shown briefly, and it has been well documented by others, that the false Babylonian religious system permeates the traditions of the church today. The infiltration of this contaminated system into the church is what was spoken of in the "Tares in the wheat" parable of Matthew 13. The implications of this are staggering.

Many of those who hold the "pre-trib" doctrine will claim as proof of their position that the "church" is not mentioned in the book of Revelation after chapter 4:1 until the end of the book, supposedly proving that the church has already been "taken out."

Sadly the contaminated *institution* [97] of the "church" is mentioned. *She is the Woman riding the Beast!*

Blinded to her identity the church has fallen into Babylonian idolatry! What is even more frightening is the realization that Isaiah chapter 14 clearly depicts none other than Lucifer as being the "King of Babylon." Is it possible that unsuspecting Christians are being tricked into actually worshipping the "King of Babylon," Satan himself?

Listen now to what another angel proclaims about this

Babylonian system: **"Come out of her, my people, lest you share in her sins, and lest you receive of her plagues. For her sins have reached to heaven, and God has remembered her iniquities. Render to her just as she rendered to you, and repay her double according to her works; in the cup which she has mixed, mix double for her. In the measure that she glorified herself and lived luxuriously, in the same measure give her torment and sorrow; for she says in her heart, I sit as queen, and am no widow, and will not see sorrow,"** Revelation 18:4-7

"I sit as a Queen, and am no widow, and will not see sorrow." Isn't this exactly the response of the church today? I have often heard it said among those in the pretribulation camp, "We are the bride of Christ, and Jesus would not put his bride through the tribulation — *we will not see sorrow.*" This is a shocking statement considering what we have discussed in this chapter!

We learn more about the fall of the Babylonian religious system in Jeremiah 50 and 51, and in Isaiah 13 and 14. From these four chapters, we learn that the ultimate fall of Babylon has not happened yet, since it is stated several times in these chapters that Babylon will never again be inhabited, and since even today there is a city of Babylon along the banks of the Euphrates River in Iraq. We also learn from Isaiah Chap 13 that the final destruction of Babylon is associated with the "Day of the Lord." (Isaiah 13:6, 9) In Jeremiah 51:45, the call goes out again, just as proclaimed in Revelation, **"My people, go out of her!"**

Tares in the Wheat

In Matthew 13, we encounter the parable of the "tares" and the wheat. A "tare" is a weed that looks like wheat when it is growing, but it is poisonous. It is not until harvest time that one can readily discern between the tare and the wheat.

Thankfully, we don't have to guess at the meaning of this parable, because none other than Yeshua himself explains it for us in Matthew 13:36-43: **"Then Jesus sent the multitude away and went into the house. And His disciples came to Him, saying,**

"Explain to us the parable of the tares of the field." He answered and said to them: "He who sows the good seed is the Son of Man. The field is the world, the good seeds are the sons of the kingdom, but the tares are the sons of the wicked one. The enemy who sowed them is the devil, the harvest is the end of the age, and the reapers are the angels. Therefore as the tares are gathered and burned in the fire, so it will be at the end of this age. The Son of Man will send out His angels, and they will gather out of His kingdom all things that offend, and those who practice lawlessness, and will cast them into the furnace of fire. There will be wailing and gnashing of teeth. Then the righteous will shine forth as the sun in the kingdom of their Father. He who as ears to hear, let him hear!"

Here we have a summary of the situation. The devil has sown his seeds into the field (the world), right alongside the seeds sown by the Son of Man. These plants that sprout from Satan's seed look like wheat, but they are poisonous! The means by which Satan has accomplished this is by contaminating the "church" with the idolatrous Babylonian religious system. At the end of the age, the Beast will turn on the woman (this Babylonian religious system) and **"devour her flesh and burn her with fire."** This will be the ultimate double cross, but it will accomplish the will of the Father (Revelation 17:17). This will happen at the end of the age, and will be part of the Great Tribulation, during which time the "love" (agape) of many will grow cold. After the tares are separated from the wheat, the reapers will harvest the wheat, **"then the righteous will shine forth as the sun in the kingdom of their Father."**

The question is — who do *you* identify with? Will you **"Come out of her my people"** and recognize your true identity? Will you acknowledge the offense of Ephraim — the offense of *idolatry*? Or, will you continue to turn a blind eye to the fact that the "church" today still holds fast to the Babylonian religious system. In the last day, you will be either the elect, or you will be part of the false religious system, the woman called Mystery, Babylon. The question of the day is: which will you choose?

"I will return again to My place
Till they acknowledge their offense.
Then they will seek my face;
In their affliction they will earnestly seek Me."

Hosea 5:14

"You have chastised me, and I was chastised, like an
untrained bull; Restore me, and I will return,
for You are the LORD my God. Surely, after my turning,
I repented; and after I was instructed, I struck myself on
the thigh; I was ashamed, yes, even humiliated, because I
bore the reproach of my youth. Is Ephraim My dear son?
Is he a pleasant child? For though I spoke against him,
I earnestly remember him still; Therefore My heart yearns
for him; I will surely have mercy on him, says the LORD."

Jeremiah 31:18-20

CHAPTER 9

So what does this mean?

Suddenly, everything has changed.

*T*he realization of just who we are in Messiah causes us to seriously reexamine the institution of the church. What's more, knowing our Israelite heritage, we are compelled to look afresh at the entire Word of God and revisit the promises given to our fathers generations ago.

We see that the "church" is largely a man made institution that is deceived and has fallen deeply into the counterfeit Babylonian system of worship. When we consider the end times in this light we are faced with a couple of shocking realizations. First, the "church," as we know it, is *not* God's vehicle for the redemption of mankind, rather, it is through His chosen people *all* Israel that God is working out His plan. Similarly, Jesus is not the "head of the church," as is commonly taught, rather He is Yeshua the Messiah the King of Israel! We see then that the event that has been called the "rapture" is not the gathering of the "church," but it is the *regathering* of Israel to the Messiah.

Understanding our identity as Israelite we no longer see the "Old Testament" as an abstract collection of stories, poems and prophecy written over 2500 years ago, rather we comprehend it as the living, breathing, Word of God written about *our* forefathers.

Instead of believing Gentiles are nothing more than an

afterthought having been granted status as an "adopted" stepchild,
we see *we are the Prodigal Son* — and we long to return to the
Father after squandering what He had given us in the land of the
Gentiles. This is the hidden meaning of the prodigal son parable in
Luke, and it is the very reason that we as believers in the Messiah
provoke the jealousy of our older brother Judah[98] when we learn
again to walk in His ways:

**Then He said, "A certain man had two sons. And the
younger of them said to his father, 'Father, give me the portion
of goods that falls to me.' So he divided to them his livelihood.
And not many days after, the younger son gathered all together,
journeyed to a far country, and there wasted his possessions
with prodigal living.**

**But when he had spent all, there arose a severe famine in
that land, and he began to be in want. Then he went and joined
himself to a citizen of that country, and he sent him into his
fields to feed swine. And he would gladly have filled his stomach
with the pods that the swine ate, and no one gave him anything.**

**But when he came to himself, he said, 'How many of my
father's hired servants have bread enough and to spare, and I
perish with hunger! I will arise and go to my father, and will say
to him, 'Father, I have sinned against heaven and before you,
and I am no longer worthy to be called your son. Make me like
one of your hired servants.'**

**And he arose and came to his father. But when he was still a
great way off, his father saw him and had compassion, and ran
and fell on his neck and kissed him. And the son said to him,
'Father, I have sinned against heaven and in your sight, and am
no longer worthy to be called your son.' But the father said to
his servants, 'Bring out the best robe and put it one him, and
put a ring on his hand and sandals on his feet. And bring the
fatted calf here and kill it, and let us eat and be merry; for this
my son was dead and is alive again; he was lost and is found.'
And they began to be merry.**

**Now his older son was in the field. And as he came and drew
near to the house, he heard music and dancing. So he called one**

of the servants and asked what these things meant. And he said
to him, 'Your brother has come, and because he has received
him safe and sound, your father has killed the fatted calf.' But
he was angry and would not go in. Therefore his father came
out and pleaded with him. So he answered and said to his
father, 'Lo, these many years I have been serving you; I never
transgressed your commandment at any time; and yet you
never gave me a young goat, that I might make merry with my
friends. But as soon as this son of yours came, who has
devoured your livelihood with harlots, you killed the fatted calf
for him.' And he said to him, 'Son, you are always with me, and
all that I have is yours. It was right that we should make merry
and be glad, for your brother was dead and is alive again, and
was lost and is found.' " Luke 15:11-32**

Now, with an understanding of the parable of the prodigal son,
let us look again at the words Jeremiah that concluded the previous
chapter of this book:

**"You have chastised me, and I was chastised, like an
untrained bull; Restore me, and I will return, for You are the
LORD my God. Surely, after my turning, I repented; and after
I was instructed, I struck myself on the thigh; I was ashamed,
yes, even humiliated, because I bore the reproach of my youth.
Is Ephraim My dear son? Is he a pleasant child? For though
I spoke against him, I earnestly remember him still; Therefore
My heart yearns for him; I will surely have mercy on him, says
the LORD." Jeremiah 31:18-20**

As the Prodigal Son, we desire to be reunited to our Father and
to dwell in His house, but we find ourselves stranded in a far away
land — hungry for our Father and yearning to return but unable to
find the way. We are sheep who have gone astray, and we are in
desperate need of the one who will lead the flock home.

As we begin to understand the deeper things of God, many
questions arise about some traditional church doctrines.

In the next two chapters we will put our end times discussion on hold to address a few pertinent issues. New insights sometimes require action. This section is by no means comprehensive but hopefully will answer some questions concerning the question, *"How does my being an Israelite effect my walk with God?"*

Wanted: the Good Shepherd

In chapter 8, we briefly examined how today's church is contaminated by the false Babylonian religious system. Although we barely scratched the surface of this issue, we see how many of our church traditions were born in the worship of false gods and we have begun to see just how misled our church leaders have been.

Sadly, we must admit that much of the church has been led astray by false prophets. I believe that most church leaders are quite sincere and well meaning, but they are badly deceived by the system in which they were raised, and only the most humble are able to receive the message this book puts forth.

Though it shocks us, we really shouldn't be surprised about the state of the church since this is the very thing that the Lord said would happen. Take a look at these next few passages. See how the very words of the prophets are today fulfilled before our eyes,

"Woe to the shepherds who destroy and scatter the sheep of My pasture!" says the LORD. Therefore thus says the LORD God of Israel against the shepherds who feed My people: "You have scattered My flock, driven them away, and not attended to them. Behold, I will attend to you for the evil of you doing," says the LORD. "But I will gather the remnant of My flock out of all countries where I have driven them, and bring them back to their folds; and they shall be fruitful and increase. I will set up shepherds over them who will feed them; and they shall fear no more, nor be dismayed, nor shall they be lacking," says the LORD. Behold, the days are coming," says the LORD, "That I will raise to David a Branch of righteousness; A King shall reign and prosper, and execute judgment and righteousness in the earth. In His days Judah will be saved, and Israel will dwell safely; Now this is His name by which He will be called: THE LORD OUR RIGHTEOUSNESS." Jeremiah 23:1-6

We see from this passage that God will raise up a few good shepherds for His sheep, but it is easy to get the feeling that the vast majority of shepherds will be of the worthless type.

Furthermore, we see just a few lines down from the above passage a warning that speaks directly to those who will be alive during the "latter days" concerning the dangers of heeding the words of the false prophets, thus proving that this passage was meant for the last generation, **"Thus says the LORD of hosts: Do not listen to the words of the prophets who prophesy to you. They make you worthless; they speak a vision of their own heart, not from the mouth of the LORD. They continually say to those who despise Me, "The LORD has said, 'You shall have peace'" and to everyone who walks according to the dictates of his own heart, they say, "No evil shall come upon you." For who has stood in the counsel of the LORD, and has perceived and heard His word? Who has marked His word and heard it? Behold a whirlwind of the LORD has gone forth in fury — a violent whirlwind! It will fall violently on the head of the wicked. The anger of the LORD will not turn back until He has executed and performed the thoughts of His heart. In the latter days you will understand it perfectly." Jeremiah 23:16-20** We see from this passage that those who **"walk according to the dictates of his own heart"** (in other words, those who *do what is right in their own eyes*) will be falsely told that **"No evil shall come upon"** them. Isn't this precisely the message the majority of the church leadership is presenting to the body in the form of pre-tribulationalism? Truly, the church is filled with unrighteous Shepherds who prophesy falsely as if they are speaking with the authority of God. Again, this should not cause dismay, for it is exactly as prophesied.

Ezekiel, also speaking of these latter day leaders of the flock also prophesied well: **"Son of man, prophesy against the shepherds of Israel, prophesy and say to them, "Thus says the Lord God to the shepherds: "Woe to the shepherds of Israel who feed themselves! Should not the shepherds feed the flocks? You eat the fat and clothe yourselves with the wool; you slaughter the fatlings, but you do not feed the flock. The weak you have not strengthened, nor have you healed those who were sick, nor bound up the** broken, nor brought back what was driven away, nor sought what was lost; but with force and cruelty you have ruled them. So they were scattered because there was no shepherd; and they became food for all the beasts of the field when they were scattered. My sheep wandered through all the mountains, and on every high hill, yes, My flock was scattered over the whole face of the earth, and no one was seeking or searching for them." Therefore, you shepherds, hear the word of the LORD; "As I live, says the Lord God, surely because My flock became a prey, and My flock became food for every beast of the field, because there was no shepherd, nor did My shepherds search for My flock, but the shepherds fed themselves and did not feed My flock" — "Therefore, O shepherds, hear the word of the LORD!" Thus says the Lord God: "Behold, I am against the shepherds, and I will require My flock at their hand; I will cause them to cease feeding the sheep, and the shepherds shall feed themselves no more; for I will deliver My flock from their mouths, that they may no longer be food for them." Ezekiel 34:1-10**

God Himself will deliver His flock from this predicament. It will not be by the hand of any great speaker or theologian. Ezekiel goes on to establish this fact, **"For thus says the Lord God: Indeed I Myself will search for My sheep and seek them out. As a shepherd seeks out his flock on the day he is among his scattered sheep, so will I seek out My sheep and deliver them from all the places where they were scattered on a cloudy and dark day. And I will bring them out from the peoples and gather them from the countries, and will bring them to their own land; I will feed them on the mountains of Israel, in the valleys and in all the inhabited places of the country. I will feed them in good pasture, and their fold shall be on the high mountains of Israel. There they shall lie down in a good fold and feed in rich pasture on the mountains of Israel. I will feed My flock, and I will make them lie down," says the Lord God. "I will seek what was lost and bring back what was driven away, bind up the broken and strengthen what was sick; but I will destroy the fat and the strong, and feed them in judgment." Ezekiel 34:11-16**

So who is this Good Shepherd that will ultimately gather the flock? None other that Yeshua himself just as He proclaimed in John chapter 10: **"I am the good shepherd. The good shepherd gives His life for the sheep. But a hireling, he who is not the shepherd, one who does not own the sheep, sees the wolf coming and leaves the sheep and flees; and the wolf catches the sheep and scatters them. The hireling flees because he is a hireling and does not care about the sheep. I am the good shepherd; and I know My sheep, and am know by My own. As the Father knows Me, even so I know the Father; and I lay down My life for the sheep." John 10:11-15**

It is discouraging, to say the least, to realize just how far off course the modern day church has been blown. We are indeed a flock of scattered sheep. We are in desperate need of the *Good Shepherd* to come and lead us back to the fold. As Yeshua proclaimed in John, however, we must "know the Shepherd," and He must "know us." Below, we will examine scripture from the New Testament that will elaborate on just what it takes to "know" Yeshua, the Good Shepherd.

As we begin to understand that to be "In the Messiah" means to be grafted (back) into the commonwealth of Israel, we realize we must reject our unintentional worship of false gods and learn to worship God in the way *He* intended. As we will see from scripture it is in this way we are able to get to *know* Him, and He to *know* us.

To Keep or not to Keep *that* is the Question…

The realization of our Israelite Identity and our need to know and be *known by God* brings many questions, the foremost of which concerns the "Law" and God's appointed and ordained method of worship. Are we to keep the Feasts of God and the Law of Moses? Or, as the church teaches, have God's instructions given through Moses been "done away with?"

Upon superficial inspection the Bible occasionally seems to contradict itself. With respect to the issue of keeping "the law" this is certainly the case. Let us take a look at a few verses to make the point:

"Do not think that I come to destroy the Law or the Prophets. I did not come to destroy but to fulfill. For assuredly, I say to you, till heaven and earth pass away, one jot or one tittle will by no means pass from the law till all is fulfilled." (Have heaven and earth passed away?) **"Whoever therefore breaks one of the least of these commandments, and teaches men so, shall be called least in the kingdom of heaven; but whoever does and teaches them, he shall be called great in the kingdom of heaven." Matthew 5:17-19**[99]

"Not everyone who says to Me, 'Lord, Lord,' shall enter the kingdom of heaven, but he who does the will of My Father in heaven. Many will say to Me in that day, 'Lord, Lord, have we not prophesied in Your name, cast out demons in Your name, and done many wonders in Your name? And then I will declare to them, <u>'I never knew you</u>; depart from Me you who practice lawlessness!" Matthew 7:21-23[100]

In this passage it almost sounds as if Yeshua is speaking about today's church. Notice that those who practice lawlessness *are not known by the Lord*. The implications here are staggering. In First John we find a similar statement, *written after the cross that* certainly seems to indicate that we ought to pay more attention to God's commandments:

He who says, "I know Him," and does not keep His commandments, is a liar, and the truth is not in him." 1 John 2:4

To be fair, we must admit we also find scripture that seemingly oppose this position:

"Therefore, the law was our tutor to bring us to Christ, that we might be justified by faith. But after faith has come, we are no longer under a tutor." Galatians 3:24-25

"But now we have been delivered from the law, having died to what we were held by, so that we should serve in the newness

of the Spirit and not in the oldness of the letter." Romans 7:6

So what are we to do? Just as we found seemingly conflicting scriptures concerning the timing of the "rapture," we now are faced with more apparent contradictions. Just as taking a step back helped us to understand our previous problem, taking a step back to consider the subject of "Law" and "Grace" will shed some light.

Law and Grace

Modern day Christians, have been preconditioned to see "Law" and "Grace" as opposite ends of a spectrum. Our understanding would have us believe that before the Messiah's sacrifice, God's people were "Under the Law" and that after the cross we are "Under Grace." We tend to see Law and Grace as something like this:

Understanding Grace

By the work of the Messiah, we are indeed beneficiaries of His Grace. We New Covenant Christians, however, tend to confuse the closely related ideas of Grace and Mercy. This in turn leads to some misunderstandings with respect to the subject of Law versus Grace.

The standard Christian theological definition for Grace is "unmerited favor." While this is the standard and accepted definition, it is surprisingly nowhere to be found in scripture. A more accurate definition of Grace would be "God's lovingkindness."

The problem with the "unmerited favor" definition is not necessarily that it is inaccurate, but that it is misleading. This is because we use the word "favor" in our vernacular to mean an *act* of kindness. For example, if I ask you to "do me a favor," I am most likely referring to an act rather than a feeling of love or of favor. In this way we can confuse the term "unmerited favor" and believe that it refers to an act that God does for us, specifically salvation, that we don't deserve.

I have oft heard it said, "Grace is the getting of something you don't deserve, and Mercy is when you don't get the very thing (punishment) you *do* deserve." While this is a quaint saying, it simply is not completely accurate and the novice will easily misunderstand this sort of loose definition. Grace is not the "Getting" of anything we don't deserve other than the "getting" of God's lovingkindness towards us (although it is true that *because* of God's lovingkindness we may "*get*" something – like mercy, or a measure of faith).

Mercy relates to his Grace since it is *because* of His Grace (His loving kindness) we are kept from the justice (punishment) we deserve.

When we extend the meaning of Grace too far, we begin to imagine we are given other things (for example salvation) on the basis of God's love for us alone, and thus nullifying any requirement on our part (for example, faith).

God's Mercy (*because of the Grace that He has for us*) covers (atones for) our sins when we don't do what the Law *still requires of us*. For example, we ought not to think of Law and Grace as opposites, but rather we ought to think of God's Law covered by His Mercy because of His Grace:

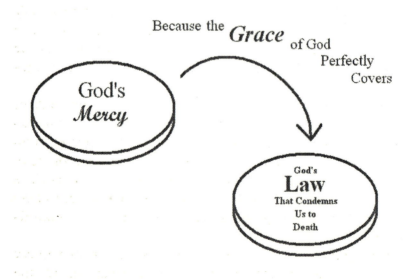

Importantly, notice God's Grace and Mercy (Because of the shed blood of the Messiah) cover God's Law — but it does not cover man's law as is graphically demonstrated below. We ought to consider carefully Yeshua's response to those who would add to God's law.

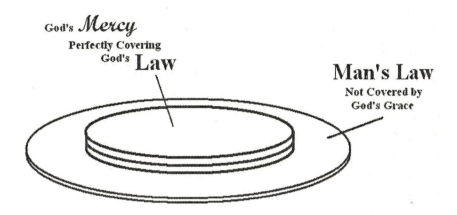

God's *Mercy*
Perfectly Covering
God's **Law**

Man's Law
Not Covered by
God's Grace

Take note now what Yeshua had to say about the practice of adding to His Word: **"Hypocrites! Well did Isaiah prophesy about you, saying: 'These people draw near to Me with their mouth, And honor Me with their lips, But their heart is far from Me. And in vain they worship Me, Teaching as doctrines the commandments of men.'" Matthew 15:7-9**

It is interesting to realize that although covering a multitude of sins, God's Grace and Mercy do not cover and atone for the breaking a commandment of man. In other words, if a church group makes a law that is not part of God's law (commandments of men), and someone breaks it, God is not even concerned about that. The fact is, it appears that God is much more troubled with our *making* our own law (and then imposing it on others) than with our *breaking* of our own law.

As we begin to explore the issue of God's Law, many will cry foul, saying that any adherence to the law is "legalism." On the contrary, adherence to God's commandments is obedience.

Imposing man made ordinances is true legalism!

We need to understand then that the term "under the Law" as used in the New Testament is *not* referring to a state of having to keep the law for salvation, for the "Law" did not save even the Old Testament saints, rather they were saved by faith. On the contrary, "Under the Law" implies being under the "curse" of the Law, and has to do with the "handwriting of requirements"[101] that is against us according to the Law, demanding our death for any deliberate sin in our lives.

In New Testament Christianity much has been written concerning Law versus Grace. To properly understand the issue, we must come to the realization that it is not the law that saves us. With this understanding we see we need not get bogged down in a list of do's and don'ts *as if that were a means to salvation.*

Law Equals Grace?

We know Yeshua came to fulfill the law (Matthew 5:17), and He kept the law perfectly. He was able to do this, because He was the physical manifestation of the Word (also known as the "Law," or the "Torah") as pointed out in John 1:1 and 1:14, **"In the beginning was the Word, and the Word was with God, and the Word was God... And the Word became flesh, and dwelt among us. And we beheld His glory, the glory as of the only begotten of the Father, full of grace and truth."**

Here we begin to get a hint that Yeshua was not only "the law fulfilled," but we also see that He was full of "Grace and Truth." We get another hint of this sort of thing when Yeshua stated, **"I am the way and the Truth and the Life"** in John 14:6.

We see also in 1 Corinthians 15:10 that the *grace* of God in the apostle Paul takes on the character of a person in that it is the *grace* of God that is laboring. Notice what Paul said here, **"But by the Grace of God I am what I am, and His grace toward me was not in vain; but I labored more abundantly that they all, yet not I, but the grace of God which was with me."** The person that was in Paul, that was laboring and that *is grace* — was Yeshua the Messiah. Yeshua is the embodiment of Grace. To receive the

Messiah, is to receive Grace. So we realize that Yeshua = the Law made flesh, *and* Yeshua = Grace. If our Savior is both the Grace and the Law made flesh, how can these two things be at opposite ends of a spectrum?

It is true that through the work of Yeshua's sacrifice, we are no longer "under the law." Again, to be "under the law" implies that one must keep the law perfectly and there is no room for error for it is written, **"Cursed is everyone who does not continue in all things which are written in the book of the law, to do them." Deuteronomy 27-26** Thankfully, the Messiah paid for our sins, because there is not a person other than He that could be declared righteous by the keeping of the law.[102] Through the work of the Messiah, we are no longer "under the Law" inasmuch as the *curse* of the law has been removed and we now have forgiveness through our faith in Yeshua.

Liberty does not equal License!

What now? Since we are saved by what *He did* and not by what we do, can we sin now because we have liberty? *Paul's adamant answer is no.* **"What then? Shall we sin because we are not under law but under grace? Certainly not! Romans 6:15**

Since we don't have license to sin, *we had better understand what defines sin*. Moreover, based on what was shown above in Matthew 15:7-9, we dare not try to define sin for ourselves. So how do we define it?

Again, it is important as we begin to understand how God defines sin we realize this is not a "Salvation" issue. In the Sermon on the Mount, Yeshua seems to indicate that even some of those who do not obey His commandments (the commandments of God) will be among those found in the kingdom of Heaven: **"Whoever therefore breaks one of the least of these commandments, and teaches men so, shall be called least in the kingdom of heaven; but whoever does and teaches them, he shall be called great in the kingdom of heaven."** The question becomes — why would one want to be the least in the Kingdom of Heaven?

Once more, to go too far in this discussion causes us to get into the realm of do's and don'ts, which is the realm of the flesh. Yeshua taught us in the Sermon on the Mount (Matthew chapters 5-7) that He is concerned with matters of the heart. This is precisely why Jeremiah speaks of a covenant that is written on our hearts. Indeed, to better understand this issue, let us return yet again to the Old Testament so that we may be able to understand the New Testament scriptures in their proper context: **"Behold, the days are coming, says the LORD, when I will make a new covenant with the house of Israel and with the house of Judah — not according to the covenant that I made with their fathers in the day that I took them by the hand to lead them out of the land of Egypt, My covenant which they broke, though I was a husband to them, says the LORD. But this is the covenant that I will make with the house of Israel after those days, says the LORD: I will put My law in their minds, and write it on their hearts; and I will be their God, and they shall be My people." Jeremiah 31:31-33**

In this passage Jeremiah seems to indicate that the "Law" written on the hearts of man under the New Covenant is the *same* "Law" that the ancient Israelites couldn't keep. God's law, referred to here as "My law" (thus indicating it is the *same* law), is to be written on the hearts of man through the empowerment of the Holy Spirit, thus giving man the ability to keep this law (not excusing lawlessness as some suppose).

Because of our sin nature, it is easy to deceive ourselves into thinking that something we are doing is right when it is contrary to the laws of God. There are plenty of examples of brethren who claim that their participating in grossly sinful or idolatrous activities has been "Okayed" by the Holy Spirit. (It is plain by our assessment of the church today in the last chapter that this commonly happens.) In order to really understand what is acceptable and what is unacceptable, what is holy and what is profane, and what is clean and what is unclean, we must turn the only source that is unchanging and uncompromising — the Word of God.

The Wrong Tree!

Considering what happened at the time of the fall of man will help us understand this issue and the reason for our problems. Recall, if you will, the name of the tree that Eve and then Adam ate from to cause the fall of man. They were deceived by Satan to partake of the "Tree of the Knowledge of Good and Evil." Pause to think about the name of this tree for a second...The Tree of the *Knowledge of Good and Evil.* When we decide for ourselves what is right and what is wrong and do that which is right in our own eyes, we employ the "knowledge" of good and evil that we received from our father Adam and we again partake of the forbidden tree. In this way, we set ourselves up to be "as God" presuming to have His wisdom and His righteousness.

This is a profound insight, and realizing this one simple point is humbling.

Hebrews 5:14 does indicate that we ought to know "good and evil," but this is in the context of the whole book of Hebrews and is made possible by us having *the law written on our heart* just as Jeremiah prophesied.[103] This ability is not something we muster up with fleshly might, but it is a gift of empowerment given by the Holy Spirit writing God's Law on our heart!

If it is true that God does not change,[104] why do we presume to think His instruction to us has changed? There is simply no explicit reference to the abolition of God's law in the New Testament. Instead, read carefully the Messiah's words again: **"Do not think that I come to destroy the Law or the Prophets. I did not come to destroy but to fulfill. For assuredly, I say to you, till heaven and earth pass away, one jot or one tittle will by no means pass from the law till all is fulfilled." Matthew 5:17**

For this reason, shouldn't we do as Paul has said and let the law be our tutor and let the *law* define sin, so that we can be brought closer to the Messiah? Since none of us are yet perfected, the law ought to retain its place as a yardstick to measure our progress and spiritual growth. When what we do naturally by the power of the Holy Spirit within us looks like the Law,[105] then we know we have attained something — yet not by our own efforts, but by Yeshua (Grace) working in us, because He has written the Law *on our hearts.*

What does the "Law" look like when it is put into action? Yeshua plainly stated that the summation of God's law was love, **"You shall love the LORD your God with all your heart, with all your soul, and with all your mind. This is the first and great commandment. And the second is like it: You shall love your neighbor as yourself. On these two commandments hang all the law and the prophets." Matthew 22:37-40.**[106] So we see that by the miracle of God's law being written on our heart, we are able to fully love as God has commanded. This all makes since when we properly see Grace as "God's Lovingkindness." We then say, for example, "I am able to Love as God commanded, yet not by my own strength, but by God's Grace (God's lovingkindness) that is within me."

When we understand Yeshua is the Law manifested as flesh and see that He is the Grace, the Love, the Truth, and the Life — we can reconcile the difficult passages that seem contradictory. We are able to see that to know the Messiah and to have his Spirit dwelling inside of us causes His law to be written on our hearts and as a natural outflow the "Fruits of the Spirit" are brought forth. This is precisely why James said **"Faith without works is dead."**[107]

But What about the Details?

Still, you might be wondering about practical matters of keeping the Old Testament law. The "Law" technically refers to the books of Moses, the first five books in the Bible. These are also known as the Torah, and can be considered God's instructions to man. Again, as we approach the Torah it is very easy to slip off into the fleshly realm of do's and don'ts — but this question of keeping the Law is precisely the question that was put to the apostles at the Jerusalem council in Acts chapter 15, so the question is legitimate. *There are practical matters about which we must have instruction.*

Not wanting to overload new converts with matters of the Law, the apostles in Acts 15 declared, **"We should not trouble those from among the Gentiles who are turning to God, but that we**

write to them to abstain from things polluted by idols, from sexual immortality, from things strangled, and from blood."

Most all New Covenant teachers stop reading at this point in this passage, but it is important to note that this is only the *starting* place.[108] As we keep reading through this section we encounter a statement that is startling in its implications. The very next verse states, **"For Moses has had throughout many generations those who preach him in every city, being read in the synagogues every Sabbath." Acts 15:21** From this we can only infer there was an expectation that new converts would continue to learn more about God's law. This is a clear indication that we ought to take heed to what the apostles recommended and continue to use the law as a yardstick to measure our growth as followers of the one who was the Law made flesh.

This book is not intended to be a resource used to determine what one ought to do as an Israelite. Suffice it to say there are many spiritual *and* practical lessons that will be learned from the careful study and application of the neglected Books of Moses. There are many resources available that will be of benefit as one realizes the value of God's instruction.

As we come to understand the importance of God's instruction and set out to honor the Father by keeping His Word, we must, however, be aware of this simple fact: By our human nature we are in rebellion against God, we are fallen just like Adam and Eve and will have a tendency toward dismissing His truth for a lie because of our rebelliousness. In our natural state, we have a tendency toward adding or subtracting from His Word because we are heirs in the flesh to those who partake of the Tree of the Knowledge of Good and Evil. We see that God's Law is good, but we must be ever diligent to avoid the pitfall of being placed under the yoke of man's law and fall into the snare of legalism. We must strive for a *balanced* and *Spirit led* walk.

A Personal Testimony

Understanding the difference between God's Laws and man's laws is crucial to a healthy walk with the Lord. Though difficult and painful for me to write about my own shortcomings, to make an important point I will share some of my own story. It is with much agonizing prayer that I have decided to share some of the details of my own life, since I do not wish to hold up my sinful past as some sort of badge of achievement. Instead, in all things I give thanks and glory to God.

My religious upbringing as a child was in a marginally non-denominational Christian family. Later, in my teenage years, my parents "quit" church for a while, and I ended up attending a denominational church with my high school girlfriend whom I married at the tender age of seventeen.

The church that she and her family attended had a significant influence on me. The doctrine of that church was very legalistic, and it was common knowledge among those believers that if you didn't attend that particular church denomination your eternal salvation was in serious jeopardy.

Legalism, once again, is doctrine that asserts *man's* laws, often making the keeping of these laws a salvation issue. (This is in contrast to the keeping of God's commands, which is called *Obedience*.) This church I attended strongly asserted *man's* laws, contending that salvation depended on, among other things, such issues as *not* having instrumental music in a worship service, partaking of communion *every* Sunday, calling the hired minister of the church a "minister' and never a "pastor," and so forth.

Unfortunately, I was able to keep the "laws of man" fairly well. I didn't drink alcohol, I didn't smoke or cuss. Generally, I felt as though I was a pretty good guy and was happy going to heaven because I was *doing* all of the things that I should, and for the most part, not many of the things that I shouldn't.

It is easy to become smug about yourself when the yardstick that is used to measure yourself by is of your own design. Because I was good at keeping man's laws, I did not realize my own need or lack and I became very judgmental of others. I had no grace for anyone less "perfect" than I. My pride was understandable. Why, after all, shouldn't one who is "perfect" expect perfection from others?

During those years, my accomplishments in life grew. I was a successful college student and had been accepted to medical school...I was proud that God wanted me to be with Him in heaven because *I was good enough*. I was a big fish in a small pond. I was completely mixed up.

Sorely lacking in grace, I became very demanding of my wife. Our young marriage was in serious trouble in spite of the fact that we were going to the *right* church and keeping man's laws just as we had been directed.

Looking back, I can honestly say there had been very little instruction in matters that could be considered "God's law" (although everything that was taught was *said* to be of God). I remember listening to many sermons espousing the "doctrine" of the church such as the evil of instrumental music in worship, but I can't remember one single time when the *Ten Commandments* were taught.

It is not as though I didn't know better, but lacking instruction, my thought life with respect to women was appalling. Yeshua, during the Sermon on the Mount, taught us that even to look upon another woman with lust in our hearts is the same as committing the very act of adultery. He was teaching one of the Ten Commandments, but teaching us that under His *New* Covenant the command would be written on the heart! The "law" had not been "done away with," but was simply *made possible* because it was to be written on the heart thereby causing a *change* of heart. The problem I had though was that I had been focused on man's laws and had rejected God's commandments as having been "done away with" because they were of the "old law."

It is not easy to write openly about what happened in my life during those years, but since I am not trying to impress anyone, I will be candid about the events that followed.

Shortly after finishing medical school in 1996 I fell into an adulterous relationship.

It remains the most devastating experience of my life. Words cannot begin to convey the grief and pain of the divorce and the events that followed.

For eight years I had very little grace for my wife, and after I disclosed my sin, I received no mercy in return.

My life was in shambles. Working as a medical intern some-times for up to one hundred hours per week, I was broken spiritu-ally, emotionally, physically and financially. Having two children whose lives I had shattered, and having broken the heart of the wife of my youth (who having full right to do so ended up re-marrying), I felt guilt and remorse beyond description.

To top it all off, based on my own theology, I *knew* I was going to hell. I was completely abandoned by my "brethren" and except from my immediate family did not receive a single phone call, or card, or letter of encouragement from any of those with whom I had attended church. I was beaten down and rejected. I became depressed and for a while I was even suicidal.

I can't really explain why God turned His face toward me after that, except to say that now *I truly* understand God's Grace (His lovingkindness). Without hope, in a moment of despair, I distinctly remember collapsing in a heap while taking a shower in 1997. I cried out loudly to the Lord, and beating my chest I was able only to utter a sobbing, "Forgive me Lord, I'm such a sinner." For the first time in my life I felt true forgiveness. It was wonderful to "come clean" with the Lord. I was a gross human being, yet He still received me. It was no longer about me and what I was doing, though; it was about Him and what He did because of His great Love.

It is difficult to explain how I got from there to where the Lord has brought me today. Through a series of events outside of my control I had to relocate several times. New towns brought new churches and new people with fresh ideas and teachings. My eyes were opened to Grace, and to Mercy, and to the gifts of the Spirit. I began to grow in the Grace and in the knowledge of the Lord. I met my wife, Dana, and God has truly turned the ashes of my life into something beautiful.

Looking back, my enthusiasm for the keeping of man's laws did not help me when temptation came. Realizing just how prideful I had become, I am actually surprised that I was even led to tempta-tion, since Satan had me right where he wanted me during those years. A spiritual principle was at work though. Pride comes before a fall and as a natural consequence of my sin, I was cut down and I crashed as hard as anyone could possibly fall.

Now, realizing my identity as an Israelite, I have since come to truly appreciate the importance of God's laws. God's laws do not save us, but they do point out our need and they certainly can protect us, perhaps even protect *our very salvation.*

My life was so devastated and shattered by my own disobedience to God's Law that I now cringe at the thought of getting away from the protection of those laws.

It is because of the love that I have for the Father (and the love that He has for me) that I *want* to do His will, and truly, I *want* to stay under His protection by following His instruction, so that I will never again end up with such tragedy in my life.

The concept of the bondservant is taught in the Torah in Exodus 21. In ancient Israel, a servant could be kept for only seven years, after which he must be set free. If, however, the servant loved his master and wanted to stay with him permanently, the servant could "bond" himself to the master by performing a ritual by which the servant would pierce his ear to the doorpost of the house with an awl. In this way he would become a "bondservant" of the master and would be a permanent member of the household and would be afforded the protection of the household.

The New Testament writers referred to themselves as "bondservants." Revelation was written to "bondservants." Not wanting to be without the protection of being of the household of God, I too have become a bondservant.

It is for this reason I have taken the penname "Obadiah," which means "bondservant of Yahweh." My given first name is "Frank" which means "freeman." Indeed, I have been set free by the blood of the Messiah, but *I love my master* and *I desire His protection*, so I *willingly* bond myself to him and again put myself back under the *protection* of His instruction. It is not as though I am under any illusion that I am obtaining salvation by the keeping of His law, but what else can I do? I love the Father, I desire His protection, and I dare not try life again without His instruction!

Because Lawlessness will abound…

Keeping in mind this book *is* meant to be a study on end times, let's take a look back at a point that was made in this book's introduction. In an effort to convince the reader that the idea of the prewrath rapture was a matter to take seriously, it was pointed out that Yeshua taught that the "Agape" of many will grow cold. In light of this chapter, another look at that particular verse is stunning: **"Because *lawlessness* will abound, the love of many will grow cold."** (emphasis mine) Here, according to the words of Yeshua, we see that the reason the love of many will grow cold is *lawlessness*.

When we see the complete lack of regard the modern church has for God's law, we realize that indeed we are seeing first hand the "falling away" spoken of by the apostle Paul in 2 Thessalonians 2:3.

Many Christians today have felt an unexplainable draw towards their "Hebraic Roots." The explanation is simple — the *Law has been written on their hearts*. We know deep down that something is not right about the traditions of the church, and we feel drawn towards the Biblical feasts. Unfortunately, most churches today are completely devoid of teaching on the law as had been the tradition **"in every city, being read in the synagogues every Sabbath"** during the first century. We find that we are drawn to the "Law" not as a means to salvation or to righteousness, but because of our *love for the Father*. Suddenly, our heart races at the sound of the Shofar blast and we look forward to the end of the week when we can enjoy His Sabbath rest. We love keeping the Law, *because we love the Father.*

"For this is the Love of God, that we keep His commandments. And His Commandments are not burdensome." 1 John 5:3

But then again:

"For what the law could not do in that it was weak through the flesh, God did by sending His own Son in the likeness of sinful flesh, on account of sin: He condemned sin in the flesh, that the righteous requirement of the law might be fulfilled in us who do not walk according to the flesh but according to the Spirit." Romans 8:3-4

CHAPTER 10

Sola Fide!

*I*n the last chapter, we examined our need for God's law and its importance even today. Because this issue is easily misunderstood, it is worthwhile to again take a step back and look at the issues of salvation and of *faith*. Let there be no misunderstanding. The means by which we are saved is faith and faith alone:

"For by Grace you have been saved, through faith, and that not of yourselves; it is the gift of God, not of works, lest anyone should boast." Ephesians 2:8-9

This famous New Covenant verse nails the point home without ambiguity. There can be no disputing this matter. In fact as we see in the above verse, not only are we saved through our faith, but also that the faith given to us was a gift that we didn't deserve in the first place — that is to say, it is *by grace* (Because of His lovingkindness towards us). The misunderstanding comes when we take this verse to mean that Grace is *how* we are saved. On the contrary, grace is not how we are saved, but rather it is *why* we are saved, and faith is *how* we attain salvation.[109]

Furthermore, it is faith *in* the messiah (the God of Abraham, Isaac, and Jacob, who manifested Himself as flesh that He might take on the transgressions of whosoever would believe in Him) that saves us. That is to say it is the *object* of our Faith, the Messiah, that saves — rather than *our* faith that saves. This is an important point to keep in mind, lest we begin to think more highly of ourselves than we ought and imagine that somehow by our own faith, as exhibited by our works, we are saving ourselves.

Salvation by Works?

As we become aware of our Israelite identity, and as we begin to agree with the apostle Paul that the "law is good,"[110] **it is easy to go overboard and begin to put our faith in the "letter" of the law rather than in the *law giver*. Paul clearly points out the folly of this kind of thinking:** "Not that we are sufficient of ourselves to think of anything as being from ourselves, but our sufficiency is from God, who also made us sufficient as ministers of the new covenant, not of the letter but of the Spirit; for the letter kills, but the Spirit gives life." 2 Corinthians 3:5-6

It is one thing to realize that we are to keep our Heavenly Father's instruction given through Moses *because of our love* for the Father and because *we believe that His instruction is good*, but it is another matter altogether to jump to the conclusion that it is by our keeping of His law that we attain our salvation.

The Misunderstanding

It is indeed easy to get carried away with the law and develop a works based righteousness mentality. On the other hand, it is also easy to mistakenly accuse brethren who are trying to be obedient out of love of having this mentality. This is because in our natural flesh we are in rebellion against God and his Commandments and there is a natural tendency within each of us to reject the law of God. It is observed, for example, that when one keeps the law (Sabbath keeping or observing the feasts) it somehow seems to point out the lack of respect for God's law in others. (though this is not the intention of the "law keeper") When this happens, light is shed on the sin of others, and there is inevitably an offense that is taken. Often, this offense is manifested by the offended one accusing his brother (who shows respect for God's instruction) of attempting to "earn salvation."

We are able to see and understand this phenomenon of causing offense as it relates to sin when we consider the interaction between non-believers and Christians. For example, it is not uncommon and in fact expected that we would offend someone living in gross sin if we pointed out some "law breaking" behavior. What is more difficult to understand is that this same phenomenon can happen within the body of the Messiah. This is precisely what happens, for example, as we begin to keep Sabbath. Sabbath keeping often becomes an offense to our brethren who are unaware of their identity and the need to keep this commandment.

As our personal revelation of God deepens through His enlightenment by the power of His Spirit, we must remain sensitive to this spiritual principle: *Man is in rebellion to God and our natural inclination is to resist His will.* When we realize this, we are able to understand our reaction to the notion that we ought to keep God's instruction and we are also able to understand the reaction of our brethren when they become offended by our keeping of the "Law."

On the other hand, when we do make the mistake of thinking righteousness somehow comes from our works, we make the exact same mistake the Pharisees made during the first century. As we begin to think that righteousness is attained by law keeping, the next logical conclusion is that we ought to have more law. After all, the more laws you keep, the more righteous you are, right? We see then why the Pharisees took the six ordinances concerning the Sabbath in the Torah and turned them into over 1000 laws! These became a true burden to those wanting to do what was right.

The truth that will "set you free" is that righteousness and salvation have *never* come by works, even in the Old Testament. We learn from the account of Abraham, that he believed God, and that his *belief* was accounted to him as righteousness.[111] Abraham didn't simply "believe" God and then rest on his laurels though; he *acted* on his faith many times. In Hebrews chapter eleven, likely the most significant chapter on faith in the entire Bible, we see the principle that "True faith leads to action." Indeed, true faith is inextricably linked to action and it is precisely for this reason that James, the brother of Yeshua, writes **"Faith without works is dead"**[112] and again, **"But be doers of the word, and not hearers**

only, deceiving yourselves."[113]

Not being properly taught in matters of Grace, Faith, Law, and Salvation, it is easy to see why many New Testament Christians are deceived. Thinking that they are nothing but a "Sinner saved by Grace" they are content to wallow in the squalor of lawlessness. They have no understanding that they have inherited the great privilege of having been given God's instruction, the Torah! Because they have not been taught this "Word of God" that Paul was referring to (the Torah) when he said **"Faith comes by hearing, and hearing by the Word of God,"**[114] their *faith* is weak. Because they are of weak faith, and because salvation is by faith, they will be easy prey for the deceiver of the whole world, and consequently, their salvation is in jeopardy!

Attaining a Saving Faith

Not long ago in the course of my daily routine in the practice of medicine, I had the opportunity to mentor a young medical student with a most interesting religious background. This young man's family was from India and was of the Hindu religion. Desiring that he would have a good education, his parents sent him to a prestigious private school that was to be Catholic. Sometime during the middle of his high school years the family moved and a new school had to be found. Apparently, at their new location the best education that could be bought happened to be at a private Lutheran school. This gentleman had received a formal education with respect to both Catholicism and Protestantism and yet he had not made up his mind about which faith to choose. His parents did not at any time attempt to influence him. As a senior in High School, he was awarded the "religion" award, the award given to the best student of religion in the entire school. Now as a young man, this medical student knew the details of the Christian faith, but had not yet been able to "hear" the Word in a way that would move him to conversion. He was able to quite readily recount the life and death of the Messiah, understood the concept of man's depravity, and understood that Yeshua "died for our sins," but he still he hadn't "heard." Why?

In my conversations with this fellow I found that he was honestly a seeker but he was somewhat turned off by the notion that one's faith must be "blind." I was struck by the fact that despite his religious education he was unable to explain where or how the "Jewish" Messiah was found in the "Old Testament."

The apostle Paul tells us in Romans 10:17 that, **"Faith comes by hearing, and hearing by the Word of God."** It seems plain that Paul in this context is speaking of the "Old Testament" when he speaks of the "Word of God." After all, the New Covenant scriptures would not be compiled for nearly a hundred years at the time Paul wrote these words. It is disturbing to realize that among our New Covenant brethren today, just like the medical student mentioned above, very few could actually present the gospel from the Old Testament alone. Yet this is precisely what was done so successfully by Yeshua and His disciples in the first century. In fact, this happens to be Peter's admonition in 1 Peter 3:15, **"But sanctify the Lord God in your hearts, and always be ready to give a defense to everyone who asks you reason for the hope that is in you, with meekness and fear."** The believer in the first century, in order to defend his faith, would be asked to prove that Yeshua was the Messiah based on the scripture *of that day*. Today, in Christianity, it is accepted at face value by many that Yeshua is the Messiah, and little effort is made to strengthen that conviction based on the same "Word of God" that Paul spoke of in Romans 10:17. In more liberal denominations, the deity of Yeshua has long ago been denied precisely for this reason. Even the "clergy" are unable to defend the hope that is within them, and so the natural consequence is to begin to doubt.

Although he believed that there must be God somewhere, my young friend, the medical student had become disenchanted with the idea that Yeshua was God incarnate because during his "Christian education" the only answer he had ever gotten to the question "Why do you believe?" was "It is a matter of faith." The "Word of God" in the Old Testament had never been presented to him as an answer to that question. So we see that the question becomes, "Why do you have such a faith?" and the answer must be something other than "*I just believe.*"

I am convinced that the masses in Christianity do indeed believe, but that their faith is really quite weak because of their lack of hearing the Word of God. Contented to speak on superficial and social issues, the faith building "Word of God" is seldom taught in churches today. It is frightening to consider what might happen to the Christian masses if their faith were seriously challenged.

Satan is carrying out a great deception. Second Thessalonians 2:3 tells us that the Day of the Lord will not come until the "falling away" comes first. Because the untaught church at large has a very weak faith that is built upon a foundation of social acceptance and peer pressure, we realize that the church is set up for a fall, just as had been prophesied. At some point in the future, the evil one will be hurling his fiery darts and we must have in our armament the shield of faith, the only way by which we can defend ourselves. This shield will protect us from Satan's attack, and is part of the essential armor spoken of by Paul in Ephesians 6:10-18: **"Above all, taking the shield of faith with which you will be able to quench all the fiery darts of the wicked one."**

In the coming chapters we will discuss events of the Great Tribulation which will be endured by all who are still alive during that time. In order to get through this awesome time, we *must* have a strong faith. Paul tells us the means by which we can attain that faith in Romans 10:17 he tells us that **"Faith comes by hearing, and hearing by the Word of God."** Again, it is interesting to note that when Paul wrote these words he could not have been talking about the New Testament, rather, he must have been talking about the only Bible that was available during his time, the Old Testament. By this we see even further reason to embrace God's Law and His Word found in the Old Testament.

Eternal Security? — How Strong is Your Faith?

When we look at the issue of Salvation and Faith in the proper light we see that indeed salvation is by faith! We can also begin to make sense of the age old argument between those who believe in "eternal security" and those who believe that we could loose our salvation. The answer to this argument is simple. "Grace" is not how we are saved; it is why we are saved. *Faith* is how we are saved. (Faith that God gives freely to those who will *hear* His Word.) If our faith is weak because it is built on a foundation of the religious traditions of man, it is easy to see how we might lose our faith, and thus our salvation if we are seriously challenged. On the other hand, if our faith is built upon the solid foundation of having *heard* the "Word of God" so much so that we are able to readily defend the "hope that is in us" by citing the "Word of God," then indeed we have a strong faith that will in fact be proven by the works that we do and the way our life is lived out.

God has given us the way to Salvation. It is a free gift, but to attain it we *must* hear His Word. As the Day of the Lord approaches, we must **"make our election sure"**[115] by feasting[116] on the Word of God and thus building our faith. Tribulation is coming, let us prepare and put on the whole armor of God.

Attaining the Messiah, *the Ultimate Goal*

Once again, it is worthwhile to take a step back from the whole debate of "Law vs. Grace" or matters of eternal security or matters of whether or not we ought to "keep the law" — and try to focus on the *big picture*. We must understand that our ultimate goal is to know and experience and enjoy the Messiah who is God in the Flesh. Because of the fall of man in the Garden of Eden, we lost our ability to commune and fellowship with God in the way that He intended. Through the sacrifice that Yeshua made the sin that separated us from God was removed and we again are able to know and experience and enjoy the fullness of God.

When we as New Covenant believers first come to the understanding of our roots in the "Olive Tree" there is a danger that we, desiring to tickle the flesh, will want to trade the Spiritual reality of our fellowship with God for the physical reality. This is because we tend to be very concrete in our thinking, and because it is our nature to be carnally minded. Because of this, we are easily duped into seeing the physical as somehow *more real* than the spiritual. Yet when we realize that the physical realm is finite, that it will end and that the spiritual realm is eternal, we understand that the spiritual is *more real* than the physical. The Biblical Feasts and the Sabbath are **"Shadows of things to come, but the substance is Christ."**[117] Keeping the Feasts and the Sabbath, and the Law of God is *not an end in itself*. Rather, the regarding of God's Word as something true and precious and worth following is the *means to the* end — that end being the Messiah.

Today, while the so called messianic movement has begun to recover many wonderful things concerning our Hebraic heritage, we tragically see a few in this movement who have forgotten this important truth. After coming to the knowledge of the truth about the importance of God's instruction some believers have subsequently denied the Messiah and have left their faith in Yeshua to embrace full Judaism. Theories abound as to why this is happening, but the simple fact is this, if we see our keeping of the "Law" as something that we are to achieve out of our fleshly might and believe that this is the *endpoint*, we set ourselves up for deception, and we miss the truth — we miss the one who *is the Torah incarnate*, the Word that was *"With God"* and that *"Was God."*[118] *May this never happen to you!* This is precisely the sort of thing that our Messiah spoke out against in John 5:39-40, **"You search the Scriptures, for in them you think you have eternal life; and these are they which testify of Me. But you are not willing to come to Me that you may have life."**

Somehow we must be made to understand that the Law's purpose, in fact the purpose of the entire Bible is to lead us to the Messiah.[119]

Therefore, when we go and slaughter a lamb and hold a Passover Feast, our eating of the physical lamb is of benefit only if our prayer of blessing and thanksgiving and praise is something like this: *"Oh Lord, this lamb is not our real Passover. You are our real Passover. Thank You that You gave Yourself to die for us that we might take You into our being for life and strength. Thank You Lord for the picture, but we thank You even more that we can have and enjoy You as the Reality of such a picture..."*

Similarly, when we honor the Creator and His commands by keeping the Sabbath, our heart ought to cry out, *"Thank You Father for Your creation and Your Sabbath rest, but thank You more for the reality of the Sabbath, the coming millennial Kingdom and our Messiah who lives within our being and gives us true rest."*

In this way we are able to see how the Messiah came to *"fulfill the Law."* [120] We are able then to experience God fully and worship Him in both *"Spirit and Truth."* [121]

CHAPTER **11**

One Stick in His Hand

*B*efore we finally get into the details of the Great Tribulation, we will explore some fascinating passages prophesy of both of the houses of Israel and show that God will indeed reunite these two brothers.

Israel and the Kingdom Parables

It is truly amazing to see the consistency of the Word of God. In the Old Testament, we see that Israel, the least of all nations, was selected by God to be His chosen people. Now, with new understanding, we are also able to see that indeed God does not change[122] and that under the renewed covenant Israel continues to be God's people. As we step back and survey God's plan, we see that it is through the chosen people of Israel that He will redeem all of mankind.

Knowing this, we now can make sense of a couple of difficult "Kingdom parables" in the gospel of Matthew that, until now, were an enigma. In Matthew 13:33 Yeshua tells us, **"The kingdom of heaven is like leaven, which a woman took and hid in three measures of meal till it was all leavened."** Before coming to an understanding of God's plan to restore the two houses of Israel and Judah, I often wondered what in world could this parable mean? When Yeshua asked his disciples if they understood what He was saying they said, "Yes, Lord." It's too bad they couldn't have asked for an explanation, but had the Lord explained, these things would not have remained hidden, and Israel would not have been blinded "in part," "until the fullness of the Gentiles have come in" as had been prophesied by Paul in Romans 11:25.

When we understand that the Kingdom of Heaven is *Israel,* it all makes sense. *Israel* is like leaven, which a woman took and hid in three measures of meal till it was "all leavened." The three measures of meal represent the world and quite possibly represent the three major groups of people who each claim they are the sons of Abraham.[123] After all, the first time the "meal offering" (three measures of *unleavened* bread) is mentioned in the Scriptures is in Genesis 18:6 when Abraham asked Sarah to prepare three measures of fine meal for "the Lord" and two companions.

The leaven, or Israel, has spread throughout the entire world, and it is quite possible that by now very large percentage of humans on earth today could have as least a trickle of the patriarch Israel's blood pumping through their veins. It is precisely for this reason that we see believers in Yeshua from every ethnic group on the face of the earth in spite of Yeshua's statement **"I was not sent except to the lost sheep of the house of Israel"** in Matthew 15:24.

When we realize that it is conceivable that anyone could claim Israelite heritage, we understand that there is no room for pride based on race or ethnicity.

Additionally, leaven usually is a "type" of sin. We see therefore that Israel was destined to miss the mark and that being "Israel" (in the flesh only and not part of the kingdom of God) is nothing really to boast about anyway. We are not anything by our own efforts, yet by the Grace of God we are *Israel,* we have been declared righteous by our faith,[124] we are *sons of the Living God — the bride of the Messiah.*

Realizing that *Israel* is the kingdom of Heaven, we also understand the parable of the Mustard Seed in verse 31-32 of the same chapter: **"The Kingdom of Heaven is like a mustard seed, which a man took and sowed in his field, which indeed is the least of all the seeds; but when it is grown it is greater than the herbs and becomes a tree, so that the birds of the air come and nest in its branches."**

Israel, therefore, is like a mustard seed, which God sowed in the field of the world. Indeed, Israel was the least of all peoples and began as a single person given a promise from God. This seed has grown into a tree that is now occupied by "birds." Typologically speaking, birds usually represent something sinister and could be compared to the tares in the wheat discussed in chapter 8. Notice as you read your Bible that every time birds are mentioned; they represent the "bad guys." This case is no exception; Israel is occupied by "birds"—tares in the wheat that cannot be distinguished from the genuine.

When we step back and take note of God's mighty hand as He has worked his will from the foundation of the world, we can only marvel. It was God's doing that the whole house of Israel was split into two kingdoms. Knowing mankind's rebellious nature, God knew that the Northern Kingdom would quickly fall into idolatry. He prophesied hundreds of years ahead of time through Moses that the nation would face judgment for her rebelliousness in Deuteronomy 28:15-68. God does nothing that He does not first reveal through His prophets as is said in Amos 3:7 **"Surely the LORD God does nothing unless He reveal His secret to His servants the prophets."**

Through His prophets God told us that He would scatter Israel among the nations, and that He would gather her back together one day. (Hosea 1:6-11, Amos 9:9-12, Zephaniah 3:8-20, Zechariah 10:6-8, Ezekiel 37:15-28, Jeremiah 31, Isaiah 65:9)

God chose to entrust His *Word* to the House of Judah.[125] On the other hand, God scattered Ephraim/Israel and in His sovereignty has filled the world with Israelites through the offspring of Ephraim just as was prophesied. It is incredibly exciting to realize that we are just now beginning to understand the extent of God's plan that was hidden from us until the veil was lifted and we are allowed to see our identity as Israel.

The Redemption of Ruth and Naomi

The book of Ruth records for our learning a beautiful story of redemption that foreshadows the Messiah's redemptive work for all mankind. Below is a summary of Ruth's story and an explanation of how the characters played out roles that typify God's people. Even the names of the characters are significant in this story.

The book of Ruth gives the account of the family of Elimelech and Naomi, who left their home in Bethlehem[126] and moved to Moab because of famine.[127] Elimelech and Naomi had two sons, Mahlon and Chilion. These sons of Elimelech married Moabite women, and the names of their wives were Ruth and Orpah.

Tragically, Elimelech and his two sons died, leaving behind Naomi and her two daughters in law, Ruth and Orpah. Following the death of the men in the family, Naomi counseled her sons' wives to leave her and to begin to build a new life of their own. Orpah followed Naomi's advice and returned to the Moabites to start again. Ruth, however, clung to her mother in law and stayed with her when Naomi returned to the land of Judea.

Back in the land of Judea, Naomi and Ruth were destitute. Elimelech had abandoned his birthright land in Judea, and because he was dead, Naomi had no inheritance to which to return.

In ancient Judea, in keeping with the law of God, the poor could follow behind the harvesters in a field and glean from the corners of the field.[128] Ruth, following the instruction of Naomi went to gather this harvest and found herself in the field of a man named Boaz. Boaz happened to be a relative of Elimelech.

Ruth found favor in the eyes of Boaz, and he instructed his men to allow her to glean even among the sheaves, the already bundled stalks of grain, and to not "reproach" her. In this way, Ruth was able to bring home a handsome amount of barley, and this pleased Naomi greatly.

When Naomi discovered that Boaz had shown Ruth favor, Naomi was very pleased and gave Ruth some interesting instruction.

Following Naomi's directions, Ruth washed and anointed herself and put on her best clothes. That evening, when Boaz had completed his days work and finished eating and drinking, he lay down to sleep for the night next to the pile of barley that had been collected and threshed. While he slept, Ruth quietly approached him and softly settled in at his feet, covering herself with the "wing" of his garment. At midnight, Boaz awoke and found Ruth at his feet. It was then that Ruth asked Boaz to perform the role of the "kinsman redeemer."

In ancient Israel, under these circumstances, a relative of a widow could take the widow for his wife and thus "redeem" her, and restore her back to her inheritance. This is the act that Ruth was requesting from Boaz.

The story of Ruth has a happy ending, because Boaz did indeed take Ruth for his wife and thus restored the inheritance of both Naomi and Ruth. Ruth, as it turns out, went on to conceive a son whose name was Obed. Obed was taken by Naomi, who became his nurse.

Obed was the father of Jesse, and so was the grandfather of King David. Yeshua is a descendant of King David making this story even more interesting because Ruth is therefore in the genealogy of Yeshua.

The story of Ruth is outstanding in its own right even when taken at face value. What is even more fascinating, though, is the deeper meaning behind this account. It is as though the entire story is a parable speaking of the redemption of God's people Israel through the work of the Messiah.

Naomi in this story is a "type" of God's people Israel, specifically the Jew (the House of Judah) who has *not* lost her identity. Naomi, whose name means "my delight" knows who she is, but having lost her husband Elimelech, whose name means God-king, she had been cut off from her inheritance.

Ruth, whose name meaning "friendship" also refers to a female companion or mate, is the daughter in law of Naomi and represents Ephraim and those who would cling to and be a friend to the people of God by following the God of Israel. Ruth therefore represents those from the Gentile nations who were once "Israelite," but having lost her husband also, were completely cut off from the commonwealth of Israel and were true Gentiles once again. Through the redemption work of Boaz, Ruth was not only brought back into Israel, but into the family of the Messiah.

On the other hand, Orpah (whose name in the Hebrew root form means "stiff-necked" as in apostasy or fleeing away) represents that portion of Ephraim who became the false church and who abandoned her roots and went "back to her people and her gods." After leaving Naomi, Orpah is not spoken of again, and is *not* restored back to her inheritance in Israel by the work of Boaz.

Boaz, who is of the "family of Elimelech," has a name that means "strength." He can be thought of, therefore, as the strength of the family of Elimelech, or strength of the God-King. Boaz, as it is well known, represents the Messiah who restores both Naomi and Ruth to their inheritance by taking Ruth as a wife.

It is fascinating to note the way Ruth "proposed" that Boaz act in the role of the kinsmen redeemer. First of all she "washed" herself. The "washing" in this story could have very well been a Mikvah bath, the Hebrew baptism ritual that John the Baptist was actually performing when preaching repentance and baptism in preparation for the first coming of the Messiah. Secondly, Ruth put on her best clothes. Typologically clothes represent our righteousness and speak of our walk with the Lord.

She then approached Boaz while he was sleeping and "covered herself" with the *hem of his garment*. When he awoke she again asked that Boaz would spread the corner of his garment over her. The writer of Ruth makes the point at least a couple of times that it was the corner of the garment that Ruth wanted to put herself under. This is significant in that the Torah specifies that tassels were to be placed on the corners of the garments. These tassels called tzit-tzit represent the written Law of Moses.

Interesting insights are gained when we look at this word picture. Ruth submitted to Boaz and showed "kindness" to him, so that Boaz agreed to "redeem" Ruth, when she put herself voluntarily under his "law" or authority when she covered herself with the corner of his garment. In the same way we ought to become bondservants (in Hebrew, Obed) and follow the commands of God, showing that we love Him, just as Yeshua instructed when He said, **"If you love Me, keep My commandments."**

The writers of the New Testament, in fact, often referred to themselves as "bondservants." Revelation was written to the "bondservants" of Yeshua the Messiah (In Greek, *Doulos* in Revelation 1:1) and it is probable that the reason certain spiritual insights remain hidden from the eyes of the unbelieving is that they are not the intended audience since they have not submitted as bondservants.

In this amazing story we also see that Naomi became a nurse to Obed, the son of Ruth. This speaks prophetically of "bondservants" coming out of Israel who, yearning for the word of God, have learned that they can be nurtured through a connection with Naomi (The House of Judah). Conversely, in the book of Ruth Obed is prophesied to become a "restorer of life age and a nourisher of your old" to Naomi. In this way, we see that the bondservant coming out of Israel will both receive nourishment from and give life to Judah!

It is fascinating to realize the traditional Jewish scripture reading holds that the book of Ruth is to be read on the Feast of Shavuot (Pentecost). It was on the Feast of Pentecost, as mentioned in Acts 2, that "proselytes" from "every nation under heaven"[129] were added to those who were being saved. We see then that, albeit unwittingly, the Jewish tradition upholds the notion that the book of Ruth speaks of the redemption of not only Israel, but also the redemption of those from among the nations.

The Woman with the Issue of Blood

In Mark 5:21-43 we are given a story about Yeshua and a miracle, actually two miracles that happen almost at the same time. It appears as though these two stories were juxtaposed in the text of Mark for a specific reason. The story relates an account of Yeshua walking along with a great multitude traveling with Him. As the story goes, a "Ruler of the Synagogue" by the name of Jairus approached Yeshua and fell at His feet. Jairus pleaded with Yeshua that He might come and lay His hands upon his daughter, who was near the point of death, and heal her. Yeshua agreed and went with Jairus; all the while the multitudes followed Him and were "thronging" him.

In the midst of this mass of humanity clutching and grasping at the Master, a woman with an "issue of blood" made her way through the crowd and touched the "Hem" of Yeshua's garment.

This poor woman had been suffering from menstrual bleeding for *twelve* years. According to the Torah, this made her "unclean." This must have been a terrible burden for her to bear. Strictly speaking, anyone she touched would be made "unclean," and thus she was likely ostracized from the rest of society. Apparently, she had spent a great deal of her livelihood on doctors, but her problem only got worse. As a physician, I can say with some authority that this poor woman was in all likelihood very pale and sickly appearing from chronic blood loss and depletion of her iron stores. I am certain that she had very little strength and that it took tremendous effort to fight through the thronging multitudes in order to get close to Yeshua.

As soon as she touched the hem of His garment (His Tzit-tzit) the **"fountain of her blood was dried up, and she felt in her body that she was healed of the affliction."** Yeshua, sensing that **"power had gone out of Him"** turned around in the crowd and said, **"Who touched My Clothes?"**

I get a chuckle out the disciples' response to this question every time I read it. Their reply was incredulous, **"You see the multitude thronging You, and You say, 'Who touched Me?'"**

The woman, fearing and trembling, fell down in front of Yeshua and told Him the whole truth. Yeshua's answer back is moving, **"Daughter, your faith has made you well, go in peace, and be healed of your affliction."**

While He was still speaking these words, a messenger came from Jairus' house with troubling news. He reported that Jairus' daughter was dead and he questioned why the Teacher should be troubled any further. As soon as Yeshua heard the words that were spoken, He said to the ruler of the synagogue, **"Do not be afraid; only believe."**

Yeshua then proceeded to the house of Jairus, allowing only Peter, James, and John and the father and the mother of the child to enter the house. The crowd outside ridiculed Yeshua, but inside, a touching seen took place when Yeshua took the child by the hand and softly said, **"Little girl, I say to you, arise."** Can you imagine the feeling of relief and gratitude that the family of this twelve year old girl felt as she stood up and walked? The text of Mark, in typical understated fashion, says that they were, **"overcome with amazement."**

While the wonderful stories of Yeshua's ministry are beautiful in their own right, like the story of Ruth, a closer look reveals a deeper level of meaning that is absolutely breathtaking.

It is no coincidence that these two miracles happened at virtually the same time and are told in this way. Both the woman with the issue of blood and the girl raised from the dead are associated with the number twelve. The woman had been bleeding for twelve years, and the girl was twelve years old.

The number twelve represents the twelve tribes of Israel, and thus these two women represent the two houses, Israel and Judah. It is a fact of history that Judah contains some of those from the house of Israel, and vise versa.

It is not hard to figure out which daughter represents Judah and which represents Israel. The daughter of Jairus (The ruler of the synagogue, whose name means "He will awaken") represents Judah. The woman who is unclean represents Israel. The story speaks to the needs of both of the two houses.

Judah, as represented by the twelve year old daughter of the ruler of the synagogue is shown to be *near the point of death*. We will show in some detail in Chapter 12, this will be the case for the house of Judah during the Great Tribulation. It will be during the darkest days of Jacob's trouble that this miracle of Yeshua will be finally completely understood. At that time, the Lord's loving admonition to the house of Judah, who will appear as dead, will simply be, **"Do not be afraid; only believe (in Yeshua)."** The house of Judah will "awaken" (Jairus means "He will awaken") to life with great joy and astonishment at the words not unlike the words of Yeshua, **"Little girl, I say to you, arise."**

On the other hand, the story of the woman with the issue of blood speaks distinctively to the need of the house of Israel. This woman, also called "daughter," is unclean and untouchable. She is defiled, sickly, and emaciated. She is in desperate need of healing and cleansing. Remarkably, she attains her healing by touching the "law" as represented by the Tzit-tzit on the hem of Yeshua's garment.

Lest anyone make the mistake of thinking that it was by her *own* effort, her *own* difficult struggle through the thronging multitude that she somehow attained her healing for herself, let us examine again the words of Yeshua, **"Daughter, your *faith* has made you**

well. Go in peace, and be healed of your affliction."

Thus, we have a perfect picture of faith in action. This woman's faith was not a mere mental ascent to some lofty ideas. She didn't just cognitively agree with the doctrinal statements penned by some religious philosophers, she was moved to action by her faith! It was by faith that she approached and touched the very thing that represents the "law," thus showing us by example what true faith is all about and showing us the deepest need of the house of Israel.

The Restoration of the Kingdom

In Acts 1:6 we have the account of the ascension of our Lord. Not yet fifty days after His resurrection, the Lord ascended into the clouds. We are told in Acts 1:11 that the Messiah's return will be in like manner.

The very last question asked of Yeshua by His disciples is noteworthy. They asked, **"Lord, will You at this time restore the Kingdom to Israel?"** Apparently, being acquainted with the Old Testament scriptures and having just spent the last three years sitting and learning at the feet of the Yeshua, the expectation of the disciples was that He would at that time begin His reign in literal Jerusalem and subdue the whole world.

God's plan was still a mystery though, and Yeshua answered back, **"It is not for you to know the times or seasons which the Father has put in His own authority. But you shall receive power when the Holy Spirit has come upon you; and you shall be witnesses to Me in Jerusalem, and in all Judea and Samaria, and to the end of the earth."** Thus the disciples began to regather the lost sheep of the Israel that had been scattered to the "end of the earth."

The mystery of God was apparently not fully made known to the disciples at the time of the ascension. Had they known God's plan to regather the flock, they would not have asked if it were time to restore the Kingdom.

The Apostle Paul speaks of this very "mystery" in Ephesians chapters two and three. Here, Paul explains that the mystery of God was that, **"The Gentiles should be fellow heirs, of the same body,** and partakers of His promise in Christ through the gospel."

Still, the disciples at the time of the Messiah anticipated an *earthly* king that would reunify the kingdom and rule on a physical throne. What was the basis for this expectation? In what remains of this book we will begin to explore some of the breathtaking Old Testament prophesies that spell out the events that must happen as this present age comes to a close. We will see that not only has Israel been grafted back into the olive tree, but that there will indeed be a true physical restoration of the Kingdom of Israel!

Ezekiel's Two Sticks

The purpose of this book is to clarify issues pertaining to the end times and to spur the reader on to a more holy lifestyle by taking into account the proper understanding of our identity as the "elect" and by highlighting the importance of God's instruction to His people.

Now, having come to an understanding of the two houses of Israel, we are at last able to also see what the end will bring. God will reunite the kingdoms that *He* separated three thousand years ago. His Word foretells it. Let's take a closer look:

Again the word of the LORD came to me, saying, "As for you, son of man, take a stick for yourself and write on it: 'For Judah and for the children of Israel, his companions.' Then take another stick and write on it, 'For Joseph, the stick of Ephraim, and for all the house of Israel, his companions.' Then join them one to another for yourself into one stick, and they will become one in you hand. And when the children of your people speak to you, saying, "Will you not show us what you mean by these?" Say to them, "Thus says the LORD God: 'Surely I will take the stick of Joseph, which is in the hand of Ephraim, and the tribes of Israel, his companions; and I will join them with it, with the stick of Judah, and make them one stick, and they will be one in My hand.'"

"And the sticks on which you write will be in your hand before their eyes. Then say to them, 'Thus says the Lord God:

"Surely I will take the children of Israel from among the nations, wherever they have gone, and will gather them from every side and bring them into their own land; and I will make them one nation in the land, on the mountains if Israel; and one king shall be king over them all; they shall no longer be two nations, nor shall they ever be divided into two kingdoms again.""

"They shall not defile themselves anymore with their idols, nor with their detestable things, nor with any of their transgressions; but I will deliver them from all their dwelling places in which they have sinned, and will cleanse them. Then they shall be My people, and I will be their God." Ezekiel 37:15-23

Ezekiel goes on to prophesy that "David" will be the King over them. Since David had been dead for many years, this is clearly a messianic idiom[130] speaking of our Messiah Yeshua, who being an heir to David's throne, is uniquely qualified to reign as the future King of Israel. This reigning of "David" over a united Israel will occur during the literal 1000 year millennial kingdom. As we read on, we see that God will **"set My sanctuary in their midst forevermore."** Vs. 26 and 28, and that **"they shall also walk in My judgments and observe My statutes, and do them"** in vs. 24. These statements indicate that God's people will follow God's Law, the Torah, during the millennial kingdom and there will be a literal temple where we will worship and meet with the Lord.

(Again, if God's elect are to follow and obey God's Law during the millennium then why are we not supposed to now? Actually, as we learned in the last two chapters, we *are* supposed to, but we are under the New Covenant, so that the righteous requirement of the law, the requirement that we pay with our lives for our inability to perfectly keep the law, has been nailed to the cross with the Messiah. Should we sin more and let grace abound then? As the Apostle Paul says, "God forbid!")

If we believe the Word and take it seriously, we realize that we (or perhaps our children) will someday live in the land of *literal* Israel. This is an incredible statement.

Would you be willing to move to Israel if God called you? If you are a believer in the True and Living God this could actually happen!

There are Christian theologians who teach that Go
with the nation Israel and that because Israel was un[
abandoned Israel and his covenant with her. A cl
Deuteronomy 29 and 30 reveals that what has happened to the
nation Israel over the millennia happened precisely as God
intended. God scattered Israel into the nations, and now just as was
prophesied by Moses, He will again bring her back into the land. In
this way we see that God did not break covenant with Israel, rather
history unfolded just as was predicted. God kept His Word, *He has
kept covenant.*

While this all sounds incredible, what is even more amazing is
the realization that this is in fact unfolding before our very eyes.
The mere fact that our brother Judah is back in the land tells us that
we are very close to the time of restoration of all things. In
Zechariah 12:7, we learn that the **"tents of Judah"** will be the first
to go up in the land of Israel — and incredibly, *this has already
happened.*

One hundred years ago the notion of Judah being back in the
land was *inconceivable*. It took the Holocaust to motivate many of
the Jews to leave their homes and immigrate back into the Promised
Land. What will it take to motivate Ephraim? Zechariah 12:1-9
appears to be happening right before our eyes, what follows, the
Day of the Lord, looks to be right around the corner. If we think
back to our discussion of the "Day of the Lord," we know that the
Great Tribulation will precede the Day of the Lord.

Remember, the Great Tribulation has also been called in the
Bible the "Time of Jacob's Trouble." Since we are part of Israel
(whose given name was Jacob), we should not expect to be
"beamed out" of this time (although we may be divinely protected).

It is during this incredible time that is about to come upon the
whole earth that many eyes will be opened — and the tares will
be separated from the wheat. It will be the time of the "Great
Tribulation."

**"At that time Michael shall stand up, the great prince who
stands watch over the sons of your people; and there shall be a
time of trouble, such as never was since there was a nation.**

Even to that time. And at that time your people shall be delivered. Every one who is found written in the book." Daniel 12:1

Daniel goes on to say in 12:3, **"Those who are wise shall shine like the brightness of the firmament, and those who turn many to righteousness like the stars forever and ever."** Notice how the language here is very similar to that of Yeshua's when explaining the tares in the wheat parable in Matthew 13:43 **"Then the righteous will shine forth as the sun in the kingdom of their Father. He who has ears to hear, let him hear!"**

So we can clearly see that it is during the Great Tribulation that God will remove the tares from the wheat. After the "weeds are pulled," the righteous will shine forth, and this will include both those who are living at the time of the resurrection and also those who partake in the first resurrection. We can make this argument based on Daniel 12:1-3 and Isaiah 26:19-20, when taken into the context of the "tares in the wheat" kingdom parable. It is very important to realize that the "tares," the counterfeit saints, are taken out first, not vice versa as is implied by those who hold to a pre-trib doctrine.

Where is the United States in Biblical Prophecy?

While much has been written about this question, the Bible is strangely quiet about the world's most powerful nation during the supposed "end times." How can this be? Simply put, the people of the earth are divided into two camps: those whose citizenship is in heaven[131] (true Israel), and those who "dwell upon the earth." When we understand God's redemption plan for mankind, we realize that the Bible is chiefly written to and about His people Israel, and that the other "nations" of the earth are of secondary interest.

Just as Paul had both Jewish and Roman citizenship, we have citizenship in both Israel and with our native country. In fact, almost every citizen of the "commonwealth of Israel" (Ephesians 2:12-13) can claim the same.

When we realize this simple fact, we begin to understand that it is not a question of whether or not a certain nation can be found in the Bible, rather, it is a question of what nation do you identify with? Do you identify with those who dwell upon the earth? Or is your citizenship in Heaven! When you realize that *you are of God's chosen people Israel*, it becomes less important what happens to the U.S. or France, or Iraq, or any other nation. We ask the question "What does the Bible say about the U.S.?" because we are curious about what will happen to us!

All of the sudden we realize that although the Bible is silent about the U.S., it has a great deal to say about *US*... Israel.

The time will surely come when a decision will have to be made.

Who will you identify with?

CHAPTER 12

The Great Tribulation and the Regathering of Israel

*T*he great tragedy of the pretribulation rapture doctrine is that it propagates the notion that we need not concern ourselves with the events of the Great Tribulation and the identity of the Antichrist, because "we won't be around to experience it." This kind of thinking is nothing short of a *lie from Satan*, so that he might deceive "even the very elect." Perhaps you too have heard such sentiments, even from the pulpit of your church. Perhaps you have even uttered such.

We must not allow ourselves to be ignorant about the times that are coming. Yeshua himself warned us about false christs in Matthew 24:25 saying, **"See, I have told you beforehand."** He plainly warns about the Antichrist in Revelation 13:18, **"Here is wisdom. Let him who has understanding calculate the number of the beast."** We have shown in previous chapters that to say that the "church" will be raptured away and that the Jew is the intended audience of these warnings is to twist the plain meaning of the scriptures. We have seen that to believe such a lie leads us right into the snare set by the evil one.

Imagine, if you will, what it might be like during the tribulation. You and your family have been trying to hide your faith from a world that has gone completely insane around you. Believers everywhere have been pulled from their homes and beheaded for their faith. Widespread famine causes hunger that is not measured by the number of meals missed, but by the number of days since you have eaten.

The entire "world" is convinced that man's suffering is due to the "intolerance" of your faith. Stories abound concerning friends who have switched to the other side; despite the difficult times, they now live a life of apparent luxury and ease while you go hungry. You even find out that a dear family member has tried to turn you over to authorities in the ultimate act of betrayal.

While a forecast such as this sounds grisly, these sorts of predictions are valid because Yeshua said that this period will be a time of tribulation such as the world has not seen up until that time — and considering world history and the famines of days gone by, we understand that the Great Tribulation will be *most unpleasant*. It could be that as your children waste away before your very eyes and cry out feebly for nourishment, you will be tempted beyond measure to relent and simply take a mark on your right hand or forehead and thus be able to feed your starving family.

Imagine further how great the temptation will be when *even your old friends from church* try to convince you, "C'mon, don't be so superstitious, this can't be the *real* 'mark of the beast', remember what Pastor said? He said *we will be gone* before all the trouble starts, now just take the mark and quit needlessly putting your family through all of this!"

I must say that I am deeply alarmed for my "pre-trib" brethren when I think of such a scenario. In fact, this very thought is in part the motivation behind writing this book.

It's *Jacobs* Trouble

Realizing that the "rapture" will be prewrath, and understanding that we believers will be going through part of the Great Tribulation, a closer look at this time period certainly seems warranted. Here are a few facts that we are able to glean from the Bible to give us some insight about this most terrible time, it is from these verses that the hypothetical scenario above was constructed:

- "They will deliver you up to tribulation and kill you, and you will be hated by all nations for My name's sake." Matthew 24:9
- "Many will be offended, will betray one another, and will hate one another" Matthew 24:10
- "Many false prophets will rise up and deceive many." Matthew 24:11
- "lawlessness will abound," and the "Love of many will grow cold." Matthew 24:12
- "Unless those days were shortened, no flesh would be saved." Matthew 24:22
- "There will be 'Great Tribulation' such as has not been since the beginning of the world nor ever shall be." Matthew 24:21
- The Antichrist will make war with the saints and overcome them. Revelation 13:7
- This time period will last 42 months (3_ years), and begin at the midpoint of Daniel's 70th week (Daniel 9:27)
- During this time, all will be required to receive a "mark" in order to buy or sell. This "mark" will cause the recipient to be eternally condemned. Revelation 13:16-17, 14:9, and 11. (Actually, it is the "false prophet" of the Antichrist that will compel all to take the mark and not the Antichrist himself.)
- Brother will betray brother, a father will betray his child, and children will rise up against parents and cause them to be put to death. Mark 13:13

Notice that the above citations are all from the New Testament. There is much more to learn about this time, however, and the Old Testament is filled with colorful accounts about the Great Tribulation.[132] Usually these Old Testament allusions are "Israel-centric": For example:

Now these are the words that the LORD spoke concerning Israel and Judah, "For thus says the LORD: We have heard a voice of trembling, of fear, and not of peace. Ask now, and see, whether a man is ever in labor with child? So why do I see every man with his hands on his loins like a woman in labor, and all faces turned pale? Alas! For that day is great, so that none is

like it; and it is the time of Jacob's trouble, but he shall be saved out of it." Jeremiah 30:4-7

Notice again that this period is called the time of *Jacob's* trouble, and not *only* Judah's. Again, this is confirmation that it will be we who are of Israel who will be going through this time called the Great Tribulation. In what will be one of the most comforting lines in the Bible during that dreadful time, we are also promised in the last line above, **"But he shall be saved out of it."**

Actually, in surveying Old Testament prophecy concerning the Great Tribulation, one comes away realizing that God *will restore* Israel, despite allowing her to go through this terrible time.[133] It will be during this time that God will truly regather His elect into the physical lands of Israel.

The "Greater Exodus" — The Return of the Prodigal Son!

It seems inconceivable to the average reader that the *whole House of Israel* will be brought into the literal Promised Land. Frankly, our unbelief is in part because most of us are "content" right here in "Egypt" and we really don't want to pull up stakes and move halfway around the world.

It is interesting to note that this attitude of complacency was the mind-set of many of the Jews at the beginning of the 20th century. World Wars I and II brought incredible suffering to the Jews, and they were compelled to leave the comforts of their homes and seek refuge in the literal land of Israel.

God's Word predicted that Judah would one day return to the literal land of Israel. The facts on the ground — the reality of existence of the nation Israel today prove that God's word concerning Judah was to be taken literally.

In the same way, we ought to take seriously God's Word concerning the scattered nation of Israel, since the prophets tell us that these too will one day join Judah in the actual Promised Land.

The "mass departure" of the remnant of Israel out of the world has been referred to as the "Greater Exodus."

Candidly, there may be those who object to the notion that

"Christian Ephraimites" will be moving to and occupying and perhaps displacing the Jew from what is now present day Israel. This scenario is not at all what is here implied. It is interesting to point out that the area currently occupied by the Palestinians includes that land that would be considered "Israelite" (the Northern Kingdom) territory. It is also important to keep in mind that the Promised Land as described by God to Abraham included what is now Lebanon, some of Syria, some of Saudi Arabia and part of Iraq with its eastern boundary at the *Euphrates River*.[134] This is a vast area that could easily contain faithful returning Israelites without dispossessing any of those from the House of Judah who have already been brought back into the land by God. Consider also that God's blessings will be upon the land and it will not likely be the barren wasteland that we know today.[135]

The "natural" response of Judah toward returning Ephraimites is to scorn them, after all the Israelites of the Northern Kingdom are the ones that fell into gross idolatry and "squandered his inheritance in the land of the Gentiles." This is just as Yeshua predicted it would be in the parable of the Prodigal Son and is the reason that many "Messianic Jews" reject the notion that born again believers could really be remnants of the scattered Northern Kingdom. Additionally, this is in part the reason why the current political climate in Israel does not allow for the returning "Ephraimite." We can assume based on the Word of God, however, that this will not always be the case and that someday an incredible event will happen that will trigger the return of the "prodigal son." Below we will explore the incident might prompt such an event.

Keeping in mind the identity of the whole House of Israel let us take a look at a couple of passages that will prove the point that *Israel* will return to the land:

"Son of man, when the house of Israel dwelt in their own land, they defiled it by their own ways and deeds; to Me their way was like the uncleanness of a woman in her customary impurity. Therefore I poured out My fury on them for the blood they had shed on the land, and for their idols with which they had defiled it. So I scattered them among the nations, and they

were dispersed throughout the countries; I judged them according to their ways and their deeds. When they came to the nations, wherever they went, they profaned My holy name – when they said of them, "Theses are the people of the LORD, and yet they have gone out of His Land." But I had concern for My holy name, which the house of Israel had profaned among the nations wherever they went. Therefore say to the house if Israel, "Thus says the Lord God: I do not do this for your sake, O house of Israel, but for My holy Name's sake, which you have profaned among the nations wherever you went. And I will sanctify My great name, which had been profaned among the nations, which you have profaned in their midst; and the nations shall know that I am the LORD, " says the Lord God, "when I am Hallowed in you before their eyes. For I will take you from among the nations, gather you out of all countries, and bring you into your own land. Then I will sprinkle clean water on you, and you shall be clean; I will cleanse you from all your filthiness and from all your idols. I will give you a new heart and put a new spirit within you; I will take the heart of stone out of your flesh and give you a heart of flesh. I will put My Spirit within you and cause you to walk in My statutes and you will keep My judgments and do them. Then you shall dwell in the land that I gave to your fathers; you shall be My people, and I will be your God." Ezekiel 36:17-28

The LORD has appeared from afar to me, saying: "Yes, I have loved you with an everlasting love; Therefore with lovingkindness I have drawn you. Again I will build you, and you shall be rebuilt, O virgin of Israel! You shall again be adorned with your tambourines, and shall go forth in the dances of those who rejoice. You shall yet plant vines on the mountains of Samaria; The planters shall plant and eat them as ordinary food. For there shall be a day when the watchmen will cry on Mount Ephraim, 'Arise, and let us go up to Zion, to the LORD our God.'" Jeremiah 31:3-6

Considering the distinction between the House of Judah and the

House of Israel, notice that the above citations refer primarily to the House of Israel. The reference to the return to the mountains of "Samaria" in the second passage above proves that what is spoken of is the Northern Kingdom and not only of the return of the Southern Kingdom of Judah. While the notion of the House of Israel's literal return to the land sounds a little incredible, the scriptural support for such a view is extensive.[136]

Jacob Returns

In Genesis 32, we are given the story of Jacob's return to the Promised Land. Jacob had been living with his uncle Laban and had been working in Haran for many years. During that time he married Leah and Rachael and through God's blessing of his efforts Jacob put together quite a herd and become rather wealthy in his own right. Still, Jacob was living in Laban's household and contention between the heads of the houses developed. Jacob wanted, therefore, to follow God's instruction[137] and return home, but there was a problem — Jacob had taken his brother Esau's birthright blessing and Esau had sworn to kill him if he returned home. Even so, Jacob yearned for his homeland, the land that God had promised to give him and he set out to return to the land of Canaan.

Upon Jacob's return we are told that he *divided* his household in order to protect them. Jacob thought that if Esau were to attack one "camp" then the other would be safe.[138] Jacob divided his house between Leah's camp (the camp of Judah) and Rachel's camp (the camp of Joseph, or later Ephraim). This occurrence prophetically foretells of God's eventual dividing of the "whole House of Jacob."

The thing that is so fascinating about this biblical story is what happens next. During the night, Jacob took his wives and the two camps and they crossed over the creek marking the boundary of the Promised Land, the ford of Jabbok.[139] It is during this night that the two camps are brought back together. It is also during this night that Jacob meets a "man"[140] who is "God"[141] and *wrestles* with him until morning. This event cripples Jacob and is rightly referred to as the time of "Jacob's Trouble."

This incident foreshadows a future occasion when God will

again contend with His people Israel — during the *Great Tribulation*. It is pertinent to again point out that the Great Tribulation is euphemistically called the "time of Jacob's Trouble" in Jeremiah 30:7. Notice that in the Genesis account, which is prophetic of the future event, it is during the time of Jacob's Trouble that the whole House of Israel is reunited and enters into the Promised Land.

Notice also that even before the time of "Jacob's Trouble" that Jacob is "afraid" and "greatly distressed."[142] This indicates that *even before* the time of the Great Tribulation, great fear and distress will come upon the Whole House of Israel.[143]

The Last Battles of This Age

At this point in our discussion of the Great Tribulation, we will attempt to begin to better define some of the events that will occur.

Technically speaking, it is important to realize that the "Great Tribulation" as defined by Yeshua Himself in Matthew 24:21 includes only the last 3 _ years of the seventieth week of Daniel.[144] The entire seven-year period is sometimes referred to simply as the "tribulation," reserving the title of "Great Tribulation" for the last half of these seven years. In order to better understand the events of the "Great Tribulation" it is useful to look at some of the preceding events.

It is apparent upon careful study of Old Testament prophecies that a series of extraordinary battles will take place as the present age comes to a close. Throughout the Old Testament, we witness the God of Israel defeating the enemies of the nation in miraculous battles. When God's timepiece resumes and the seventieth week of Daniel begins to unfold, we will again see the Hand of God intervene in a mighty way. It appears that there will be at least three major battles as this age comes to a close. In each of these, God will intercede, each time with increasing severity so as to eventually bring the entire world into submission.[145]

The Gog-Magog Invasion

It appears that the first of these end time battles will be the Gog-Magog battle of Ezekiel 38-39. Here in these two chapters of Ezekiel, God reveals the names of the countries that form an alliance and attack Israel. For many years now, based mainly on the work of Hal Lindsey and company, most contemporary theologians have taught that the coalition of countries in the Gog-Magog invasion refer to an alliance of nations led by the Soviet Union. It seems likely that this interpretation grew out of consideration of the political climate at the time this position was formed.

We ought to be careful not to interpret scripture based on the status quo geo-political situation, rather, we ought to interpret the scriptures first at "face value," and then perhaps we can speculate more authoritatively.

There is good reason to believe that rather than being a "Soviet" coalition, that the countries and peoples identified by their *historic* names likely represent a coalition of Middle Eastern countries led by a man referred to as "Gog of Magog," the "Rosh" (Hebrew for prince) of Meshech and Tubal. The ancient regions of Meshech and Tubal spoken of here are readily identifiable by anyone with internet access and the inclination to research the topic.

These geographic regions correspond roughly to the area just south of and along the Caucasus Mountains between the Caspian Sea and the Black Sea. The area of Magog *includes* Mechech and Tubal. This region is present day Georgia, Armenia, and Azerbaijan which are just to the north of and border Iran. Older Biblical geographic maps have this area actually extending to the south into Northern Syria, Northern Iran and Northern Iraq.

The narrative of Ezekiel 38-39 tells us that this coalition will include Libya (thought to include that part of Northern Africa that is mostly Arabic), Togarmah and Gomer (Turkey), Persia (Iran), and Ethiopia (this may include Sudan, Ethiopia, and Somalia). Led by the "Prince of Magog," the entire coalition will invade the "unwalled villages" in the mountains of Israel.[146] Interestingly, the area prophesied to be invaded is presently where the poorly defended Jewish Settlements are located. This whole scenario does not seem all that far-fetched given the current political situation in the Middle East.

Admittedly, it seems a little strange that the land of Babylon is not specifically named in this coalition. Now that Babylon (Iraq) is under U.S. control though, this makes sense. It is interesting that *Northern* Iraq, which includes some of the ancient land of Magog, has proven very difficult for the U.S. to subdue, and in fact this is where Sunni loyalists have a stronghold and anti American sentiments run deep.

In trying to build a workable end times scenario, it is not inconceivable that the U.S. invasion of the middle east could spill over into Syria precipitating a regional war. If a regional war were to break out, new alliances would likely form and it is easy to imagine how the named coalition in Ezekiel might unite so as to be a more formidable opponent to what would appear to the Muslim world as a Western invasion. Interestingly, there is a lot of political upheaval in the Republic of Georgia and in fact in November 2003 the President of Georgia was forced to resign amid heated protests and political pressure.

It is also interesting to note that Syria, Lebanon, Saudi Arabia, Egypt, and Afghanistan are not *specifically* named in this Muslim coalition. Could this be because the invasion into Iraq will spread into and thus overthrow Syria and Lebanon? (Saudi Arabia and Kuwait are roughly Sheba, Dedan, and Tarshish — who stay out of the battle according to the Ezekiel account). Egypt also appears to be sitting this one out. Why? Only time will tell.

According to the account in Ezekiel, God will intervene in this major battle and Israel will be overwhelmingly victorious. The net result will be a realization among the *whole House of Israel scattered among the nations* that YHWH is the true and Living God.

"So the house of Israel shall know that I am the Lord their God from that day forward. The Gentiles shall know that the house of Israel went into captivity for their iniquity; because they were unfaithful to Me, therefore I hid My face from them. I gave them into the hand of their enemies, and they all fell by the sword. According to their uncleanness and according to

their transgressions I have dealt with them, and hidden My face from them. Therefore thus says the Lord God: "Now I will bring back the captives of Jacob, and have mercy on the whole house of Israel; and I will be jealous for My holy name."'
Ezekiel 39:22-25

The spectacular victory by the hand of God during the Gog-Magog invasion will be a signal to those among the House of Israel that it is time to return home. It is likely that the political climate in Israel will change to allow the influx of the House of Israel, possibly because of greatly expanded borders.

Presently, the Middle East is in much turmoil but it appears as of early 2005 that a few things must happen before the Gog-Magog invasion could take place. Exactly how long it might take for such a scenario to unfold is uncertain, but given the instability of the region, it is not hard to see how these events could unfold in a matter of a few months

It is a little speculative, but I believe that this battle will occur immediately before the seven year covenant is confirmed by the Antichrist. I believe this because I think that such an event would pave the way for such a treaty, both in terms of humbling the Arab nations around Israel and because the destruction of the invading forces will be so dramatic and lop-sided that the nations of the world will demand "peace and security" and some kind of assurance from Israel that they will not further expand their borders. The Antichrist will burst upon the scene and broker this deal and thus the seventieth week of Daniel will begin.[147]

Further support for this position comes with the realization that in Ezekiel 39:9 we are told that Israel will gather the weapons of the invading forces and use them for fuel for *seven* years. The only way this makes sense is if the captured weapons are *nuclear*. With more and more rouge countries possessing nuclear capabilities this certainly seems plausible. The reason this period is limited to seven years is because after this battle the seven year "covenant with death" will be ratified and there will only be seven years left until the end of the age. By this we can deduce that the Gog-Magog battle of Ezekiel 38-39 will occur just before Daniel's 70th week.

The Joel Confrontation

The second major conflict that will occur during the seventieth week of Daniel is the one spoken of in Joel 2. This situation will occur *after* the midpoint of the 70th week,[148] and involves a threatening army from the North[149] and not from the countries that surround present day Israel.

It will be in the midst of the worst days of the Great Tribulation[150] and after the famine and pestilence of the seal judgments that Israel will be threatened by this army.[151] This is in contrast to the Ezekiel 38-39 invasion that will come against a people who "dwell safely."[152]

The army from the "North" in Joel is the same army spoken of in the sixth trumpet judgment in the book of Revelation and will be a fearsome sight.[153] In fact, careful comparisons between Joel 1:15 through 2:11 and the trumpet judgments reveal these sections of scripture to be parallel passages.[154] This turns out to be another very important piece of our "prophecy puzzle." It is important to note, however, that the events in Joel 1:15 through 2:11 are spoken as warnings and *don't actually happen* to those who call a sacred assembly and fast and repent as shown in Joel 2:12-17:

"Now, therefore," says the LORD, "Turn to Me with all your heart, With fasting, with weeping, and with mourning." So rend your heart, and not your garments; return to the LORD your God, For He is gracious and merciful, slow to anger, and of great kindness; and He relents from doing harm. Who knows if He will turn and relent, and leave a blessing behind Him — A grain offering and a drink offering for the LORD your God? Blow the trumpet in Zion, consecrate a fast, call a sacred assembly; gather the people, sanctify the congregation, assemble the elders, gather the children and nursing bless; let the bridegroom go out from his chamber, and the bride from her dressing room. Let the priests, who minister to the LORD, weep between the porch and the altar; Let them say, 'Spare your people, O LORD, and do not give Your heritage to reproach, hat the nation should rule over them. Why should they say among the peoples, "Where

is their God?" ' "

As this Northern army bears down on Israel, and as it appears the Day of the Lord is approaching it will seem like an impossible situation[155] for all Israel.

At the last moment, when it appears that all hope is lost, the whole House of Israel will acknowledge their ways, repent, and seek the face of the Lord just as shown in the above passage and also in Hosea:

"For I will be like a lion to Ephraim (Israel), and like a young lion to the house of Judah. I, even I, will tear them and go away; I will take them away, and no one shall rescue. I will return again to My place till they acknowledge their offense. Then they will seek My face; in their affliction they will earnestly seek Me. Come, and let us return to the LORD; for He has torn, but He will heal us; He has stricken but He will bind us up. After two days He will revive us, on the third day He will raise us up, that we may live in His sight." Hosea 5:14-6:2

Before the coming of the great and awesome Day of the Lord there will be signs in the sun and the moon and the stars.[156] The elect will be gathered together.[157] Then the Lord will come roaring in to personally fight this battle[158] and thus the Day of the Lord and the events of the trumpet Judgments will begin.

Armageddon

As the end of the 70th week comes to a close, Satan will muster his troops for one last futile attempt and will gather on the plain of Megiddo.[159] The 3rd and final great battle of the end of the age will occur and it will be the "mother of all battles," the Battle of Armageddon. This battle will occur after the rapture and the resurrection and is the climax of God's Wrath. Revelation records that it will be during this battle Satan is captured and will be bound for 1000 years.

The Beginning of the End

From Daniel 9 we learn that the last 7 years of this age coincide with a seven-year peace treaty "confirmed" by the Antichrist. While one might be inclined to think that the ratification of this treaty will be obvious when it happens, history has proven there may be "red herrings."

The Olso accord was a seven-year agreement between Israel and the Palestinians that was thought by some to be the covenant spoken of by Daniel in chapter 9. This mistaking of the Olso accords for the real "covenant with death" has perhaps unfairly hurt the credibility of some excellent Bible teachers. On account of this, and because I am not sure the Antichrist will *openly* broker the deal,[160] I am not optimistic that we will be able to discern with certainty the *beginning* point of the 70th week of Daniel based on the signing of a 7 year treaty.

It is possible, however, that we may be able to identify it based on the occurrence of the Gog-Magog invasion. Additionally, for reasons described below we may be given hints as to the start date since we can expect 70th week of Daniel to begin on the Biblical Holiday Yom Kippur. Furthermore, although the start day of this treaty may be a little vague, we will most certainly be able to pinpoint the beginning of the *Great* Tribulation when we see a certain incident occur.

As incredible as it may sound, we can actually pinpoint the beginning of the Great Tribulation to an *obvious event*. Yeshua himself tells us the start point of this 3½ year period: **"Therefore, when you see the 'abomination of desolation,' spoken of by Daniel the prophet, standing in the holy place"** (whoever reads let him understand), **"then let those who are in Judea flee to the mountains. Let him who is on the housetop not go down to take anything out of his house. And let him who is in the field not go back to get his clothes. But woe to those who are pregnant and to those who are nursing babies in those days! And pray that your flight may not be in winter or on the Sabbath. For then there will be great tribulation, such as has not been since the beginning of the world until this time, no, nor ever shall be. And unless those**

days were shortened, no flesh would be saved; but for the elect's sake those days will be shortened." Matthew 24:15-22

In this passage, Yeshua points us to the prophet Daniel, specifically to Daniel 11:31 and to Daniel 9:27. In this section of Daniel we find reference to this yet future event. As pointed out in chapter 5, this is an example of a "near/far" prophecy. In approximately 166 B.C.E., this prophecy was fulfilled for the first time. We can look at this first occurrence to help us understand what must happen in the future.

The Abomination of Desolation

After the untimely death of Alexander the Great at thirty years of age, the Greek Empire was split into four parts, each part going into the hands of one of Alexander's four most powerful Generals. For many years thereafter these four powers fought against each other in an effort to enlarge their territory. Geographically caught in between the Seleucid Empire (former Assyria) and the Ptolemaic Empire (former Egypt), the tiny province of "Judea" changed hands multiple times. The history of this era was beautifully spelled out in advance in Daniel 11.

In around B.C.E 166 there arose in the Northern Kingdom (the Seleucid Empire) a vile man by the name of Antiochus Epiphanes. This king gained power in Jerusalem and stopped the daily sacrifices, offered up a sow on the altar, and erected a statue of Zeus in the Holy of Holies.

The righteous men of Judea were so enraged by this abominable act that they revolted. Under the leadership of the Maccabees, the yoke of Antiochus Epiphanes was thrown off in a miraculous battle. The temple was rededicated, and in a miracle one day's worth of oil burned for eight days. This is the origin of the Jewish Festival Hanukah, and happens to be what Yeshua was observing in John 10:22.

Yeshua pointed to this specific event (that occurred many years before His time) as a signpost marking the beginning of the Great Tribulation. We know therefore, that something like it must occur again. As mentioned in the first chapter of this book many of those who hold to the amillenialist/preterist position believe that this happened in 70 A.D. While Josephus records that Titus did in fact erect his own pagan gods *outside* the temple during the siege of Jerusalem in A.D. 70, nothing like the abomination that causes desolation (of the temple) during the time of Antiochus Epiphanes took place, because the temple was burned to the ground. Furthermore, the siege of Jerusalem that caused so much suffering happened *before* Titus erected his pagan gods outside the walls of Jerusalem and *not after* an abominable act as Yeshua warned in Matthew 24.

The War in Heaven

A step back from the details of the Great Tribulation helps us to understand what is happening and why. As you may recall, in Revelation 12, Michael and his angels succeed in expelling Satan from heaven. The question is though, why didn't God just order Michael to do this sooner? This may be a good time to review just what has happened to the universe so that it now requires our Messiah's redemptive work.

In the beginning, God gave dominion over the Earth to Adam,[161] and God gave the highest honor in heaven to Lucifer.[162] Because of pride Lucifer "fell," yet we learn from the book of Job that he still has access to heaven. By deceit Satan took the right of dominion over the Earth from Adam. This is alluded to by the fact that Paul called Satan the "god of this world." Further proof of this is the fact that Yeshua did not dispute the Devil's *rightful* ownership of the world when Satan offered the world to Yeshua in exchange for His worship.[163] When we look at the temptation of the Messiah in that light, we realize that Satan was trying to deceive Yeshua into giving His authority and legitimate right to the title King of the universe to Satan, just as the serpent had deceived Adam in the garden. Thankfully, Yeshua was not deceived, and so He was able to become the perfect unblemished substitutionary sacrifice.

Because our Creator is perfectly righteous and just, He will not just simply seize control back from Satan as that would amount to stealing something back that was legitimately granted by Adam.

Since Yeshua was a man not of Adam's seed, but conceived of the Holy Spirit, He can rightfully in a legal sense make the claim that Satan and sin have no control or legal right over Him. When we die to this world and receive the Messiah, we too receive that right by becoming adoptive sons of the Living God, and thus become one of the Messiah's and are saved from the curse that came through the partaking of the tree of the knowledge of good and evil — that curse being death!

In Revelation chapter four we encounter the story of John seeing a scroll written "within and without" (both sides are written on, this being typical of a legal document in that day). This scroll is the "title deed" to the universe. The seals that are on it represent Satan's grip on this title. John weeps much when **"No one was found worthy to open and read the scroll, or to look at it."** But praise and honor to Yeshua, the Lamb of God who was found worthy to open the scroll!

Now back to the tribulation. Satan, you see, is still allowed in Heaven. There he accuses the brethren before the throne of God.[164] Because Yeshua has prevailed, Satan will be evicted from before the throne in a great war in Heaven.[165] Michael the Archangel will be the leader of the angels that defeat the Devil in this heavenly war.

In this light, perhaps we ought to revisit the issue of the "restrainer" from 2 Thessalonians 2. In Daniel 12:1 we read, "at that time Michael shall stand up" marking the beginning of the Great Tribulation. The word for "stand up" in this verse is amad, which according to Strong's concordance can mean "arise" or "stand still." I believe that in this context it means to both "stand still" from his earthly duties which involve the protection of the nation of Israel,[166] and "arise" into the heavens to fight the battle of Revelation 12:7.

When Satan is kicked out of Heaven, he has **"great wrath, because he knows his time is short."** He is enraged with the woman (Israel) so he makes war with her and the rest of her offspring (the "church"). He is given 3_ more years of authority here on earth, and he is really, really angry (Revelation 12). Since the Archangel Michael will not be on the earth to protect Israel, Satan will have free reign to persecute God's elect like never before.

In what will be his first act,[167] he will indwell the man who is the Antichrist, and the "man of sin" will be revealed. He will **"oppose and exalt himself above all that is called God or that is worshipped, so that he sits as God in the temple of God, showing himself that he is God."** 2 Thessalonians 2:4

Satan's original sin was to presume to be **"like the Most High."**[168] This act of setting himself up in the temple of God is merely a natural consequence of this desire, since the earthly temple is a replica of Heaven and the dwelling place of God.[169] Thus the "Great Tribulation" will begin.

What will follow this abominable act will be a time of indescribable persecution — The Great Tribulation. Many will die. The sheer severity of the situation will force everyone on the face of the earth into one of two camps — those who belong to the true and living God, and those who belong to Satan.

How will we make it through this???

By now, you may be wondering just how it will even be possible for anyone to make it through the Great Tribulation. Indeed, according to scripture, many will make the ultimate sacrifice and be martyred for their faith.

In Revelation chapter 3, we gain fascinating insight into this important question through the promise given to the Church in Philadelphia. The Church in Philadelphia and the Church in Smyrna are the only churches with nothing negative said about them. We notice as we read about the Philadelphian church that they have **"kept My Word"** and have **"not denied My Name"**[170] vs. 8. Note also that because they **"kept My Command to persevere"** they will be **"kept from the hour of trial which shall come upon the whole world to test those who dwell on the earth."** The Greek in this sentence implies that the Church in Philadelphia will be kept from the "hour of trial" while remaining *within* the trial,[171] and not removed out from the trial. (As a pre-trib rapture would imply). This verse shows that there will be those who by their works (vs. 8) and by their keeping of the Word and by their not having denied the Name and by perseverance somehow attain the right to enjoy God's divine protection during the "hour of trial." It is interesting to note that today's church seems to emphasize God's Grace and seems to frown on the notion of "earning" anything. Here we see clearly that our "works" could be rewarded with God providing His divine protection. Those who are unworthy will have to go through the fire of testing. What is equally fascinating is this notion of keeping the "Word" of God as being something that could save us. Again, Paul hints at the very same concept in 1 Corinthians 10:11 when he explains that the things that were written about the Israelites during the wilderness wanderings were written for the admonition of those *"upon whom the ends of the ages has come."* This certainly indicates that our keeping of God's Word,[172] God's instruction that was written for our learning,[173] will help us make it through the difficult days that lay ahead.

Putting it all Together

As the Great Tribulation unfolds, thousands will turn to the true and Living God and be martyred for their beliefs, and sadly, scripture tells us many will also turn away from God. Intense pressure will be put on the nation of Israel just before it appears that the Antichrist will finally succeed at annihilating God's chosen people and her offspring, and a national repentance will take place. A wonderfully descriptive account of the time period during the Great Tribulation and just before the return of Yeshua can be found in the book of Joel. It will be during the throws of tribulation that Judah will finally recognize the one "who has been pierced,"[174] and Ephraim will "acknowledge his ways"[175] and repent of his idolatries.[176] Many from Ephraim will return to the Land of Samaria.

As was shown in chapter 4 of this book, the events described above dovetail perfectly with the book of Revelation chapter 6 and 7. In Revelation, the opening of the sixth seal results in the sign in the sun and the moon, and then the kings of the earth hide themselves **"For the great day of His wrath has come, and who is able to stand?"**

Then, in Revelation 7:9 the "gathering together" occurs when there is the sudden appearance in Heaven of those who have washed their robes in the blood of the lamb and have "come out of the Great Tribulation."

It should also be pointed out that in a parenthetical portion of Revelation this event is reviewed again from a different perspective. This occurs in Revelation 14:14-16. Note here that our Lord is depicted as "one like the Son of Man, having on His head a golden crown, and in His hand a sharp sickle," is sitting on a cloud and "harvests" the earth.[177] Notice again how it is immediately after the gathering of the "elect" that the "wrath" of God is started (we see this in both Revelation chapter 7, and again in the parenthetical overview of Messiah's return in Revelation chapter 14).

And so, here are the major end time events (puzzle pieces) put together *in order* as best as can be determined at this point:

- In the context of Middle East unrest a great battle will take place that will set up a seven year treaty. This will be the battle described in Ezekiel 38 and 39. The Nation of Israel will begin to receive not only those returning from the land who are Jewish, but this event will trigger a political change that will allow those from the "House of Israel" to also return. Many of the House of Israel will begin to immigrate into the Land of Israel from all the nations of the world. Ezekiel 39:21-29.
- The scroll is taken by the lamb and the seals are broken (this likely starts the 70th week of Daniel). Revelation 5
- On the heels of the Gog-Magog battle, a seven year covenant is made between Israel and her enemies. This covenant will be "confirmed" by the Antichrist. Daniel 9:27
- The four horsemen are allowed to go forth — wars, disease, and famine follow. One third of mankind will die.
- Daily sacrifices will resume, presumably in a rebuilt Temple.
- Satan is kicked out of Heaven by Michael at the midpoint of Daniel 70th week.
- Satan is granted 3_ more years of authority here on earth.
- Satan indwells the Antichrist.
- The Antichrist sits as God in the Temple of God, (the abomina-

tion that causes desolation), and the Great Tribulation begins.
- he ministry of the Two Witnesses begins here on the Earth.
- Persecution of the elect will accelerate. The "Mark of the Beast" is instituted. This likely coincides with the opening of the 5th seal. Many will betray one another and the "Agape" of many will grow cold.
- The Nation of Israel, at this time now composed of members of both the House of Judah and the House of Israel is well into the throws of tribulation. (Joel 1) Under incredible pressure they will be besieged by the Northern Army and the situation will be exceedingly grave (Joel 2:3-11). Finally, both Ephraim and Judah will acknowledge their ways, repent, and seek the face of the LORD. (Joel 2:12-27) God will then pour out His Spirit on those who are in Israel. (Joel2:28-29)
- Sixth Seal – The sign in the sun and the moon and the stars. (Joel 2:30-32, Matthew 24:29-30, Mark 13:24, Mark 21:25, Revelation 6:12-13)
- God will defend Israel in the Valley of Jehosephat. (Joel 3:12)
- Messiah returns, the elect are gathered from the four corners of the Earth. (1 Thessalonians 4:16-17, Matthew 24:29-31, Revelation 7:9 Revelation 14:14-16.)
- The *Wrath of God* follows as outlined by the 7 trumpet judgments and the 7 seal judgments.
- The seven bowl judgments and the "Battle of Armageddon" (Revelation 16:12-16 and then picking up in Revelation19:11) occur just after the close of Satan's 42 month reign.
- The millennial kingdom is established for 1000 years.
- At the end of the millennial kingdom, Satan is loosed and deceives the world one more time, the Gog-Magog battle of Revelation 20:8 reoccurs[178] and the wicked are again destroyed.
- The final judgment takes place and Satan is cast into the lake of fire.
- The New Jerusalem is brought forth.

Prewrath or Post-Trib?

There are many who believe that the "gathering together" will actually be post-tribulational (after the completion of the 70th week of Daniel). This position can be a little confusing and perhaps some clarification is in order: Revelation chapter 12 indicates that Satan will be given authority for 3_ years; and so one might be inclined to think the elect will go through the entire 1260 days of Great Tribulation.

Additionally, since Paul states, **"We shall not all sleep, but we shall all be changed — in a moment, in the twinkling of an eye, at the last trumpet. For the trumpet will sound, and the dead will be raised incorruptible, and we shall be changed." 1 Corinthians 15:51-52**

Based primarily on this verse, many excellent Bible teachers believe that the rapture will happen at the seventh (last?) trumpet of the trumpet judgments in the book of Revelation. In order to explain this possibility, those who hold the post-tribulation view contend that the seventh seal, seventh trumpet, and seventh bowl all happen at the *same time.* (sometimes called "symphonically")

One problem with this line of thinking is comes with the realization that the feasts of God (including the feast of trumpets) will be kept throughout the millennium. Since that is the case, the seventh trumpet in the book of Revelation is not really the "last trump" that will ever be blown.

As will be explained below, the Feast of Trumpets is very significant in our end times study, and it is entirely possible that in this statement Paul is alluding to the Feast of Trumpets and is perhaps speaking of a final ceremonial trump that is blown on this God ordained feast.

Furthermore, the book of Revelation was given to John long after Paul's death, and in order to make Paul's "last trump" the seventh trumpet of Revelation we have to assume that Paul was given the same revelation as John. There is simply no biblical or extra-biblical basis for this assumption.

To shed a little more light on this complicated issue, let us again return to our "prophecy puzzle" analogy. Recall that by comparing Matthew 24, Revelation 6, we see that the "rapture" occurs at the opening of the seventh seal — *the seal that unleashes the wrath of God.*

Realizing the trumpet judgments *follow* the opening of the 7th seal, we can deduce that the rapture must happen *before* the end of the 70th week of Daniel. The logic is as follows: Since the Trumpets follow the seals, and since the 5th trumpet unleashes a plague that will last for five months, and since all of the trumpets happen *before* the end of the 70th week of Daniel (The 7th trumpet happens right at the end of the 7 year time period right when the two witnesses are resurrected), we can infer that the "rapture" must happen *at least* five months before the end of the Great Tribulation. Thus arguing against a pure post-trib rapture.

Given that the opening of the seventh seal unleashes the Wrath of God contained in the trumpets and bowls let us take note again at the scriptural agreement concerning the wrath of God:

"Much more then, having now been justified by His blood, we shall be saved from wrath through Him." Romans 5:9

"And to wait for His Son from heaven, whom He raised from the dead, even Jesus who delivers us from the wrath to come." I Thessalonians 1:10

"For God did not appoint us to wrath, but to obtain salvation through our Lord Jesus Christ." I Thessalonians 5:9

The prophets agree:

"Your dead shall live; Together with my dead body they shall arise. Awake and sing, you who dwell in dust; For your dew is like the dew of herbs, and the earth shall cast out the dead. Come, My people, enter you chambers and shut your doors behind you; for a little moment, until the indignation is past. For behold, the LORD comes out of His place to punish the inhabitants of the earth for their iniquity; The earth will also disclose her blood, and will no more cover her slain." Isaiah 26:19-21

> ...e LORD, all you meek of the earth, who have
> justice. Seek righteousness, seek humility. It may be
> ...ill be hidden in the day of the LORD's anger."
> ...2: 3

Again, in order to explain a "post-tribulation" position (a rapture event following the 70th week of Daniel), some propose that the seals, trumpets, and bowls of Revelation occur "symphonically," arguing that these unfold simultaneously and staggered over each other temporally. This notion simply does not fit with the face value (pashat) reading of the book of Revelation. Revelation 15:7 and 16:1 describe the bowls as "bowls of wrath." We see from the above verses that the elect will not experience this wrath. Therefore we see that the "bowl judgments" *cannot* happen during the same time as the seal judgments as those who put forth a "symphonic" arrangement of seals, trumpets and bowls purport.

Furthermore, when one realizes that Matthew 24 presents a summary of the seven seals of Revelation chapter 6, yet there is *no mention of any of the events that occur during the trumpet or bowl judgments* in Yeshua's overview of the end times in the Olivet discourse, one must conclude that the seals, trumpets, and bowls occur sequentially and not "symphonically." The trumpets follow the seals, and the bowls *follow* the trumpets. The bowls, it turns out, occur *after* the close of the 70th week of Daniel as will be explained below.

Further proof that God's elect will not suffer through the events of the trumpet judgments comes with the realization that Joel 1:15-2:11 is a parallel passage to the events of the trumpet judgments of Revelation. Joel 2:12-17 makes it clear that the events of the trumpet judgments as warned of in Joel 1:15-2:11 will *not* take place because national repentance will happen. This realization is in its own right an excellent argument against a pure post-tribulation rapture that would place the "gathering together" after the trumpets judgments and the entire seventieth week of Daniel.

For these reasons, we see then that for those raptured, the Great Tribulation will be "shortened" (for the elect's sake[179]) agreeing with Paul's statement that, **"we are not appointed unto wrath."**[180]

Thus the "Elect" will not have to endure the entire 42 month period.[181] The elect *will* be subject to the terrible events that occur during the opening of the seals (the wrath of Satan), but not the wrath of God contained in the trumpet and bowl judgments. In a manner of speaking the rapture *will* be "post-trib," however, since those who are gathered together out of the Great Tribulation will have just gone through some exceptionally great tribulation.

Truthfully, those who would continue hold a post-tribulation position have much in common with what I have presented as a modified "prewrath" view thus far. It is my opinion that this is an area with which we ought to have much grace and that this is not a valid reason to divide the body of Messiah. The alarming problems of the pretrib and amillennial positions, namely that they leave the body of believers woefully unprepared for the end times, are not inherent to the post-trib position since the post-trib viewpoint has the elect experiencing "Great Tribulation" just as Yeshua foretold.

The proposals that are laid out in this book is will be strengthened by a study of the feasts of God and by the typology found in the account of Noah's flood. Below we will see how the "Feasts of God" fit into a prewrath scenario.

The Feasts of God

A deeper study of the books of Moses affords some amazing insight into the prewrath rapture view. While a *complete* study of the feasts could take a lifetime and is beyond the scope of this book, what follows is a brief survey that the reader may find compelling.

In the Torah we find instruction concerning God's "appointed" feasts. These feasts days turn out to be incredibly relevant. Through Moses, God instructs, **"These are the feasts of the LORD, holy convocation which you shall proclaim at their appointed times" Leviticus 23:4**

Here, the Hebrew word translated as "feast" is "moedim" — which actually means "appointed time." The word translated as "convocation" is the Hebrew word "mikrah" which means a "public gathering" but carries with it's meaning the idea of a "rehearsal." By looking historical events, we are able to see that the appointed

Biblical feasts are indeed rehearsal feasts to help us remember not only events of the past, but also future yet unfulfilled events.

To further explain this, let's take a look at the feasts which appear to have been fulfilled. The spring feasts were fulfilled during the first coming of the Messiah. Yeshua was crucified on the Passover, He was resurrected on the Feast of First Fruits, and the Holy Spirit was given on the Biblical Feast of Shavuot, also known as Pentecost.

Given God's history of causing major events to occur on His appointed feast days, it is reasonable to surmise that Yeshua's return will be on one of the remaining Biblical feasts.

There are a total of seven Biblical feasts that God has ordained in the Old Testament. In addition to the four feasts mentioned above, there are three remaining moedim, which occur in the fall of the year, and the prophetic significance of these fall feasts are as yet unfulfilled. These feasts include the Feast of Trumpets, Yom Kippur, and the Feast of Tabernacles. For several reasons explained below the Messiah will likely return and gather the elect into heaven on the Feast of Trumpets.

The Feast of Trumpets, also known as Yom Teruah, marks the beginning of the Jewish Civil New Year. This Feast is also known by other names[182] including the "Day of the Awakening Blast," the "Day of opening Gates" (in heaven), and the "Day of Hiding." Yom Teruah is preceded by thirty days of introspection and repentance during the entire month of Elul on the Jewish calendar. Notice how the euphemistic names for this feast implicate it as the feast during which the rapture and the resurrection will occur.

The start date and time for the Feast of Trumpets is a little unclear. It can occur anytime over a two day period because it begins with the uncertain event of a New Moon sighting. In ancient Israel, two witnesses were selected by the Sanhedrin to go out of the city and watch, waiting for the sliver of the New Moon to appear at dusk in the Western Sky. Upon seeing crescent moon, they would signal the Sanhedrin, and trumpets would sound indicating the official start of the New Year. Because of the vague start time for this ordained festival of God, it is said that "No one knows the day or the hour" of the start time of the Feast of Trumpets from year to year.

This is fascinating in light of Yeshua's response to the question of when He would return: **"But of that day and hour no one knows." Matthew 24:36** With this amazing statement, Yeshua seems to be saying *"I will return on the Feast of Trumpets, but you will not know the day or hour of my coming, just like you don't know the day or hour of the start of the Feast of Trumpets!"*

Ten days after the Feast of Trumpets the high holy day of Yom Kippur occurs. Yom Kippur is also known as the "Day of the LORD." It is thought of as the day when the "books close" on the judgment and is preceded by 10 days of more focused introspection and repentance called in traditional Judaism the "days of Awe."

Five days after Yom Kippur comes the seven days long Feast of Tabernacles. This is a joyous time of feasting and fellowship and is thought to foreshadow the wedding feast of the Lamb and the Bride of the Messiah.

As in the Days of Noah

Perhaps the best typological example of God's wrath and judgment found in the Bible occurs in the account of Noah's Flood. Yeshua, in fact, compared His second coming to the Great Flood in Matthew 24:37, **"But as the days of Noah were, so also will the coming of the Son of Man be."**

During the Flood, God's judgment upon the Earth lasted exactly one year and ten days: **"In the six hundredth year of Noah's life, <u>in the second month, the seventeenth day of the month</u>, on that day all the fountains of the great deep were broken up, and the windows of heaven were opened." Genesis 7:11** and, **"It came to pass in the six hundred and first year, in the first month, the first day of the month, that the waters were dried up from the earth; and Noah removed the covering of the ark and looked, and indeed the surface of the ground was dry. And <u>in the second month, on the twenty seventh day of the month</u>, the earth was dried. Then God spoke to Noah, saying, 'Go out of the ark, you and your wife, and your sons and your sons' wives with you.'" Genesis 8:13-16**.

It is speculative, but highly provocative to consider that perhaps God's second judgment upon the earth, the judgment with fire, will likewise last for a total of one year and ten days. If this is true, then we are able to begin to construct a timetable that will lay out the events that will occur during the seventieth week of Daniel.

First we must make a couple of valid assumptions. Assuming the 360 day year of the book of Revelation,[183] and assuming the rapture will happen 370 days before the end of the 70th week of Daniel, if the Messiah's return occurs as outlined above on the Feast of Trumpets, then God's Wrath would occur for the next year and ten days (fitting the model of the flood), and will be finished on Yom Kippur one year and ten days after the "rapture." This defines the "Day of the Lord" therefore, as being the last year of Daniel's 70 week prophecy.

Incredibly, counting backwards 3½ years from the "end" of this seven year period brings us to the midpoint of the 70th week of Daniel, and happens to fall on the tenth of Nisan.[184]

It makes sense that it will be at this time that the great counterfeiter himself, Satan, will triumphantly enter Jerusalem, just as the true Messiah did on this *same date* (see chapter 2) almost 2000 years ago. On this occasion, however, the Antichrist will set himself up to be worshipped as God, in the Temple of God, showing himself that he is God,[185] and thus perform the "abomination of desolation."

This event will appear to the uninitiated as a sign that the Antichrist is the true God. Satan will try to deceive as many people as possible by trying to fulfill the symbolism of the Passover, just as the Messiah did. It is conceivable that a counterfeit death and resurrection will likewise take place since Revelation 13:3 and 13:14 speak of a "deadly would that has been healed."

Remarkably, in the traditional celebration of Passover a plate is always set for the prophet Elijah, since there is an expectation that he will return as predicted in the Old Testament[186] during the Feast of Passover. This is very interesting since most Bible scholars believe that Elijah is one of the two witnesses that will be seen prophesying during the Great Tribulation. The two witnesses will speak out for the three and one half years concurrent with the last half of the Great Tribulation. If the Great Tribulation ends with the "Day of Atonement" as I am suggesting, then the Jewish tradition has merit and Elijah will appear on Passover!

If the 70th week of Daniel ends on the Day of Atonement (Yom

Kippur), then it also begins on this day, (or technically the day after since the 70th week is seven years long and not seven years and one day). This amazing fact gives us something to look forward to every year as this day approaches. If the modern day leaders of Israel make a "treaty" for peace and security following a miraculous military victory on the day after Yom Kippur... then LOOK OUT! This could be the beginning of the end!

Rabbinical Judaism teaches that the ten days between Yom Teruah and Yom Kippur are a time for deep repentance and retrospection. It is possible that given the euphemisms for both the Feast of Trumpets, (Awakening Blast, Open gates) and Yom Kippur (Closed judgment books, closed gates to Heaven, Judgment, Day of the Lord) that it will be during these ten days of true "Awe" that many will still be allowed to turn from their ways and follow the true and living God. It is speculative, but it could be that those who are "Left Behind" after the initial gathering of the saints will be given ten more days to prove they are worthy of entering the Kingdom. It could be that the deep repentance that takes place in Joel 2:12-17 occurs during this time period, seeing as a call for a **"Fast, a sacred assembly"** is consistent with the themes of Yom Kippur.

It is possible, therefore, that there will be those who will miss the "wedding night(s)" (following the rapture) and will be outside in the "dark" "gnashing their teeth." The tradition of the Jewish wedding is interesting in this light. In the ancient Jewish tradition, after a bride had been selected and betrothed, the groom would go and build a house (This is reminiscent of Yeshua's words, **"In My Father's house are many mansions; if it were not so, I would have told you, I go to prepare a place for you. And if I go and prepare a place for you, I will come again and receive you to Myself; that where I am, there you may be also." John 14:2-3**). When the house was complete, the Father would then give the bridegroom permission to go and get his bride. Typically, the groom would arrive with a great shout and would sweep his bride away, carry her off to their chambers, and their union would be consummated. The bride and the groom would stay in the chambers for seven days.

Interestingly, there are *seven* full days between the two days of the Feast of Trumpets and the Day of Atonement. Additionally, in the Genesis flood account, God required Noah to "Come" into the ark exactly seven days[187] before God poured his wrath upon the earth in the first judgment.

This seems to relate to the ten virgin parable in Matthew Chapter 25:

"Then the kingdom of heaven shall be likened to ten virgins who took their lamps and went out to meet the bridegroom. Now five of them were wise, and five were foolish. Thos who were foolish took their lamps and took no oil with them, but the wise took oil in their vessels with their lamps. But while the bridegroom was delayed, they all slumbered and slept. And at midnight a cry was heard: 'Behold, the bridegroom is coming; go out to meet him!' Then all those virgins arose and trimmed their lamps. And the foolish said to the wise, 'Give us some of your oil, for our lamps are going out.' But the wise answered, saying, 'No, lest there should not be enough for us and you; but go rather to those who sell, and buy for yourselves.' And while they went to buy, the bridegroom came, and those who were ready went in with him to the wedding; and the door was shut. Afterward the other virgins came also, saying, Lord, Lord, open to us!' But he answered and said, 'Assuredly, I say to you, I do not know you.' Watch there fore, for you know neither the day nor the hour in which the Son of Man is coming." Matthew 25:1-13

So what is the oil? I have seen many opinions offered, but consider this, Yeshua didn't just pull this lamp idiom out of thin air. He used phrases and terminology familiar to the Hebrew ear. Keeping this in mind, consider the words of the Psalmist, **"Your word is a lamp to my feet and a light to my path." Psalm 119:105** Again, this fits the profile of the church at Philadelphia, **"who have <u>kept My word</u> and have not denied My name."**

The ten days of awe are a time period of deep introspection. If one were to miss the coming of the bridegroom, it seems likely that there would be a lot of soul searching as to the reason why. This soul searching would crescendo as one knew the "Day of the closing of the books" (the day of atonement) was approaching.

It *could be* then that those who miss the wedding and the consummation will still have an opportunity to make it into the kingdom. It is possible that some of these must choose, however, with their lives. This whole scenario may be what is spoken about to the "Church in Smyrna" in Revelation 2:10, **"The devil is about to throw some of you into prison, that you may be tested, and you will have tribulation <u>ten days</u>. Be faithful until death, and I will give you the crown of life."**

Again, this also could be what is spoken about in Joel 2:12-17, **"Now, therefore," says the LORD, "Turn to Me with all your heart, With fasting, with weeping, and with mourning." So rend your heart, and not your garments; return to the LORD your God, For He is gracious and merciful, slow to anger, and of great kindness; and He relents from doing harm. Who knows if He will turn and relent, and leave a blessing behind Him — A grain offering and a drink offering for the LORD your God? Blow the trumpet in Zion, consecrate a fast, call a sacred assembly; gather the people, sanctify the congregation, assemble the elders, gather the children and nursing bless; let the bridegroom go out from his chamber, and the bride from her dressing room. Let the priests, who minister to the LORD, weep between the porch and the altar; Let them say, 'Spare your people, O LORD, and do not give Your heritage to reproach, hat the nation should rule over them. Why should they say among the peoples, "Where is their God?" ' "**

(On the other hand, this is getting into some highly speculative conjecture and I wouldn't count on having any opportunities for repentance after the "gathering together" of the saints. It would be far better to be prepared, having your lamp filled with oil as did the five faithful virgins in the parable of Matthew 25:1-13)

The Jewish festival of Hanukah may also play a role in the end time scenario. Hanukah is the feast celebrating the rededication of the temple following its defilement by the hand of Antiochus Epiphanes. It occurs 75 days following Yom Kippur, and is apparently what is spoken of by Daniel when the prophet writes there will be days added on to the 1260 (the last half of the 70th week),

"Blessed is he who waits, and comes to the one thousand three hundred and thirty five days." Daniel 12:12

Following the bowl judgments and the cleansing of the Earth, the new Temple of the millennial kingdom will be rededicated in a great ceremony, thus fulfilling the Jewish festival of Hanukah.

Graphically presented, the final seven years and the overlay of the feasts of those years will likely look like this:

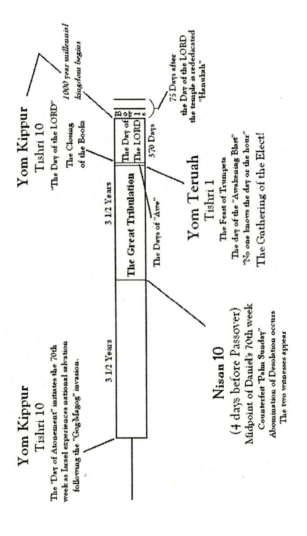

Trumpets and Bowls — the Grand Finale

After the gathering together of the saints on the Feast of Trumpets, Satan will be left on earth with the unbelievers and will have authority for the last year and ten days of the 3_ years, but those "gathered together to the Messiah" will be gone. Ten days after the removal of the elect on the Feast of Trumpets the real battle on earth will intensify as the Wrath of God is poured out on those who remain upon the Earth.

With the exception of the 144,000 there is no mention of any believers being on the Earth during the trumpet judgments or the bowl judgments, thus solidifying the case for the prewrath gathering together. The identity if the 144,000 is discussed below.

By virtue of the following it can be established that the bowl judgments do not occur within the 3_ year time period:

- The resurrection of the two witnesses occurs at the sixth trumpet.
- The two witnesses' ministry exactly overlaps the time period of the Great tribulation. (The last 3 _ years)
- The bowl judgments *follow* the trumpet judgments.

Because of the above, the bowl judgments must occur *after* the 3_ years are completed. Bowls signify cleaning, and it will be through the bowl judgments that God will clean up what is left of the Earth. These judgments will happen in rapid succession and are what occurs during the "extra days" added onto the 1260 spoken of by the prophet Daniel in 12:11, **"And from the time that the daily sacrifice is taken away, and the abomination of desolation is set up, there shall be one thousand two hundred and ninety days."**

Graphically presented the tribulation Period looks like this:

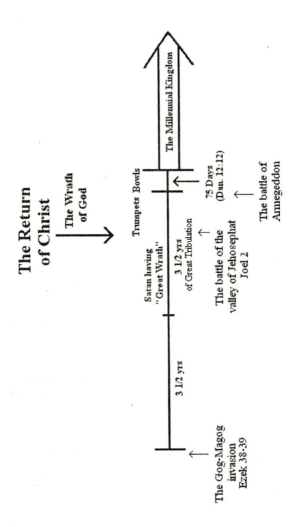

The 144,000 Israelites

Scripture indicates there will be two groups of believers that are redeemed by the blood of the Lamb. Simply put, these two groups are those spoken of in Revelation 7 and are the elect "from every tribe and nation and tongue" in Revelation 7:9, and the 144,000. So far we have mostly blurred the lines between these two groups and haven't discussed them separately. It is clear these two groups are different.

In Matthew 24:31, the "elect" are gathered from the four corners of the Earth, and so it can be assumed that not all of these are "gathered" from the land of Israel. We can infer then that not all of those who are *of Israel* and "elect" will actually return to the Land (Just as not all "Jews" have returned to Israel in modern times). This "elect" that are "raptured" will consist of both the faithful living and the faithful dead. This group, again, is mentioned in Revelation 7:9 and is an innumerable multitude. While no one can judge but the Messiah Himself I am of the opinion that this group will include the countless number of saints who do not understand their Israelite identity because they have been deceived by the prince of this world. These, despite their lack of knowledge, love the Lord and will be saved by the amazing Grace of God.

On the other hand, we see in Revelation 14:1 and Ezekiel 9 that those numbered among the 144,000 are not gathered from the "four corners of the earth" but are gathered together with the Lord *from Jerusalem* and taken to Mt. Zion, a physical place in the land of Israel.

The 144,000 are made up of 12,000 from *each of the tribes of Israel* (excluding the tribe of Dan and instead counting 12,000 for each of Joseph's two sons). According to the accounts in both Ezekiel 9 and in Revelation 7, these are sealed on the forehead by an angel *just before* the Wrath of God is poured out upon the Earth. It seems plausible that the 144,000 represent the *most faithful* of the remnant of all Israel.

The 144,000 are not mentioned as having been taken up to heaven but are given God's divine protection here on the Earth through the time of the Wrath of God. This assertion is based on the fact that Revelation 9:4 shows that the 144,000 will be present during the trumpet judgments, which are part of the wrath of God. It is logical, therefore, to conclude that the 144,000 do not have "resurrection bodies."

Given that Yeshua said that after the resurrection we will not be married,[188] we can reason that those resurrected and raptured will *not* be the ones who repopulate the earth during the millennial kingdom. Those who are raptured will be able to enjoy the millennial Kingdom and partake of the great rewards of dwelling with the Messiah (Rev7:15-17), but will not be given the distinct honor of repopulating the earth.

While it is a little speculative, I believe this is the role of the 144,000 — to populate the planet with Israelites after the wrath of God has come and the unbelievers are destroyed.

It is possible there are Bible teachers who misunderstand God's plan for the end times and believe in a pure "post-trib" gathering together because they lump the 144,000 from each of the tribes of Israel together with the "elect" spoken of in Revelation 7:9.

It is entirely possible there are brethren, who *properly* interpret the prophetic Word, but do so from the standpoint of *being one of the select 144,000* (and perhaps *they are* part of this group) rather than being one of the "elect" in Matthew 24. This select group of 144,000 from each of the twelve tribes of Israel will be on the Earth and will experience the horror of *entire* three and one half years of the Great Tribulation, but they will be divinely protected by the seal of God. For these saints the Messiah's return *will* be truly "post-trib" since after all is fulfilled they will testify that the "Return of the Messiah" to set up His Earthly Kingdom *came not only after* the "Great Tribulation," but that they had to endure the entire 70th week of Daniel.

Problems arise when one tries to apply the arguments for a post-trib (Post seventieth week of Daniel) return of the Messiah to the *entire* saved body of believers. The group of raptured and resurrected believers is mentioned in Revelation 7:9 and is distinct from the 144,000. It is clear from a comparison of Matthew 24 with Revelation 6 and a comparison between the trumpet judgments and the warnings given in Joel 1:15-2:11 that those raptured will be gathered to the Messiah just before the Wrath of God is poured out on the unbelieving.

Again, to say one believes in the prewrath "gathering together" is to agree that the return of Messiah will be *in a way*, post-tribulational. For the elect, you see, it *will* be in a way post-tribulational, because these will have had to endure tribulation, it is just that the tribulation period will have been "shortened."[189]

To be a member of the 144,000 will be a great honor. A quick calculation (6 billion divided by 144,000) shows that only about 1:40,000 people will be part of this blessed assembly. The qualifications and disqualifications are found in Revelation 14:4-5 and in Ezekiel 9. Ezekiel 9:4 is particularly fascinating as it identifies just who will be marked: **"Go through the midst of the city, through the midst of Jerusalem, and put a mark on the foreheads of the men who sigh and cry over all the abominations that are done within it."** This verse is in direct reference to the preceding chapter, Ezekiel 8, where these "abominations" are described and are none other than **"women weeping for Tammuz"**[190] (for example Lent) and **"men with their backs toward the temple of the LORD and their faces toward the east, and they were worshiping the sun toward the east."**[191] This passage is utterly astounding considering the influence of sun worship that is prevalent in the church today.

It is probable that the sealing of this group will happen on a major feast day, since their sealing takes place in Jerusalem and since it is a command of God to be physically present in Jerusalem three times per year for the Major biblical feasts. These feasts include the Feast of Unleavened Bread (when Passover occurs), Shavuot (also called the Day of Pentecost), and the Feast of Tabernacles.

The Great Tribulation will be the time when the tares will be separated from the wheat. It will be a time when many will fully turn to the Lord, and a time when many will turn away. As we begin to see the importance of keeping the commandments of God and keeping His appointed feast days, we will also again begin to see the need to pay attention to the admonition written to us almost two thousand years ago, **"not forsaking the assembling of ourselves together** (On these major feast days) **as is the manner of some, but exhorting one another, and so much the more as you see the Day approaching." Hebrews 10:25**

Could it be as the Day of the Lord approaches, that a call will go out to those who are of the 12,000 from each of the tribes of Israel?

For there shall be a day
When watchmen will cry on Mount Ephraim,
Arise, and let us go up to Zion,
To the Lord our God.
Jeremiah 31:6

CHAPTER 13

The Coming World Leader

*A*t this juncture, we will now delve into an area that by nature can be quite fascinating — the characteristics of this mysterious person we call the Antichrist. As pointed out in the last chapter, proponents of a pre-trib rapture hold the position that believers will not be around to experience the "Wrath of Satan" and persecution by the hand of the Antichrist. It is for this reason I have heard on several occasions, from the pulpit, such statements as, "You don't need to concern yourself with the identity of the Antichrist because you will not be around to experience these things."

The Bible, however, teaches otherwise with statements that directly contradict the notion that we ought not to concern ourselves with his identity:

"Here is wisdom. Let him who has understanding calculate the number of the beast, for it is the number of a man: His number is 666." Revelation 13:18

While it appears from this verse that some speculation about the identity of the antichrist is authorized, we most likely will not be able to *positively* identify the Antichrist until he is "unveiled," as alluded to in 2 Thessalonians 2:3, **"Let no one deceive you by any means; for that Day will not come unless the falling away comes first, and the man of sin is <u>revealed</u>, the son of perdition."**

Overview of Antichrist Passages

Since we are given signs in the scripture that warn us about the one that will be the antichrist, we will now take a brief look at these since this book is a study on the end times.

Most of what we know about the one that will be called *the* Antichrist is found in the books of Revelation and Daniel. Presented below is an overview of some of the scriptures that have been attributed to the Antichrist. Most of these scriptures use highly figurative language. The interpretations, therefore, often are varied since often there is no clear plaintext meaning that is understandable. Although it is a little cumbersome, I will insert my own commentary in the verses presented below in an attempt to make these difficult passages more understandable:

We will start in Daniel Chapter 7. Here the antichrist is mentioned as being the ruler of the fourth great world empire.[192]

"After this I saw in the night vision, and behold, a fourth beast (this beast is thought to be the "fourth empire" seen by Daniel in the vision and is thought by most scholars to be the Roman Empire)**, dreadful and terrible, exceedingly strong. It had huge iron teeth; it was devouring, breaking in pieces, and trampling the residue with its feet. It was different from all the beasts that were before it, and it had ten horns** (In this passage, horn represent kings or kingdoms of this fourth beast empire). **I was considering the horns, and there was another horn** (thought to be the Antichrist), **a little one coming up among them, before whom three of the first horns were plucked out by the roots. And there, in this horn, were eyes like the eyes of a man, and a mouth speaking pompous words." Daniel 7:7-8**

It is from the above passage that many scholars believe the "antichrist" will come from the revived Roman Empire, thought by some to be the modern European Union. We see also that this man will be a great orator, "speaking pompous words." Daniel continues on with some more detail about the antichrist in verses 20-22:

"And the ten horns that were on its head, and the other *horn* which came up, before which three fell, namely, that horn which had eyes and a mouth which spoke pompous words, whose appearance was greater than his fellows. I was watching; and the same horn was making war against the saints, and prevailing against them,** (this clearly indicates as argued extensively in this book the "saints" will suffer the persecution of the Antichrist) **until the Ancient of Days came, and a judgment was made *in favor* of the saints of the Most High, and the time came for the saints to possess the kingdom." Daniel 7:20-22** Here we see another proof of a prewrath rapture and proof that the "saints" of the Most High will be on the earth until the time came for the saints to possess the kingdom. Daniel continues on, explaining more detail:

"Thus he said: 'The fourth beast shall be a fourth kingdom on earth, which shall be different from all other kingdoms, and shall devour the whole earth, trample it and break it in pieces. The ten horns are ten kings who shall arise from this kingdom. And another shall rise after them; he shall be different from the first ones, and shall subdue three kings. He shall speak pompous words against the Most High,** (this is thought by many to be during the abomination of desolation when the Antichrist will sit in the Temple of God, showing himself that he is God)**, shall persecute the saints of the Most High, and shall intend to change times and law** (Below we will see that the Antichrist will cause the daily sacrifice to cease). **Then the saints shall be given into his hand for a time and times and half a time** (this is another way to say three and one half years). **But the court shall be seated, and they shall take away his dominion,** (his dominion was given for a time, times and one half a time, or 3 _ years, but will be "taken away," indicating this dominion will not last for the entire time allotted. The time that the saints are given into the hand of the Antichrist is cut short "for the elect's sake." This dovetails perfectly with the "prewrath" argument.), **to consume and destroy it forever. Then the kingdom and dominion, and the greatness of the kingdoms under the whole heaven, shall be given to the**

**people, the saints of the Most High. His kingdom is an everlasting kingdom, and all dominions shall serve and obey Him.' "
Daniel 7:23-27**

The next chapter in Daniel, chapter 8, also gives us some more hints about the antichrist and his exploits:

"And out of one of them came a little horn which grew exceedingly great toward the south, toward the east, and toward the Glorious Land. And it grew up to the host of heaven; and it cast down some of the host and some of the stars to the ground (this is of course reminiscent of Revelation chapter 12)**, and trampled them. He even exalted himself as high as the Prince of the host; and by him the daily sacrifices were taken away, and the place of His sanctuary was cast down** (again, the abomination of desolation)**. Because of transgression, an army was given over to the horn to oppose the daily sacrifices; and he cast truth down to the ground. He did all this and prospered. Then I heard a holy one speaking and another holy one said to that certain one who was speaking, "How long will the vision be, concerning the daily sacrifices and the transgression of desolation, the giving of both the sanctuary and the host to be trampled underfoot?' And he said to me, 'For two thousand three hundred mornings and evenings; then the sanctuary shall be cleansed.' " Daniel 8:9-14**

This entire prophecy speaks both of the coming of Antiochus Epiphanes at the time of the Maccabean revolt in 166 B.C., and of the coming of the Antichrist. Yeshua pointed to the event that occurred at the time of Antiochus Epiphanes as yet being in the future, and so we can conclude that this is a "near/far prophecy."

The 2300 "mornings and evenings" represent 2300 days. This passage indicates the sacrifices and offerings will be officially opposed by the Antichrist for 2300 days. Assuming 360 day (twelve 30 day months) prophetic years, we will see this day occurs a mere 220 days into the seventieth week of Daniel.

Based on this prophecy, the Antichrist will likely come out with a political position that is opposed to the daily sacrifices. The average Christian will find himself in agreement with the Antichrist on this issue, since the commonly held view among the church is that the sacrifices have all be "done away with" because of the sacrifice of Christ. As we will show below, you absolutely do not want to be on the side of the antichrist on this issue!

As we continue on with passages that deal with the Antichrist we learn that, **"And in the latter time of their kingdom, when the transgressors have reached their fullness, a king shall arise, having fierce features, who understands sinister schemes.** (this may indicate the Antichrist will have connections to the occult) **His power shall be mighty, but not by his own power** (indicating he will have great authority, but more importantly, he will have a great deal of influence over those who have power and they will give their power over to his disposal)**; he shall destroy fearfully, and shall prosper and thrive; he shall destroy the mighty, and also the holy people.** (Yet another indication the Antichrist will prevail against the saints!) **Through his cunning he shall cause deceit to prosper under his rule; and he shall exalt himself in his heart** (he will "show himself that he is God" as is said in 2 Thessalonians 2:4). **He shall destroy many in their prosperity. He shall even rise against the Prince of princes** (the true Messiah, Yeshua)**; but he shall be broken without human means." Daniel 8:23-25**

Daniel's famous "70 week prophecy" also gives us some detail about the Antichrist:

"Seventy weeks are determined for your people and for your holy city, to finish the transgression, to make an end of sins, to make reconciliation for iniquity, to bring in everlasting righteousness, to seal up vision and prophecy, and to anoint the Most Holy. Know therefore and understand, that from the going forth of the command to restore and build Jerusalem until Messiah the Prince, there shall be seven weeks and sixty two weeks; the street shall be built again, and the wall , even in troublesome times. And after the sixty-two weeks Messiah shall

be cut off (an obvious reference to the crucifixion)**, but not for Himself** (He allow himself to be sacrificed for us)**; and the people of the prince who is to come shall destroy the city and the sanctuary** (The people who destroyed the city and the sanctuary were the Romans in 70 A.D., thus the Antichrist will come from the Roman Empire. The European Union is thought by many to represent the "Revived" Roman Empire and in fact uses many symbols formally used by the ancient Roman Empire). **The end of it shall be with a flood, and till the end of the war desolations are determined. Then he** (the antichrist) **shall confirm a covenant with many for one week; but in the middle of the week** (3 _ years) **he shall bring an end to sacrifice and offering. And on the wing of abominations shall be one who make desolate, even until the consummation which is determined is poured out on the desolate." Daniel 9:24-27**

Again, it is important to understand that Daniel chapter 11 speaks of the Antichrist using "near-far" prophecy. These verses also speak of both Antiochus Epiphanes and the "Antichrist," as is evidenced by Yeshua's pointed warning in Matthew 24:15, **"Therefore, when you see the abomination of desolation spoken of by the prophet Daniel."** Yeshua pointed to the event involving Antiochus Epiphanes that occurred almost two hundred years before His time as being an event that was yet in the future, thus proving the prophecy has both *near* and *far* applications.

Daniel 11 goes on to say about the antichrist: **"And in his place shall arise a vile person** (the Antichrist)**, to whom they will not give the honor of royalty** (he will not get the royal title here on earth that he desires)**; but he shall come in peaceably, and seize the kingdom by intrigue.** (The rider of the white horse in Revelation 6 had a bow with no arrows, this speaks of the Antichrist and how he comes to power.) **With the force of a flood they shall be swept away from before him and be broken, and also the prince of the covenant. And after the league is made with him** (this speaks of the seven year peace treaty that the Antichrist will broker or enforce) **he shall act deceitfully, for he shall come up** and become strong with a small number of people. He shall enter peaceable, even into the richest places of the province; and he shall do what his fathers have not done, nor his forefathers..." Daniel 11:21-24

"For ships from Cyprus shall come against him; therefore he shall be grieved, and return in rage against the holy covenant, and do damage. So he shall return and show regard for those who forsake the holy covenant. (Those Christians who deny that God's law is still pertinent and important are those who "forsake the holy covenant." The Antichrist will befriend these, and show regard for them *by flattery*. It is in this way that the Antichrist will deceive many and lead them astray.) And forces shall be mustered by him, and they shall defile the sanctuary fortress; then they shall take away the daily sacrifices, and place there the abomination of desolation. Those who do wickedly against the covenant he shall corrupt with flattery; but the people who know their God shall be strong, and carry out great exploits. And those of the people who understand shall instruct many; yet for many days they shall fall by sword and flame, by captivity and plundering. (Yet once more, this indicates the saints will fall under the persecution of the Antichrist!) Now when they fall, they shall be aided with a little help; but many shall join with them by intrigue. And some of those of understanding shall fall, to refine them, purify them, and make them white, until the time of the end because it is still for the appointed time. Then the king shall do according to his own will; he shall exalt and magnify himself above every god, shall speak blasphemies against the God of gods, and shall prosper till the wrath has been accomplished; for what has been determined shall be done. He shall regard neither the God of his fathers nor the desire of women, nor regard any god; for he shall exalt himself above them all." Daniel 11:30-37

Antichrist passages are not limited to the Old Testament. Paul wrote explicitly of the Antichrist in his second letter to the Thessalonians:

"Let no one deceive you by any means; for that Day will not come unless the falling away comes first, and the man of sin is revealed, the son of perdition, who opposes and exalts himself above all that is called God or that is worshiped, so that he sits as God in the temple of God, showing himself that he is God. Do you not remember that when I was still with you I told you these things? And now you know what is restraining (As we pointed out in Chapter 3, this is Michael the archangel)**, that he** (the Antichrist) **may be revealed in his own time. For the mystery of lawlessness is already at work; only he who now restrains will do so until he is taken out of the way. And then the lawless one will be revealed** (Again, this seems to indicate the Antichrist will not be *revealed until* the midpoint of the 70th week of Daniel, since it is at the midpoint when Satan is cast out of heaven by Michael and his army of angels in Revelation 12.) **whom the Lord will consume with the breath of His mouth and destroy with the brightness of His coming. The coming of the lawless one is according to the working of Satan, with all power, signs, and lying wonders, and with all unrighteous deception among those who perish, because they did not receive the love of the truth, that they might be saved. And for this reason God will send them strong delusion, that they should believe the lie, that they all may be condemned who did not believe the truth but had pleasure in unrighteousness." 2 Thessalonians 2:3-2**

Wow! Don't let Paul's last point here escape you. Those who "have pleasure in unrighteousness" are sent a "strong delusion" *by God Himself.* To have "pleasure in unrighteousness" is to be *lawless.* This is indeed a sobering reason to recognize the "law" is good.

The book of Revelation, of course, also has some pertinent information concerning this man of sin: **"Then I stood on the sand of the sea. And I saw a beast rising up out of the sea, having seven heads and ten horns,** (this is the same fourth kingdom spoken of by Daniel. The beast only has seven horns because three were "plucked up" by the Antichrist as pointed out in Daniel 7:8) **and on his horns ten crowns, and on his heads a blasphemous name. Now the beast which I saw was like a leopard, his feet were like the feet of a bear, and his mouth like the mouth of a**

lion. The dragon gave him his power, his throne, and great authority. And I saw one of his heads as if it had been mortally wounded, and his deadly would was healed. And all the world marveled and followed the beast. So they worshiped the dragon (Satan) **who gave authority to the beast; and they worshiped the beast** (the Antichrist), **saying, 'Who is like the beast? Who is able to make war with him?' And he was given a mouth speaking great things and blasphemies, and he was given authority to continue for 42 months. Then he opened his mouth in blasphemy against God, to blaspheme His name, His tabernacle, and those who dwell in heaven. It was granted to him to make war with the saints and to overcome them. And authority was given him over every tribe, tongue, and nation. All who dwell on the earth will worship him, whose names have not been written in the Book of Life of the Lamb slain from the foundation of the world." Revelation 13:1-8**

Isn't the consistency of the word amazing? Now that we have been through some of the passages in Daniel, the Book of Revelation is suddenly less mysterious.

What follows the above passage in Revelation 13 is another passage detailing the works of the "False Prophet." Satan, as we have seen, is a great counterfeiter. Just as John the Baptist came and proclaimed Yeshua, a great false prophet will arise *showing great signs and wonders.* It will be this false prophet who will compel the world to receive the "mark of the Beast," a mark on the right hand or forehead that will demonstrate allegiance to the Antichrist and will allow those with the mark to buy or sell. Taking of this "mark" will result in eternal damnation. **"Then I saw another beast coming up out of the earth, and he had two horns like a lamb and spoke like a dragon. And he exercises all the authority of the first beast in his presence, and causes the earth and those who dwell in it to worship the first beast, who's deadly wound was healed.** (This statement hints that the antichrist will possibly perform a counterfeit resurrection) **He performs great signs, so that he even makes fire come down from heaven on the earth in the sight of men. And he deceives those who dwell on the earth by those signs which he was granted to do in the sight of the** beast, telling those who dwell on the earth to make an image to the beast who was wounded by the sword and lived. He was granted power to give breath to the image of the beast, that the image of the beast should both speak and cause as many as would not worship the image of the beast to be killed. He causes all , both small and great, rich and poor, free and slave, to receive a mark on their right hand or on their foreheads, and that no one may buy or sell except one who has the mark of the name of the beast, or the number of his name. Here is wisdom. Let him who has understanding calculate the number of a man: His number is 666." Revelation 13:11-18**

We see then from the prophecies of the Bible the Antichrist and his false prophet will cause much havoc on the Earth. Thankfully, we also can know the ultimate end of these two men who will do the devil's bidding, **"Then the beast was captured, and with him the false prophet who worked signs in his presence, by which he deceived those who received the mark of the beast and those who worshiped his image. These two were cast alive into the lake of fire burning with brimstone." Revelation 19:20**

This survey of the passages that speak of the Antichrist is not exhaustive, but should give the reader a good feel for what this person's role on earth will be. This person will do the bidding of his master, Satan, and many believe will actually be indwelt by Satan after the abomination of desolation at the midpoint of the 70th week of Daniel.

We can see from the above that the abomination of desolation is a major event and is spoken of or alluded to many times. This event will trigger the Great Tribulation just as Yeshua warned in Matthew 24. We also see clearly from the above passages the Antichrist will prevail over the saints and many will suffer at his hand.

Identifying the Son of Perdition

Most of the church today ignores the large body of prophecy text that speaks of the Antichrist, instead preferring to believe these words do not apply to the modern church. Despite this, there has always been speculation as to the identity of the Antichrist.

Apparently, we will not know with certainty the identity of this man until he is "revealed" as stated in 2 Thessalonians 2:3. We were given a few hints about him though, and so some speculation is authorized, particularly if the conjecture is based on the numerical calculation of names, since this is the major sign to look for according to the book of Revelation.

It seems like almost every major world leader has been accused at one time or another of being the "Antichrist" at one time or another. Recently, I have heard and read "expert" speculations that include George Bush, Tony Blair, Bill Clinton, Former U.N. Secretary Boutros Boutros-Ghali, Gorbachev, Saddam Hussein, JFK, and even a resurrected Adolph Hitler. Most of these speculations are based on whimsical ideas and anecdotal information. None of these listed satisfy the apparent criteria of the name calculation as defined in Revelation 13, **"Here is wisdom. Let him who has understanding calculation the number of a man: His number is 666."**

Of note, there is one theory that has been put forth by author Tim Cohen that does present a case for Prince Charles being the Antichrist in a scenario apparently satisfying the numerology requirement. Presented in his book *The Antichrist and a Cup of Tea*, Cohen makes a compelling argument.[193] In the first edition of *The Watchmen's Cry*, I more thoroughly outlined the details of this case, but have decided after some good counsel by some respected brethren that a presentation of these details may be a little too sensationalistic and may detract from the truths presented so far in this book. For a brief overview of some of the arguments presented by Tim Cohen, please see the above endnote.

British Israelism and False Doctrines

Often times we find Satan the deceiver polluting the truth with a lie. Regrettably, this has happened with the truth of Ephraim being scattered among the nations. Even though the Bible explicitly says that Ephraim would become many nations, there are many who would deny this truth simply because there have been fringe groups who also espoused this view. Both the Jehovah's Witness and the Mormon Church promote the idea of the "lost tribes of Israel" and perhaps because of this, many have rejected the truth of this understanding.

Satan knows the truth about Israel, and he does not want the truth to "get out." To pollute the truth with a lie is the classic method of operation of the deceiver. When tempting Yeshua, Satan quoted scripture, and in the garden Satan told Eve several bits of truth to get her to believe the lie. When it comes to the "two house" teaching (The understanding that God cast Israel to the nations and in the last day He is bringing them back together with Judah) Satan has polluted the truth with false doctrines of men and now most Christians simply "throw out the baby with the bath water."

In the 20th century a movement called the "Worldwide Church of God" gained popularity under the leadership of Herbert Armstrong. Again, like the Mormon Church and the Jehovah's Witness, this group originally held to some odd beliefs that may have hurt the credibility of the legitimate truth concerning the "lost tribes of Israel."

One particularly troublesome doctrine held by some in the Worldwide Church of God is the doctrine of "British Israelism." This belief claims that Ephraim *became* Great Britain and the rights to the *throne of Jerusalem*, which are found only in the lineage of King David, have been *transferred* to the British Monarchy. It is easy to see how this line of thinking could bolster the argument that a British Monarch could be the "true" messiah, since only those of the "Royal Line" have a bloodline supposedly going back to King David — a requisite to claiming the messiah title.

Whoever the Antichrist is, we must be on alert, and we must be prepared for the "hour of trial" that will come upon the whole earth. Most believers today have been lulled to sleep under a false sense of security. They are spiritually and physically unprepared. We say we are rich, yet we are poor and blind and naked. We are truly living during the age of the Laodician Church.[194]

The Lawless One

Keeping in mind that there are spiritual principles at work in addition to the physical, a point *must* be made. While we realize that according to the testimony of scripture the Antichrist will be a real person who defiles a physical Temple of God, there are some deeper spiritual applications that can be made.

Since *we* are now the "Temple of God,"[195] and the Spirit of God dwells in us, could it be that by our own lawlessness (as has been previously pointed out) that we are somehow performing an "abomination that makes desolate?" After all, Paul refers to the Antichrist as the "lawless one."[196]

In chapter four of this book, we spent a fair amount of time showing the correlation between Matthew 24 and Revelation 6. It was pointed out that the first four seals have been happening at a low level since the crucifixion of the Messiah. In light of this chapter and these last few conclusions, another look at Matthew 24 is warranted.

In Matthew 24:5, Yeshua warned that, **"Many will come in My name saying 'I am the Christ,', and will deceive many."** This statement of Yeshua was shown to correlate with the coming of the first seal and the appearance of the antichrist. John, however, as shown below, tells us that even in the first century, many antichrists had already come.

"Little children, it is the last hour; and as you have heard that the Antichrist is coming, even now many antichrists have come, by which we know that it is the last hour." 1 John 1:8

In order to reconcile the above passage with the notion that a specific end times antichrist, *the* Antichrist, will appear as suggested by the events described in the opening of the first seal, we must realize that the events of the first four seals have been happening since Yeshua's sacrifice. Just as there have been many wars and rumors of wars (red horse), famine in various places (black horse), and disease and pestilence (pale horse), there have been many who have come in "My name" saying "I am the Christ." It appears that just as with a woman in labor, these birth pangs will crescendo as the Day of the Lord approaches. These seal judgments describe the death of one third of mankind, and so we can also conclude that we haven't seen the fullness of the seal judgments.

What's more, as we ponder the meaning of Matthew 24:5 we would do well to realize that the original manuscripts did *not* include punctuation. In light of this fact, let's look one more time, this time closely, at this passage.

There are quotation marks that have been placed in our English Bibles that are not found in the Greek. So we have to ask ourselves, which is correct? Is it correct that Yeshua, implying that many will proclaim themselves as the messiah, said:

"Many will come in My name saying 'I am the Christ,', and will deceive many."

Or, without added quotation marks, did Yeshua *really* say:

"Many will come in My name saying *I* am the Christ and will deceive many."

Think about this for a moment. If Yeshua said as above that many will come in *His* name (in the name of Yeshua or Jesus) saying *He* (Yeshua) is the Christ and will deceive many, how might these believers in the Christ be deceived? And, how does that relate to the coming of *the* Antichrist in the opening of the first seal?

I submit that second rendering of Matthew 24:5 is correct and that *the* deception concerns the notion that God's Torah has been done away with, and that we as believers in Yeshua need not concern ourselves with God's everlasting instructions.

After all, since the first century we have indeed seen wars, famine, and pestilence. Yet, can we honestly say that we have seen many false christs who also claimed the *name* of Jesus? On the contrary, we have *not* seen these false messiahs. Instead, the testimony of history is that we have seen many coming in the name of Jesus, proclaiming that Jesus is the Christ, but deceiving many with a religious philosophy opposing Yeshua's words:

"Do not think that I come to destroy the Law or the Prophets. I did not come to destroy but to fulfill. For assuredly, I say to you, till heaven and earth pass away, one jot or one tittle

will by no means pass from the law till all is fulfilled. Whoever therefore breaks one of the least of these commandments, and teaches men so, shall be called least in the kingdom of heaven; but whoever does and teaches them, he shall be called great in the kingdom of heaven." Matthew 5:17-19

Thus, as the seal judgments fully come forth we will likely see *the* Antichrist teaching and adhering to a great deal of what mainstream Christianity *already* falsely teaches. Daniel confirms this notion with his prophetic words, **"he shall return and show regard for those who forsake the holy covenant" and "those who do wickedly against the covenant he shall corrupt with flattery."** In this way the Antichrist will further deceive many. Revelation agrees that it is for the sake of keeping the commandments of God that the Antichrist will persecute the elect during the Great Tribulation, **"And the dragon was enraged with the woman, and he went to make war with the rest of her offspring, who keep the commandments of God and have the testimony of Jesus Christ." Revelation 12:17**

Incredibly, our assessment of the modern church demonstrates that Satan has already laid the groundwork for this great deception and we see the fulfillment of Yeshua's prophecy in *our* day, before our very eyes. Paul knew too well that this would happen, and he expressed his fear in the following heartrending verse:

"But I fear, lest somehow, as the serpent deceived Eve by his craftiness, so your minds may be corrupted from the simplicity that is in Christ. For if he who comes preaches another Jesus whom we have not preached, or if you receive a different spirit which you have not received, or a different gospel which you have not accepted – you may well put up with it!" 2 Corinthians 11:3-4

Indeed, in modern times myriads of preachers and evangelist bring the flock to an understanding of *who* the messiah is (they come in the name of Jesus saying that He is the Christ), only to abandon their new disciples, leaving the flock hungry and in desperate need of instruction as had been the custom, **"In every**

city, being read in the synagogues every Sabbath." [197]

In our day the modern day institution of the church has rejected God's instructions and has instead embraced man's idolatrous traditions. Seeing this causes one to stop and think… (And shudder).

Therefore:

"Let no one deceive you with empty words, for because of these things the wrath of God comes upon the sons of disobedience." Ephesians 5:6

"Little children, it is the last hour; and as you have heard that the Antichrist is coming, even now many antichrists have come, by which we know that it is the last hour."

How close are we? In the concluding section of this book we will examine some of the "signs of the times" that indicate we are indeed living in the last days!

EPILOGUE

A Call to Holy Living

Signs of the Times

$\mathcal{B}$y now we have hopefully shown why it is so important to understand the truth about God's prophetic Word. We see that we ought not to allow ourselves to be swept up in a tide of "feel good" theology. There will be no pre-tribulation rapture. The elect will be here on earth to endure Satan's Wrath, the Antichrist, and the Great Tribulation. Our identity must be with Israel and we must not be a part of the Woman riding the Beast.

We must be prepared. While it may be impossible to prepare physically for such a time — we *must* be prepared spiritually. For centuries many have proclaimed the imminent return of the Lord and so far they all have been wrong! I will make no predictions as to the timing of the Lord's return, but by looking at God's Word we realize the end of the age is on the horizon — perhaps in this generation. What follows is a partial list of reasons we could be living in the last days.

Israel is in the Land

Isn't it interesting that Sir Robert Anderson came under fire in the late 1800's for proclaiming the Messiah's return was not imminent because there was no nation of Israel in the Promised Land?

We showed in chapter 2 that God's timepiece apparently stops when Israel is either in apostasy or out of the Promised Land. Today, through a series of miraculous wars and overcoming incredible odds, the Nation of Israel is a reality. In most all of the scriptural references to the Day of the Lord, Israel is literally in the Land.

The Sabbath Millennium

As we learn to embrace our Hebraic roots, we realize God's Law is not merely a set of do's and don't but it is also a set of teachings that lead us to the Messiah. The keeping of the Sabbath, one of the Ten Commandments, is no exception. This Law is not meant to be a burden, but a delight. It was indeed meant for man's enjoyment — but there is more. It not only looks back to Creation, but it is prophetic of the millennial kingdom.

Sometime in the not too distant future, we will enter the 7th millennium. Some even advocate we entered the seventh millennium on the Jewish New Year 2001. The Jewish New Year fell in September in the year 2001. As you may remember, September 2001 was an eventful month. History may yet mark the destruction of the World Trade Center in that month as the event that led to WWIII.

No one can precisely know where God's clock is right now. Tables of biblical chronology differ at many points. In fact, the first Bible I ever remember owning was an old King James Version with a table in the back comparing three different versions of biblical chronology.

It is provocative to use Sir Robert Anderson's theory of a 360 day prophetic year as it points us to some interesting speculation. If the Messiah's first coming came at the close of 4th millennium as some suppose,[198] and we then add two thousand (360 day) years to His first coming, (1972 yrs + 32 A.D.) we end up somewhere in the neighborhood of Fall 2004.

Reportedly there has also been some interesting work done correlating astronomical data and the historical and biblical records that purports the 6001 year from creation occurring in 2007.

The Jubilee Generation

In a very interesting proposal, Angus Wooten points out that we live in a biblical jubilee generation. In the Bible every 50th year had special significance and all debts were cancelled. Why would God ordain such a law? Could it be as a foreshadowing of future events? As it turns out 50 is an important number biblically. Apparently, Yeshua came in the 50th generation following the flood, and 1996 began the 50th generation after the first coming of the Messiah.[199] Could this be a coincidence?

The World's Population

Let us consider also the term the "fullness of the Gentiles" used by the Apostle Paul. Paul stated that **"blindness in part has happened to Israel until the fullness of the Gentiles is come in."** [200] This term the "fullness of the Gentiles" is very interesting since it implies there has been a preset number that must be reached before Israel is unblinded. In the not too distant future the world's population will approach 7 billion. Seven billion is 7 times 1000, times 1000, times 1000. Anyone with even a superficial understanding of the significance of numbers can understand the significance. Seven is the number of divine perfection, or completion. To multiply seven times 1000 cubed certainly seems interesting, particularly if one believes that possibly the whole face of the earth is filled with Israelites.

The Example of the Unfaithful Spies

In Numbers 14, we learn that although God through Moses had miraculously delivered the young nation of Israel from the hand of the Egyptians, the nation was greatly afraid of "giants in the land" and rejected the report of Caleb and Joshua. Because of their unbelief, the nation had to wait another 40 years before entering into the Promised Land.

In June of 1967, the Nation of Israel was again miraculously delivered from the hand of the "Egyptians." They were again led by a man named Moses.[201] After capturing the most holy spot in all of Judaism they again were afraid of "giants in the land" and gave up the rights to the Temple Mount. It is conjecture, but I look for Israel to again assume authority over the Temple Mount 40 years after 1967. This will be roughly in 2007. We have shown that the Antichrist will sit "as God, in the Temple of God" at the time of the abomination of desolation. This requires a temple or at least some sort of tabernacle to be in place. It seems unlikely this would occur anywhere but on the temple mount. Look for Israel to regain control 40 years after 1967. In any case preparations for a new Temple on the Temple Mount have been underway for many years. Priests and sacrificial instruments are prepared and are waiting for the time and place.

Israel the Fig Tree

It is indeed amazing to realize that although highly improbable, Israel is again a nation in the promised land after being exiled for almost 1900 years. In Luke 21:29 we have the parable of the fig tree, which is commonly held to be symbolic of the nation Israel. **"Look at the fig tree, and all the trees. When they are already budding, you see and know for yourselves that summer is now near. So you also, when you see these things happening, know that the kingdom of God is near. Assuredly, I say to you, this generation will by no means pass away till all things take place. Heaven and earth will pass away, but My words will by no means pass away."**

According to David, writing in Psalms a generation is 70 years. Seventy years added to 1948, the year of the birth of the modern nation of Israel, bring us to the year 2018. Many believe the "fig tree" represents Israel, and accordingly, "all these things" (the second coming of the Messiah spoken of in Luke 21) will have taken place by 2018.

The Rise of the European Superstate — the Revived Roman Empire

Incredibly, we are witnessing the birth of the European Union. The land mass covered by this new entity is roughly the same as the Roman Empire. Daniel 9:26 tells us it is the "people of the prince who is to come" will destroy the sanctuary. We know the Temple was destroyed in 70 A. D. by the Romans. The Romans are the "people" and the "prince who is to come" is the Antichrist. The Antichrist must come from the "Romans." Look for the Antichrist to be put into a position of great power in the European Superstate.

Knowledge Will Increase

In Daniel 12:4 we learn concerning the time of the end, **"Many shall run to and from, and knowledge shall increase."** Certainly we live in a day unlike any other. With the rapid transfer of information we have seen a literal explosion of knowledge. One thousand years ago our clothes were made from agricultural products such as cotton and wool and we traveled and communicated at the speed of horseback. Just 100 short years ago the situation was virtually the same. Today we are able to manipulate molecules of petroleum products and we clothe ourselves in synthetic products such as nylon and rayon. We travel at the speed of sound and communicate at the speed of light. It certainly sounds like we are living in the end times according to this passage.

One particular piece of technology that is presently under development is the implantable microchip. This technology will begin to make perfect sense as "white collar" computer crime increases, child abductions become more publicized, and as the worldwide terror threat worsens. Microchip implants are already being placed in Mexico and as has already been mentioned has been placed into the right hands of some members of the British Royal Family. Look for the system to be a functional system that solves many problems before it is misused to persecute believers. *Do not under any circumstances* take a mark in your right hand or forehead that allows you to buy or sell.[202]

Increasing Knowledge…Knowledge of the Name

One obscure but rather provocative prophecy concerning the "day of affliction" has to do with the emerging knowledge of the eternal name of God. In Jeremiah 16:19-21 we find a prophecy concerning the restoration of Israel and Judah during the last days of this age:

O LORD, my strength and my fortress, My refuge in the day of affliction. The Gentiles shall come to You from the ends of the earth and say, "Surely our fathers have inherited lies, worthlessness and unprofitable things. Will a man make gods for himself, which are not gods?" "Therefore behold, I will this once cause them to know. I will cause them to know My hand and My might. And they shall know that My name is …"

Here, most all widely accepted translation fall well short of the true meaning and say, **"My name is the LORD."** The interesting thing to note is that many are beginning to come to the knowledge of the true name of the Almighty Creator, the God of Abraham, Isaac, and Jacob.

God's name is most definitely not "the LORD." "Lord" is a title. The word "Baal" is rightly translated as "Lord." God has a name and the third commandment instructs us not to bring it to nothingness. We take the commandment **"Do not take the name of the LORD God in vain"** to mean not swearing or cursing. Incredibly, a more careful study of the Hebrew indicates the Command ought to read something like this… "I am YHWH your Elohim, do not bring my name to nothingness." This makes sense when we understand that to do something *in vain* is to do it for nothing. Amazingly, for centuries most people have not even realized that God has a name and instead have used the label "God" or the title "Lord." *God's name is YHWH*, and although the exact pronunciation may be in dispute, the mere fact that more and more people are becoming aware of His name indicates we are getting closer to the end times based on this prophecy of Jeremiah that rightly ends…

"And they shall know that My name is YHWH"

The Stage is Set

When one takes a step back and looks at the current political climate in the world it is not hard to see how someone could burst on the scene and solve many problems. This person will be trusted by Jews, Christians, and Muslims. He will bring in world peace and because of his great ability he will be worshipped. It may take more war and suffering before the world is ready to receive such a man, but rest assured, God's plan will be accomplished. Imagine for a moment what the world would be like if an all out World War broke open. We are on the verge of that right now. The Middle East is a powder keg waiting to explode. North Korea is led by an insane man with nuclear weapons. India and Pakistan have nuclear weapons pointed at each other. Most of the entire Continent of Africa is embroiled in ethnic and religious hatred. The European Superstate is rising to power. And importantly, precedent has been set for the "World Government" to interfere in the internal conflicts of small countries, setting the stage for World Government interference in the Israeli-Palestinian conflict.

How might it all happen?

Although speculative, a possible end time scenario could go something like this: World War III breaks out in full force. It is short, but massive worldwide famine and disease follow the nuclear carnage.[203] It is possible the "Gog-Magog" battle of Ezekiel 38-39 could be a part of this war.[204] Ezekiel 39:9 tells us that the captured weapons used during this war will burn for "seven years." This implies the Gog-Magog battle of this world war could (along with the peace treaty that will follow such a battle) could signify the beginning of Daniel's 70th week.

The European Union, under the leadership of the Antichrist will then be in a position to restore order to the rest of the world, in part based on the treaty the Antichrist enforces between Israel and the Islamic world. (This may imply the U.S. is severely crippled because it is not featured prominently in the prophetic end times picture in the Bible.) These events would encompass the first four seals of Revelation chapter 6.

The Antichrist, because of his exploits and political savvy, is revered by all. People will begin to actually worship him and he will be proclaimed the messiah by many false prophets, including a major false prophet who will be seen as the worldwide leader of the "church."

The peace that follows is shaky and is held together by the constant threat of violence. Because of the incredible victory of the Gog-Magog battle and as part of the seven year treaty that is enforced by the Antichrist in the "covenant with Death,"[205] Israel will regain control over the temple mount. Sacrifices will then resume in the Temple that will be quickly rebuilt by the Jews.

At the midpoint of the seven year period the Antichrist will be indwelt by Satan himself after he is kicked out of heaven in a great battle with Michael the Archangel. Satan, having great wrath will begin intense persecution of believers. The Antichrist will likely blame believers for all of the world's turmoil. Even marginal Christians will be subject to this terrible persecution. The world will be in chaos. The Antichrist will muster support for his oppressive policies. The worldwide leader of the "church," the False Prophet, will require everyone to prove there alliance to the Antichrist by taking a mark, likely a microchip, in either their hand or forehead.

Faith will be tested as never before. The tares will be separated from the wheat. It is not difficult to imagine how this might come to pass. Even today, any "religious fundamentalist" is already cast in a bad light in the modern media. The world will hate the true believer and will try to purge those who shine a light on the darkness. The events of the Great Tribulation as outlined in the previous chapter will then follow. Under intense persecution the House of Israel and the House of Judah will be regathered together in the literal land of Israel where upon seeing all hope is lost when the armies of the Antichrist are bearing down on them, they will acknowledge their ways, and seek the face of the True and Living God, and true repentance will take place. Then, praise the LORD! Relief will come when our Messiah returns to avenge and restore the kingdom.

Prepare! Sound the Alarm!

One cannot begin to overstate the importance of getting your "house in order" and preparing spiritually for the events that lay ahead. Knowing the truth about having to go through the tribulation is only part of the preparation. Learning to live a holy or set apart life during the present time is essential.

As we begin to understand the importance of God's instruction (His Torah) we are able to see why Paul stated in 1 Corinthians 10 that the things that happened to the Israelites during the wilderness wanderings **"happened to them as examples, and they were written for our admonition, upon whom the ends of the ages have come."** Being untaught in God's instruction, how do "New Covenant Brethren" expect that we will be able to stand up against the wiles of the Devil during the Great Tribulation, not living a holy life now? Following Paul's admonition, we must study carefully the mistakes made by our ancestors so we do not make the same mistakes as the time of His glorious return approaches.

We have learned it is because *"lawlessness abounds"* that the Agape of many will grow cold. Our constant prayer should be that the Lord would not let our Agape grow cold. To this end then, we must embrace God's Law — His instruction for a holy life, His Torah. Once again, we do this not as a means to salvation per se, but because we love the Father *so much* that we agree with His Word, and believe that His instruction is good and holy.

We realize then, it is not as though simply following God's Law saves us in a *legal* sense, for salvation is by faith. Paul tells us, however, that **"Faith comes by hearing, and hearing by the word of God."** James adds further to this by saying, **"But be doers of the word and not hearers only, deceiving yourselves."** We realize therefore, that obedience to God's law saves us in a very real and practical way by *building our faith* in and leading us to the only one that can *truly* save us, Yeshua the Messiah.

We must see that the *entire* Word of God points us to our Savior and that attaining Him is the only worthy goal. To that end, let us do away with the doctrines of man that **"have the appearance of wisdom in self-imposed religion but are of no value against the indulgence of the flesh."**[206] We must therefore recognize it is lawlessness to continue in the idolatrous practices we learned from our forefathers.[207]

We must not let "lawless abound,"[208] supposing by this we are letting "grace abound." We must understand that God alone defines what is holy and what is profane; therefore, let us return to *His* instruction and turn away from the Tree of the Knowledge of Good and Evil so we may do *His* will and not ours. In *this* way we will be able to *know* Him and thus strengthen our faith preparing for the days that lay ahead.

And So:

Father in Heaven, whose name is above all names, we bow our hearts unto You. You are worthy of glory and honor and praise. This marvelous work You are doing here on the Earth is glorious beyond measure. It is truly amazing that you will restore your bride, Your nation set apart unto You. Father, I earnestly pray, that for Your glory You would reveal this awesome handiwork to those who love you. Increase in each of us the knowledge of You. Grant that we would have discernment and Wisdom. Father, the enemy of this world is a master deceiver – and he has spread his lies and blinded many. I pray, O Father in Heaven, O Mighty Creator, that you would open the eyes of those who love you. Help us all to comprehend the knowledge surpassing love of our Messiah. Help us all to understand Yeshua's redemptive work. Help us to see how the evil one is deceiving the earth, and grant us the strength to respond to the Truth of Your Word with actions. Grant that we would have a renewed love for you and your Word. Grant that we could fully embrace your Law – Your instruction. Write your law fully on the hearts of those who love you, that we might be able to live a truly set apart life unto you. Grant to us by the Power of your Holy Spirit that the Agape Love within us would remain strong. Grant that the Love You gave us that we might Love You and that we might Love one another, Your Agape Love – will never grow cold. We pray that if we still are living upon the earth during the Great Tribulation, we would be found worthy to receive Your divine protection and provision just as You protected and provided for our fathers in the wilderness. Prepare us now that we might not fall away, but that we would enjoy eternity with You. Father, hold us in Your hand and let no one snatch us away. Strengthen and increase our Faith that we might be able to withstand the fiery darts of the evil one. Increase in each of us a hunger for Your Word, that our Faith may also be nourished. Now to Him who is able to do exceeding abundantly above all that we ask or think, according to the power that works in us, to Him be glory by Messiah Yeshua to all generations, forever and ever. Amen.

Shalom,

Obadiah Frank

Endnotes

[1] The Author has chosen to use the generic designation "God" for the eternal creator, YHWH, the God of Abraham, Isaac and Jacob to foster communication with readers who may be unfamiliar with the eternal names Yahweh or YHWH. Our Messiah and Savior Yeshua will be referred to in this text as Jesus Christ for the same reason. The issue of the name will be addressed briefly in a later chapter.

[2] World Magazine Dec 7, 2002, p.5

[3] Revelation 2:7,11,17,29,3:6,13,22

[4] Revelation 13:18

[5] The "Day" here speaks of the "Day of the Lord," the coming of our Lord Jesus Christ as outlined in Matthew 24

[6] The complicated issue of "eternal security" is beyond the scope of this introductory chapter and will not be dealt with specifically. The controversy is pointed out to raise the question and promote interest in the topic of prophecy. Eternal security will be specifically addressed in chapter 10.

[7] These four levels are called PaRDeS. The Hebrew word PARDES is spelled in Hebrew without vowels as PRDS. PaRDeS refers to a park or garden, especially the Garden of Eden. The word appears three times in the Aramaic New Testament (Luke23:43, 2 Corinthians 12:4, Rev 2:7) PRDS comes from P=Pashat (simple), R=Remez (hint), D=Drash (search), and S=Sod (hidden).

[8] That God often uses "symbols" found in stories and prophecy is proven by His word in Hosea 12:9

[9] I Corinthians 2:7-16, **"But we speak the wisdom of God in a mystery, the hidden wisdom which God ordained before the ages for our glory, which none of the rulers of this age knew; for had they known, they would not have crucified the Lord of glory. But as it is written: "Eye has not seen, nor ear heard, nor have entered into the heart of man the things which**

God has prepared for those who love Him." But God has revealed them to us through His Spirit. For the Spirit searches all things, yes the deep things of God. For what man knows the things of a man except the spirit of the man which is in him? Even so no one knows the things of God except the Spirit of God. Now we have received, not the spirit of the world, but the Spirit who is from God, that we might know the things that have been freely given to us by God. These things we also speak, not in words which man's wisdom reaches but which the Holy Spirit teaches, comparing spiritual things with spiritual. But the natural man does not receive the things of the Spirit of God, for they are foolishness to him, nor can he know the, because they are spiritually discerned. But he who is spiritual judges all things, yet he himself is rightly judged by no one. For "who has known the mind of the LORD that he may instruct Him? But we have the mind of Christ."

[10] Marvin Rosenthal, *The Prewrath Rapture of the Church* (Thomas Nelson Publishers, 1990),49

[11] *Josephus, the Complete Works*, translated by William Whiston, A.M. (Thomas Nelson Publishers), 1998 The War of the Jews Book 5 and 6

[12] *Josephus, the Complete Works*, translated by William Whiston, A.M. (Thomas Nelson Publishers), 1998 The War of the Jews 6.3.4.207

[13] *Josephus, the Complete Works*, translated by William Whiston, A.M. (Thomas Nelson Publishers), 1998 The War of the Jews 5.10.5

[14] The thousand year millennial kingdom is mentioned four times in the first five verses of Rev 20

[15] This will be fully elaborated in Chapter 4 of this book

[16] Scholars agree that John received the vision of the Book of Revelation around A.D. 95

[17] In Genesis Chapter 15, God makes his covenant with Abraham and his descendants. Only God is required to pass between the divided carcasses of the sacrificed animals indicating that God made a unilateral covenant with Abraham and his descendents.

[18] Genesis 17:8, **"Also I give to you and your descendants after you the land in which you are a stranger in all the land of Canaan, as an everlasting possession; and I will be their God."**

[19] 2 Corinthians 4:4, **"whose minds the god of this age has blinded, who do not believe, lest the light of the gospel of the glory of Christ, who is the image of God, should shine on them."**

[20] Matthew 7:14 **"Because narrow is the gate and difficult is the way which leads to life, and there are few who find it."**

[21] John F Walvoord "The fact is that neither posttribulationism nor pretribulationism is an explicit teaching of the Scriptures. The Bible does not, in so many words, state either" The Rapture Question, 1st ed. (Findlay, Ohio 1957) p.148

[22] Sir Robert Anderson, *The Coming Prince*. Reprint 1957 from 10th ed. (Kregel Publications, Grand Rapids)

[23] this decree to rebuild the city of Jerusalem is what the conversation is about in Nehemiah 2:1-5, **"And it came to pass in the month of Nisan, in the twentieth year of King Artexerxes, when wine was before him, that I took the wine and gave it to the king. Now I had never been sad in his presence before. Therefore the king said to me, "Why is your face sad, since you are not sick? This is nothing but sorrow of heart." So I became dreadfully afraid, and said to the king, "May the king live forever! Why should my face not be sad, when the city, the place of my fathers' tombs, lies waste, and its gates are burned with fire? Then the king said to me, "What do you request?" So I prayed to the God of heaven. And I said to the king, "If it pleases the king, and If your servant has found favor in your sight, I ask that you send me to Judah, to the city of my fathers' tombs, that I may rebuild it."**

[24] Chuck Missler, Study Notes to *Expositional Commentary of Daniel* 7-12, p.15. (Koinonia House 1994)

[25] there is good evidence to argue for a different order of events on Passion Week and would refer to this as "Palm Sabbath, believing that this occurred on Saturday rather than Sunday.

[26] This event is referred to as the triumphal entry and is recorded in Luke chapter 19, John 12:12, and Matthew 21.

[27] John 7:8, 7:30

[28] Chuck Missler, Study Notes to *Expositional Commentary of Daniel* 7-12, p.23. (Koinonia House 1994)

[29] We can deduce this from Genesis 12:4 and Galatians 3:17

[30] Genesis 16: 16 tells us that Abraham was 86 years old when Hagar bore Ishmael, therefore Abraham was 85 when he and Sarah decided to take matters of God's promise into their own hands. Genesis 21:5 explains that Abraham was 100 when Isaac was born. This leaves 15 years when Abraham was walking in apostasy, according to the flesh.

[31] This time period began in 1Kings 6-8, and was completed in 1 Kings 6:38

and lasted a total of 601 years. The Israelites were captive as noted in Judges for the follow intervals that total 111 years: Mesopotamia 8 years (3:8), Moabites 18 years (3:12-14), Canaanites 20 years (4:2,3), Midianites 7 years (6:1), Ammonites 18 years (10:7,8), and the Philistines for 40 years (13:1). Total years of captivity = 111 years.

[32] 2 Chron 36:21, **"To fulfill the word of the LORD by the mouth of Jeremiah, until the land had enjoyed her Sabbaths, As long as she lay desolate she kept Sabbath, to fulfill seventy years."**

[33] Matthew 18:22, **"I do not say to you seven times, but up to seventy times seven."**

[34] see vs. 9:26 **"the end of it shall be with a flood"** — the word Diaspora, which is the word commonly used for the dispersion of the Jews in 70 A.D. actually means flood!

[35] Isa 28:15, **"Because you have said, 'We have made a covenant with death, and with Sheol we are in agreement. When the overflowing scourge passes through, it will not come to us, for we have made lies our refuge, and under falsehood we have hidden ourselves.'"**

[36] Other Day of the Lord Passages can also be found at the following: Psalms 110:5, Isa 2:12, 13:9, 22:5, Jeremiah 46:10, Ezekiel 7:19, 30:3, Joel chapters 2 and 3, Zephaniah 1;2-5,Mal 3:2, 4:5, 1 Corinthians 1:8, 5:5.

[37] We see this event in Acts Chapter 2. It was prophesied to happen in Jeremiah 31:33, **"But this is the covenant that I will make with the house of Israel after those days. Says the LORD: I will put My law I their minds, and write it on their hearts; and I will be their God, and they shall be My people."**

[38] notice how this sounds a lot like Matthew 24: 21, **"For then there will be great tribulation, such as has not been since the beginning of the world until this time, no, nor ever shall be."**

[39] Strong's 5975

[40] Daniel 11:31-36, Mark 13:9, Luke 21:12

[41] Rev 13:7

[42] John 3:16

[43] Studies have purportedly shown that fully fifty percent of teenagers who are "born again believers" will deny their faith after only one year of college.

[44] 1 Corinthians 10:11 indicates that the things that happened to the Israelites in the wilderness were written for the admonition of those **"on whom the ends of the ages has come."** This indicates that a detailed understanding of

the wilderness wanderings of the Israelites will be essential to us who will have to endure the Great Tribulation. This aspect of spiritual preparedness is grossly overlooked in the modern Church.

[45] Hosea 12:10 **"I have also spoken by the prophets, and have multiplied visions; I have given symbols through the witness of the prophets."** Here God points out that He has spoken to us using symbols, proof from the Word that the study of "types" is very legitimate.

[46] Genesis 7:4

[47] Since the events in Matthew 24 include the abomination of desolation spoken of by Daniel, then Daniel's 70th week must have already begun at this time.

[48] 2 Thessalonians 2:1-4

[49] The fifth seal in Rev 6

[50] The sixth seal in Rev 6

[51] Revelation 1:3

[52] This fascinating passage is elaborated in Joel 2:1-11 where Joel vividly describes the events of the fifth and sixth trumpets. He begins with a description of the sixth trumpet, and we are able to see that these events occur during the Day of the Lord, **"Blow the trumpet in Zion, and sound an alarm in My holy mountain! Let all the inhabitants of the land tremble; For the day of he Lord is coming, for it is at hand: A day of darkness and gloominess, a day of clouds and thick darkness, like the morning clouds spread over the mountains. A people come, great and strong, the like of whom has never been; nor will there ever be any such after them, even for many successive generation. A fire devours before them, and behind them a flame burns; the land is like the Garden of Eden before them and behind them a desolate wilderness; surely nothing shall escape them. Their appearance is like the appearance of horses; and like swift steeds, so they run. With a noise like chariots Over mountaintops they leap, like the noise of flaming fire that devours the stubble, Like a strong people set in battle array."** Joel 2:1-5

Events of the fifth seal are described in the following passage Joel 2:6-11, **"Before them the people writhe in pain; all faces are drained of color. They run like mighty men, they climb the wall like men of war; every one marches in formation, and they do not break ranks. They do not push one another; every one marches in his own column. Though they lunge between the weapons, they are not cut down. They run to and** from in the city, they run on the wall; they climb into the houses they enter at the windows like a thief. The earth quakes before them, the heavens tremble; the sun and moon grow dark, and the stars diminish their brightness. The Lord gives voice before His army, for His camp is very great; for strong is the One who executes His word. For the day of the Lord is great and very terrible; who can endure it?"

[53] Revelation 15:1

[54] Strong's no. 972

[55] Strong's no.977

[56] This is reminiscent of Romans 8:14: "**For as many as are led by the Spirit of God, these are sons of God.**"

[57] The combined Houses of Israel and Judah are sometimes collectively referred to as the "House of David." To avoid confusion between Israel, the original Kingdom, and the "House of Israel," the Northern Kingdom, the Bible sometimes refers the Northern Kingdom as Ephraim.

[58] The term "Jacob's Trouble" originally comes from Genesis 32:22 when Jacob "wrestled with God." It is most interesting to note that just prior to this event Jacob divided his house (Genesis 32:7) so as to protect them from his brother Esau. This is a foreshadowing of the two "houses" of Israel having been divided into the "House of Judah" and the "House of Israel." Jacob divided his house but they were brought back together when they re-entered the Promised Land.

[59] Judah, from whom we derive the word "Jew," is but one tribe of Israel (Jacob).

[60] For a full treatise on this subject, I highly recommend "*Who is Israel*" by Batya Wooten, Key of David publishing, St. Cloud, FL

[61] Also known as the Great Tribulation

[62] Chuck Missler, *The Expositional Commentary of Ezekiel.* P.221 (Koinonia House, 1998)

[63] Romans 4:22, Genesis 15:6

[64] Acts 7:18

[65] See 1 Kings 11:11-13, 31-35, 12:24

[66] vs. 64-68, "Then the LORD will scatter you among all peoples, from one end of the earth to the other, and there you shall serve other gods, which neither you nor your fathers have known – wood and stone. And among those nations you shall find no rest, nor shall the sole of your foot have a resting place; but there the LORD will give you a trembling heart, failing

eyes, and anguish of soul. Your life shall hang in doubt before you; you shall fear day and night, and have no assurance of life. In the morning you shall say; Oh, that it were evening!' and at evening you shall say, 'Oh, that it were morning!' because of the fear which terrifies your heart, and because of the sight which your eyes see. And the LORD will take you back to Egypt in ships, by the way of which I said to you, 'You shall never see it again.' And there you shall be offered for sale to your enemies as male and female slaves, but no one will buy you" (this last verse was literally fulfilled during the Holocaust when shiploads of Jews were rejected at every port and eventually sent back to Hitler's camps).

[67] Jeremiah 25:12

[68] King Hiram, the King of the Phoenician city-state of Tyre was friends with David and Solomon and in fact helped to gather supplies to build the Temple of Solomon. See 1 Kings 5:1

[69] Stephen M. Collins, *The "Lost" Ten Tribes of Israel...Found!* P. 51,(CPA Books, Boring, OR 1995)

[70] (As a parenthesis, let's read on....) **All the sinners of my people shall die by the sword, who say, 'The calamity shall not overtake nor confront us'** " (could this be speaking to those who believe that there will not be a 'tribulation' or who believe that we will be raptured out of it?) **" 'On that day I will raise up the tabernacle of David** (David ruled over the *whole House of Israel*), **which has fallen down, and repair its damages; I will raise up its ruins, and rebuild it as in the days of old; That they might possess the remnant of Edom, and all the Gentiles who are called by my name,' Says the LORD who does this thing." Amos 9:10-12.**

[71] A must read in this context is also Ezekiel 35:11-31

[72] We must distinguish here between being "Israelite" and being "Jewish." All Jews are Israelites, but not all Israelites are Jewish. (Just as all Texans are Americans, but not all Americans are Texans.)

[73] **As He says in Hosea: "I will call them my people, who were not my people, and her beloved, who was not beloved. And it shall come to pass in the place where it was said to them, 'you are not My people,' there they shall be called sons of the living God." Romans 9:25-26**

[74] **"Yet the number of the children of Israel shall be as the sand of the sea, which cannot be measured or numbered. And it shall come to pass in the place where it was said to them, "You are not My people," There it shall be said to them, "You are the sons of the living God." Hosea 1:10**

[75] Ephesians 2:15, Galatians 3:28

[76] Yeshua is the Hebrew name for the Messiah, Jesus Christ. Now that the reader is familiar with his or her Israelite roots, the author will begin to use this designation for Jesus frequently through the rest of this book. Similarly, instead of using the word "Christ," the designation "the Messiah" will be used.

[77] Ephesians 2:11-19

[78] This is the generally accepted date.

[79] This takes into account the fact that there was no year zero.

[80] Zechariah 8:23, "Thus says the LORD of hosts: 'In those days ten men from every language of the nations shall grasp the sleeve of a Jewish man, saying, "Let us go with you, for we have heard that God is with you" '" — the "ten" men here represent the ten northern tribes that have been scattered to the nations.

[81] Amazingly Judah's punishment was accurately predicted as well. Judah did not learn from Israel's mistakes and so was given the punishment of both Israel's 390 years and Judah's 40 years. The combining of the punishment is detailed in the prophecy of Ezekiel 23 in the context of the two harlot sisters Aholah and Aholibah. The combined years of punishment = 430 years. Four hundred and thirty 360 day years equals just over 423.8 365 day years. Sometime during the reign of Zedekiah the anger of the LORD was kindled enough that He **"cast them out from His presence"** (2 Kings 24:20), and Zedekiah rebelled against Babylon, who had already sacked Jerusalem once and had set up Zedekiah as a vassal king. Zedekiah's reign was from 595 to 585 B.C. If we add our 423.8 years to this time period we end up at the time of the Maccabean Revolt, when under the leadership of the Maccabees, the nation of Judah regained control of the temple from Antiochus Epiphanes. This author asserts that the start date for this prophecy given in Ezekiel was an undocumented time when God "cast them out from His presence."

[82] Jeremiah 31:19

[83] Dave Hunt, *A Woman Rides the Beast* ch.18 (Harvest House, Eugene, OR) 1994

[84] These quotes were taken from *How Long, O Lord, How Long? A History of Antisemitism in Christianity* written by Luana Fabri. This is a well documented essay on Church History as it relates to anti-Semitism, and is highly recommended. This is a hard to find book in the United States. To obtain this book write to Luana Fabri, P.O. Box 80, Paradise Point, Q 4216, Australia. Or Email at lfabri@bigpond.net.au

85 Daniel Juster, *Jewish Roots* pp.142-143, (Destiny Images, Shippensburg, PA) 1995

86 The standard theological position justifying a "Sunday Sabbath" is based on an erroneous translation of Acts 20:7. Here, Paul is said to have met and "broke" bread on the "first day of the week." The word *day* in this phrase is added as is indicated in most English translations by the use of brackets or italics. Furthermore a correct translation of the Greek manuscript "mia ton sabbaton" used in Acts 20:7 reads on "one of the sabbaths" and not on "the first [day] of the week" as has been erroneously taught for hundreds of years. Furthermore, our misunderstanding of the Jewish way to reckon time has caused us to assume that the phrase "on the first of the week" in Acts 20:7 means Sunday, rather than Saturday night (the evening after the Sabbath is completed) when in keeping with Jewish tradition, those who gathered in the Synagogue for a day of study and worship would break bread and fellowship after the meeting.

87 Acts 17:2

88 Matthew 12:40

89 Jer16:19, "**O LORD, my strength and my fortress, my refuge in the day of affliction, the Gentiles shall come to You from the ends of the earth and say, "Surely our fathers have inherited lies, worthlessness and unprofitable things."**

90 Alexander Hislop, *The Two Babylons*, p.97 (Kessinger Publishing, LLC) 1916

91 Alexander Hislop, *The Two Babylons*, p.102 (Kessinger Publishing, LLC) 1916

92 Alexander Hislop, *The Two Babylons*, p.103 (Kessinger Publishing, LLC) 1916

93 Alexander Hislop, The *Two Babylons*, p.103 (Kessinger Publishing, LLC) 1916

94 Strong's Dictionary

95 Richard Rives, *Too Long in the Sun*, Partakers Publications, Charlotte, 2003

96 Genesis 11:6

97 Not the brethren, but the *institution*.

98 Rom11:14

99 A point worth making here is this: Is not Jesus the greatest in the Kingdom of Heaven? Since He is, could He possibly have been trying to teach us to do away with the law? According to this verse, He must have been teaching us to uphold the law otherwise there is a great contradiction here.

100 This correlates well with John 14:7-24 where we learn that those who love Jesus keep His commandments (vs. 15), and that by doing this we will receive the Spirit of Truth, the Holy Spirit. It is by this Spirit that we know

God and are known by God.

[101] Colossians 2:14

[102] Romans 3:23

[103] Jeremiah 31:31-34, Hebrews 8:8-12

[104] Hebrews 13:8, Mal 3:6

[105] The Law as defined by the Torah, and not by man's additions to God's instruction.

[106] Jesus was quoting the Torah here. Deuteronomy 6:5

[107] James 2:17

[108] Notice also the reference to idolatry. This obviously has significance in light of what was discussed in Chapter 8.

[109] See also Romans 5:1-2

[110] **"Therefore the law is holy, and the commandment holy and just and good." Romans 7:12, "For I delight in the law of God according to the inward man." Romans 7:22**

[111] Galatians 3:6

[112] James 2:17

[113] James 1:22

[114] Romans 10:17

[115] 2 Pet 1:10

[116] Matthew 4:4, Luke 4:4

[117] Colossians 2:17

[118] John 1:1-2

[119] Hebrews 10:7 Christ is quoted here as saying, **"Behold, I have come. The volume of the book is written of Me."**

[120] Matthew 5:17

[121] John 4:24

[122] Mal 3:6

[123] Jews, Christians, and Muslims

[124] Even our faith is not of ourselves - Ephesians 2:8

[125] Romans 3:1-2 **"What advantage then has the Jew, or what is the profit of circumcision: Much in every way! Chiefly because to them were committed the oracles of God."**

[126] Bethlehem means "house of Bread"

[127] It is a little ironic that Elimelech moved from the "house of Bread" because there was nothing to eat.

[128] Leviticus 19:9, 23:22

[129] Acts 2:5

[130] This is an example of a Remez or "hint." See Chapter One.

[131] As a side note, it is interesting that the New Jerusalem has 12 gates, each named after one of the tribes of Israel. This implies that only those from the tribe that the gate(s) are named for may enter.

[132] Daniel 12:2, Isa29, Joel 1, Amos 1-6, 9:1-10, Obad 10-14, Micah 1, Zephaniah

[133] Isaiah 27-29, Daniel 12:1, Hosea 14, Joel 1-3, Amos 9, Jeremiah 23:7-8

[134] Genesis 15:18

[135] Prior to the return of Judah into the Promised Land, the land was a barren wasteland and considered by many to be uninhabitable.

[136] Deuteronomy 29, 30, and 31:29-32:43, (this is the "song of Moses" of Rev 15:3), Hosea 12:9, 14, Ezekiel 36:17-24, Jeremiah 3:18, Jeremiah 30 and 31, Isa 11:2, Isa 65:9, **Jeremiah 23**, Amos 9:11-15, Micah 4:6-7-20. Zechariah 10:7. These passages clearly demonstrate the regathering of *both* houses of the Nation of Israel during the time of the great tribulation. It is highly probable that the Biblical Feast of Tabernacles is a reminder of not only the past exodus, but also the future *"Greater Exodus"* that will occur when the truly "elect" of God are regathered by God from "all of the nations" into the *literal* land of Israel, this may be why Hosea 12:9 speaks of again making Jacob to dwell in "tents."

[137] Genesis 32:9

[138] Genesis 32:8

[139] Jabbok means empty, indicating that Jacob's house was in an emptied out state.

[140] Genesis 32:24

[141] Genesis 32:30

[142] Genesis 32:7

[143] This is likely what Jesus spoke of when He said, **"You will hear of Wars and Rumors of wars. See that you are not troubled; for all these things must come to pass, but the end is not yet."** Matthew 24:6

[144] We realize this when we understand that the abomination of desolation happens at the midpoint of Daniel's 70th week.

[145] Romans 14:11, Philippians 2:10-11

[146] Ezekiel 38:11, 39:2

[147] Daniel 9:27

[148] Notice that the grain offering and the drink offering have been "cut off" in

Joel 1:9

[149] Joel 1:6, 2:20

[150] Joel chapter 1

[151] Notice famine in Joel chapter 1

[152] **"You will say, 'I will go up against a land of unwalled villages; I will go to a peaceful people, who dwell safely, all of them dwelling without walls, and having neither bars nor gates.'"** Ezekiel 38:11

[153] Note the similarities between the Revelation passage discussing the fifth and sixth trumpet and Joel 2:1-11, **"Then the fifth angel sounded: And I saw a star fallen from heaven to the earth. To him was given the key to the bottomless pit. And he opened the bottomless pit, and smoke arose out of the pit like the smoke of a great furnace. So the sun and the air were darkened because of the smoke of the pit. Then out of the smoke locusts came upon the earth. And to them was given power, as the scorpions of the earth have power. They were commanded not to harm the grass of the earth, or any green thing, or any tree, but only those men who do not have the seal of God on their foreheads. And they were not given authority to kill them, but to torment them for five months. Their torment was like the torment of a scorpion when it strikes a man. In those days men will seek death and will not find it; they will desire to die, and death will flee from them.**

The shape of the locusts was like horses prepared for battle. On their heads were crowns of something like gold, and their faces were like the faces of men. They had hair like women's hair, and their teeth were like lions' teeth. And they had breastplates like breastplates of iron, and the sound of their wings was like the sound of chariots with many horses running into battle. They had tails like scorpions, and there were stings in their tails. Their power was to hurt men five months. And they had a king over them, the angel of the bottomless pit, whose name in Hebrew is Abaddon, but in Greek his has the name Apollyon. One woe is past. Behold, still two more woes are coming after these things."

Then the sixth angel sounded: And I heard a voice from the four horns of the golden altar which is before God, saying to the sixth angel who had the trumpet, 'Release the four angels who are bound at the great river Euphrates.' So the four angels, who had been prepared for the hour and the day and month and year, were released to kill a third of mankind.

Now the number of the army of the horsemen was two hundred million; I heard the number of them. And thus I saw the horses in the vision: Those who sat on them had breastplates of fiery red, hyacinth blue, and sulfur yellow; and the heads of the horses were like the heads of lions; and out of their mouths came fire, smoke and brimstone. By these three plagues a third of mankind was killed — by the fire and the smoke and the brimstone which came out of their mouths. For their power is in their mouth and in their tails; for their tails are like serpents, having heads, and with them they do harm. But the rest of mankind, who were not killed by these plagues, did not repent of the works of their hands, that they should not worship demons, and idols of gold, silver, brass, stone, and wood, which can neither see not hear nor walk. And they did not repent of their murders or their sorceries or their sexual immorality or their thefts."

"Blow the trumpet in Zion, and sound an alarm in My holy mountain! Let all the inhabitants of the land tremble; For the day of he Lord is coming, for it is at hand: A day of darkness and gloominess, a day of clouds and thick darkness, like the morning clouds spread over the mountains. A people come, great and strong, the like of whom has never been; nor will there ever be any such after them, even for many successive generation. A fire devours before them, and behind them a flame burns; the land is like the Garden of Eden before them and behind them a desolate wilderness; surely nothing shall escape them. Their appearance is like the appearance of horses; and like swift steeds, so they run. With a noise like chariots Over mountaintops they leap, like the noise of flaming fire that devours the stubble, Like a strong people set in battle array." Joel 2:1-5

Events of the fifth seal are described in the following passage Joel 2:6-11, "Before them the people writhe in pain; all faces are drained of color. They run like mighty men, they climb the wall like men of war; every one marches in formation, and they do not break ranks. They do not push one another; every one marches in his own column. Though they lunge between the weapons, they are not cut down. They run to and from in the city, they run on the wall; they climb into the houses they enter at the windows like a thief. The earth quakes before them, the heavens tremble; the sun and moon grow dark, and the stars diminish their brightness. The Lord gives voice before His army, for His camp is

very great; for strong is the One who executes His word. For the day of the Lord is great and very terrible; who can endure it?"

[154] In both passages we see, the grass and trees burned, the water dried up or contaminated, people writhing in pain, and a massive army of horsemen with a noise like chariots.

[155] Joel 2:2-11

[156] Joel 2:30-32, Matthew 24:29-30, Mark 13:24, Mark 21:25, Rev 6:12-13

[157] Matthew 24:31, Rev 7:9

[158] Joel 3:1-17

[159] Rev 16:14-16, 19:11-21

[160] It is possible that the *unveiling* of the Antichrist will not happen until the abomination of desolation event.

[161] Genesis 1:26

[162] Ezekiel 14:28-29

[163] Matthew 4:8-10

[164] Rev 12:10, Job 1

[165] Rev 12:7

[166] Daniel 10:21

[167] The abomination of desolations happens at the midpoint of the 70th week of Daniel and so does the kicking of Satan out of heaven. This is because both events happen with only 3 1/2 years left until the end of the age. Since both happen at the midpoint of the 70th week, we can infer that this is the first thing that Satan will do after his banishment from heaven.

[168] Isa 14:14

[169] Hebrews 8:5

[170] The second commandment instructs us to not "take the LORD's name in vain." To do something "in vain" means to do it "for nothing" or for no benefit. God (YHWH) gave us His name yet how many of our fellow brethren even know it? We have done precisely what we were commanded not to do and have taken the Lord's name for nothing and instead use the title "Lord" or the generic word "God." Our heavenly father has desired a personal relationship with us and the intimacy that goes with using one's name.

[171] Marvin Rosenthal, The Pre-Wrath Rapture of the Church, p.232-233 (Thomas Nelson Publishers, Nashville)1990

[172] Specifically the Torah in this example that Paul speaks about in 1 Corinthians 10

[173] Paul was referring specifically to the Torah here.

[174] Zechariah 12:10

[175] The offense of Ephraim is idolatry. See Chapter 8

[176] Hos5:15, Matthew 24:29-31, Joel 3

[177] Matthew 13:43

[178] It appears the Gog-Magog scenario will happen twice, the second time at the end of the millennial kingdom, and instead of being a near-far prophecy this could be called a far-farther prophecy.

[179] Matthew 24:22

[180] 1 Thessalonians 5:9

[181] the 144,000 will be on earth for the duration of the 42 months, but will be divinely protected and "sealed."

[182] *The Seven Festivals of the Messiah,* Eddie Chumney, Strasburg Ohio

[183] Admittedly, assumptions of a "prophetic" 360 day year are used to make these speculations. Rev 12 and the Genesis account of the flood indicate that God operates on a 360 day calendar. How these events will correlate with either the Gregorian calendar or the Jewish Calendar is not understood by the author. It is possible the length of the year and months will change, since the Antichrist is prophesied to "change the times and the seasons" in Daniel Chapter 12.

[184] Using 360 day prophetic years

[185] 2 Thessalonians 2:4

[186] Mal 4:5

[187] Genesis 7:1,4,10

[188] Matthew 22:30

[189] Matthew 24:22

[190] Ezekiel 8:14

[191] Ezekiel 8:16

[192] Most theologians agree that that the fourth great empire outlined in this chapter is the Roman Empire. This is based on the whole of the Book of Daniel. There are several dreams and visions in the book of Daniel outlining the four great world empires (Daniel Chapters 2, 3, and 7). These world empires are in order the Babylonian, Medo-Persian, Grecian, and Roman.

[193] In an amazing body of work, The *Antichrist and a Cup of Tea,* Tim Cohen presents a case for one particular Antichrist candidate who apparently does meet the numerology criteria. For the reader's information, I will present some of this information and yet make no claims otherwise. *If what follows turns out to be in error, it by no means detracts from the truth of God's Word previously presented. We cannot know with certainty the identity of the*

Antichrist until the abomination of desolation occurs. It is possible, since God knows when the Day of the Lord will occur but Satan does not, that Satan has a man prepared in every generation who could be the person known as the Antichrist.

Here is a partial overview of the evidences pointing towards Prince Charles as being the Antichrist. Again, for a thorough treatment of the subject, I do recommend Timothy Cohen's work, *The Antichrist and a Cup of Tea.*

Prince Charles claims lineage back to King David, and in fact it has been announced on Israeli Television Channel 2 that this is the case. Lineage to King David is a prerequisite for the title of the Jewish Messiah, and will likely also be claimed by the counterfeit.

It is shown by Mr. Cohen that Charles has incredible "behind the scenes" power and is able to manipulate world governments with his influence. According to Cohen, he is also deeply involved in the occult and in the new age movement and has authority over Freemasonry and the Illuminati world-wide.

Additionally, the Royal family has enormous wealth and through his holdings could, if desired, control the world's food supply. It is shown by Mr. Cohen that Charles is an accomplished military man, having piloted fighter aircraft and captained naval vessels and that despite Charles' media exposure has already exceeded that of every other man in history and yet he is still looked upon favorably by the press.

The Antichrist and a Cup of Tea also shows that Prince Charles steers the environmental ethics and business agendas of the word's most powerful multinational corporations. The book also purports that Prince Charles and his sons have already taken a traceable biochip implant into their right hands and that Charles has officially requested of the European Union to be named the "King of Europe." Apparently, Charles is the heir to the title "King of Jerusalem," being heir to the British throne he is actually heir to the highest physical throne in existence on the earth today.

According to Cohen, Prince Charles' "Coat of Arms" is full of allusions to biblical satanic imagery. For example, it includes a creature that has the head of a lion, the body of a leopard, and the feet of a bear." Rev13:2 His coat of arms evidently has a prominent Red Dragon and a coded statement that reads, "I the Black prince serve the Red Dragon." There are much more detail of the Coat of Arms than can be included here in an endnote. Furthermore, according to Mr. Cohen, Charles' genealogy includes seem-

ingly almost everyone who has ever been anyone including most all of
European royalty, Russian royalty, and occult bloodline supposedly to
Yeshua and Mary Magdalene. (as a side note, the popular fiction book The
DiVinci Code, by Daniel Brown, is based on this blasphemous theory and
may be laying the groundwork for the rise of the Antichrist.), King David,
and even to the prophet of Islam – Mohammad. (In Islamic Eschatology, the
"Muslim messiah" the Imam Mahdi must be of the tribe of Mohammad!) He
is related to many former presidents including Bush, Clinton, JFK, and
George Washington but he actually appears to be a descendant of the tribe of
Dan.

Cohen points out that Charles, means "Man" (reread Rev 13:18, it is the
number of "a man").

And most incredibly, according to Mr. Cohen, Charles' official name (title –
Prince Charles of Wales) scripturally calculates to 666 in both the Hebrew
and in the English.

[194] Revelation 3:14-22

[195] 1 Corinthians 3:16, **"Do you not know that you are the temple of God and that the Spirit of God dwells in you?"**

[196] 2 Thessalonians 2:8, **"And then the lawless one will be revealed, whom the Lord will consume with the breath of His mouth and destroy with the brightness of His coming."**

[197] Acts 15:21

[198] Avi Ben Mordechai, *Signs in the Heavens*, p.216 (Millennium 7000 Communications, Int'l)1999

[199] Angus Wooten, Restoring *Israel's Kingdom*,p.179 (Key of David Publishing, Saint Cloud)2000

[200] Romans 11:25

[201] Moshe Dayan was the minister of Defense during the Six Day War in 1967.

[202] Rev 13:16-17, 14:11

[203] This will coincide with the opening of the first four seals in Rev 6.

[204] Gog-Magog is also mentioned in Rev 20 and is to occur at the end of the millennium. This is likely another example of a "near-far" prophecy.

[205] Isa 28:15

[206] Colossians 2:23

[207] Jer16:19-21

[208] Matthew 24:12

Printed in the United States
28472LVS00004B/55-510